TRANSITIONS OF AGING

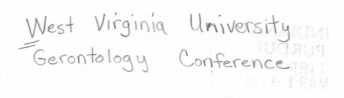

TRANSITIONS OF AGING

Edited by

Nancy Datan

Department of Psychology
West Virginia University
Morgantown, West Virginia

Nancy Lohmann

School of Social Work
West Virginia University
Morgantown, West Virginia

1980

ACADEMIC PRESS
A Subsidiary of Harcourt Brace Jovanovich, Publishers
New York   London   Toronto   Sydney   San Francisco

ACADEMIC PRESS, INC.
111 Fifth Avenue, New York, New York 10003

United Kingdom Edition published by
ACADEMIC PRESS, INC. (LONDON) LTD.
24/28 Oval Road, London NW1 7DX

Library of Congress Cataloging in Publication Data

West Virginia University Gerontology Congress,
 1st, 1979.
 Transitions of aging.

 Includes bibliographies and index.
 1. Gerontology––United States––Congresses.
2. Aged women––United States––Congresses. 3. Aged
policy––United States––Congresses. I. Datan, Nancy.
II. Lohmann, Nancy. III. West Virginia. University.
IV. Title.
HQ1064.U5W47 1979   305.2'6   80–528
ISBN 0–12–203580–1

PRINTED IN THE UNITED STATES OF AMERICA

80 81 82 83   9 8 7 6 5 4 3 2 1

lw
3-19-81

For Louise Burr Gerrard

Contents

List of Contributors

Numbers in parentheses indicate the pages on which the authors' contributions begin.

NANCY DATAN (57), Department of Psychology, West Virginia University, Morgantown, West Virginia   26506

CAROL BOELLHOFF GIESEN (57), Department of Psychology, West Virginia University, Morgantown, West Virginia   26506

BRIAN GRIFFIN (119), Department of Psychiatry and Behavioral Sciences, Northwestern University Medical School, Chicago, Illinois 60611

JEROME GRUNES (119), Department of Psychiatry and Behavioral Sciences, Northwestern University Medical School, Chicago, Illinois 60611

DAVID GUTMANN (119), Department of Psychiatry and Behavioral Sciences, Northwestern University Medical School, Chicago, Illinois 60611

GISELA LABOUVIE–VIEF (3), Institute of Gerontology, Department of Psychology, Wayne State University, Detroit, Michigan   48202

M. POWELL LAWTON (171), Philadelphia Geriatric Center, Philadelphia, Pennsylvania   19141

NANCY LOHMANN (27), School of Social Work, West Virginia University, Morgantown, West Virginia   26506

HELENA ZNANIECKA LOPATA (93), Center for the Comparative Study of Social Roles, and Department of Sociology, Loyola University of Chicago, Chicago, Illinois   60626

ANDREW OSTROW (41), School of Physical Education, West Virginia University, Morgantown, West Virginia   26506

GRAHAM D. ROWLES (153), Department of Geology and Geography, West Virginia University, Morgantown, West Virginia   26506

GAYLE B. THOMPSON (133), Division of Retirement and Survivors Studies, Office of Research and Statistics, Social Security Administration, Washington, D.C.   20009

SHELDON S. TOBIN (195), The School of Social Service Administration, The University of Chicago, Chicago, Illinois   60637

LILLIAN E. TROLL (75), Department of Psychology, Rutgers University, New Brunswick, New Jersey   08903

Preface

The contributors to this volume, the proceedings of the First West Virginia University Gerontology Conference, represent a range of disciplines from clinical psychology to geography, from physical education to economics. This breadth is a natural outcome of the interdisciplinary nature of gerontology; it is also a reminder that the transitions of aging can be made by a healthy mind in a healthy body; that aging, like all developmental processes, is a social phenomenon as well as a biological phenomenon; that physical health can be made better, and so can the health of the social, spatial, and economic environment in which we grow older.

This conference has given particular attention to two populations often described as special—the rural aged and aging women. The rural aged are, of course, to be the focus of research carried out at the West Virginia University Gerontology Center; they are also a population insufficiently studied by gerontologists. Above and beyond the immediate mission of our center, however, and in addition to the scientific common sense which would suggest the study of an understudied population, we suggest that the rural aged may have lessons to teach us about healthy aging in communities where the extended family remains a strong bond and age grading has not disrupted the developmental ties of the family life cycle.

The attention to women has a very different explanation. Statistically, women *are* the aging population, outliving men and outnumbering them increasingly with each advancing decade of life. Yet the transitions characteristic of the later life of women have not received scientific attention proportionate to women's statistical domination of the aging population, although there have been recent efforts to correct past oversights: Special programs and task forces have been devoted to the special problems of aging women. It is our contention, however, that the aging woman's problems are not "special" but in fact are the normative problems of later life; it is in this spirit that we have addressed such topics as widowhood and the economic problems of women in later life.

This volume opens with a chapter on adaptive dimensions of adult cognition; and the process of adaptation—physical, intellectual, interpersonal, environmental—is a recurrent theme throughout the book. Underlying the theme of adaptation is the assumption that the individual is more than the sum of the environmental influences on development: Active adaptation characterizes individual development throughout the life span and through all the transitions of aging. Not all the news is good news, of course; this volume is not a paean to successful aging, for not all aging is successful. Yet even those authors who address problem areas do so with the expectation that things can be changed for the better, and that the first step to change is understanding.

This book is dedicated to the memory of Dr. Louise Burr Gerrard, who believed, as we and our contributors do, that the transitions of aging are good and can be made better. She served the state of West Virginia for 10 years as the executive director of the Commission of Aging, and in that position she greatly expanded the quantity and quality of services available to older West Virginians. For us and others in the gerontological community, she served as an example of scholarship in action. With her death, we have lost a colleague and a friend.

Acknowledgments

The first West Virginia University Gerontology Conference has had the support of many members of the university community. As always, the lion's share of our financial support was provided by our favorite lion, Ray Koppelman, Vice President for Energy Studies, Graduate Programs, and Research; additional support came from our colleagues, Anita Harbert, Director of the West Virginia University Gerontology Center, and Ralph Nelson, Acting Dean of the School of Social Work. Special thanks are due to our husbands for their countless efforts behind the scenes. The graduate student hosts from the Department of Psychology, Laura Carstensen, Jeanne Thomas, and Dean Rodeheaver, carried on the tradition of hospitality initiated at the Life-Span Developmental Psychology Conferences; we owe many thanks to them for their remarkable success at making the difficult look easy.

PART I

PERSONAL TRANSITIONS OF AGING

Chapter **1**

Adaptive Dimensions of
Adult Cognition[1]

GISELA LABOUVIE–VIEF

A cursory familiarity with the vast literature on adult cognition (for recent reviews, see Botwinick, 1978; Horn, 1970; Labouvie-Vief & Chandler, 1978) can create a degree of cognitive conflict for those who are interested in defining adaptive characteristics of adult and later-life intellectual changes. On the surface, the case for regression and decrement as a main defining element of cognitive aging appears so firmly established that to present an alternative may be considered a hopeful but blind denial of an inevitable deteriorative course of later-life development. And yet, a conflict seems to exist in the minds of many recent writers. Perhaps it may best be explained with the aid of a metaphor, taken from a file by François Truffault. The film's name is "The Wild Child," and its theme is the real-life story of a boy, the wild child of Aveyron, who had grown up wild in the forests of southern France and was eventually captured there. The boy was held in a prison cell until an eminent scientist from the Institute for the Deaf and Mute in Paris sent for him. The boy's caretaker accompanied him to Paris, and upon their arrival they were both led to the scientist's office. They were sitting there with the scientist and his assistant, when, by accident, the office door suddenly slammed shut with a loud bang. The scientist

[1] Preparation of this chapter was supported by Research Career Development Award, NIA Grant 5 KO 4 AG00018-02.

TRANSITIONS OF AGING

cried out excitedly "Did you see this?": To reaffirm his observation he went to the door, opened it, and again slammed it. The boy showed absolutely no reaction to the loud noise. Amazed by this absence of reaction, the scientist said to his assistant: "Write down: Is insensitive to noises in his environment." Upon which the caretaker interjected: "But Sir, I've seen him turn around if somebody only cracked a nut behind him!" The scientist reflected on this for a moment, then told the assistant, "Write down: Does not react to significant sounds, but may react to more insignificant ones."

This chapter argues that the ambiguity of interpretation suggested by this episode carries more than metaphorical value, and that our notions of cognitive regression in later life are partly due to the fact that researchers in adulthood and aging have tended, figuratively speaking, to listen to the sounds of slamming doors rather than cracking nuts. Rather than judging intellectual competence by a generalized standard of adaptation, and notions of growth and regression as departures from either side of this apogee, I propose that interpretations of increments and decrements are inherently relative. Whereas models of aging and models of development have tended to become juxtaposed, a more valid and heuristic view may be one in which processes of growth and regression are interwoven at all points of the life span. Normative aging, in this view, can be conceptualized as a mere logical extension of earlier developmental processes. Thus it takes on the status of another stage that follows in a logical and progressive fashion the earlier stages of the life course, and that brings unique adaptive integrations.

The chapter is organized into three sections. The first section gives a brief overview of some of the interpretive tensions that have arisen in the field of psychogerontology as a result of the juxtaposition of notions of growth and aging. The second and main section proposes an outline of a life-span model that integrates these dualistic tensions. The third section points out several avenues of research that are integrated within this model.

Dualistic Tensions in Models of Cognitive Aging

The literature on developmental processes in cognitive and mnemonic functioning throughout the life span has presented a confusing and controversial picture, and a number of recent reviews (Baltes & Labouvie, 1973; Botwinick, 1973, 1977; Craik, 1977; Horn, 1976; Labouvie-Vief, 1977) have pointed out several divergent potential conclusions. The attempt to understand the theoretical significance of apparent decrements throughout the adult life span in the individual's ability to effectively and efficiently utilize and organize information has been the core of these various writings. Current interpretations of this attempt have polarized around two sources of possible variance of such deficits. Decrement has been attributed by some to a regressive restriction of the efficiency of biophysical brain structures, referred to as "fluid" or "mechanistic." This interpretation has been challenged by the view that such deficits are only apparent and reflect differential age-related familiarity with certain knowledge structures from which assessment tasks are derived.

The argument over which portion of age-related variance in memory and cognition to attribute to a deficit in "knowledge," and which to one in "mechanistic" processes, has been clouded by the fact that adult cognitive development has not been as yet sufficiently guided by a set of developmental principles important to adulthood change. Paraphrasing Wohlwill (1973), the research tradition still prevalent in this area is one of experimental gerontology rather than life-span analysis, and this heritage has shaped our current view of how to assess the competencies of adults.

The still young discipline of geropsychology was launched from a variety of theoretical orientations not uniquely developmental in focus: anthropometric and psychometric assessments, laboratory studies of decision making and reaction time, learning and memory, problem solving and complex cognitive operations, as well as much evidence relating to changes accompanying senility and imminent death (see Riegel, 1977). The conglomeration of these orientations, with their focus on specific tasks and explanatory hypotheses, led to an early view of the aging of certain cognitive and mnemonic functions as the result of inner biological changes that were seen as manifestations of primary, inherent, universal, and irreversible biological concomitants of aging.

Yet ever since the first life-span studies of intellectual development (see Jones, 1959; Riegel, 1977 for review), it was apparent that this integration offered only a partial solution. In research on aging, both decrement and stability were the rule: Whereas fluid-type abilities showed relatively robust decrement functions, another group of abilities appeared to show profound correlations with sociocultural variables such as socioeconomic status, level of education, and cohort membership (see Baltes & Labouvie, 1973; Labouvie-Vief & Chandler, 1978; Schaie & Labouvie-Vief, 1974).

Whereas this body of evidence has presented a rather stable picture, interpretations of it have tended to vary over the years. The most widely accepted interpretation has been of the type suggested by Cattell(1963) and by Horn (1970, 1978) in the model of fluid and crystallized intelligence. This model proposed two distinct kinds of intelligence, fluid and crystallized, each associated with somewhat distinct sources of causation (i.e., biophysical in the former case, and social–structural in the latter). From the dualistic action of these two sources, the disparate life-course development of fluid and crystallized abilities was seen to arise:

> At first (fluid intelligence) and (crystallized intelligence) are indistinguishable. . . ; The accumulation of CNS injuries is masked by rapid (neurological) development in childhood, but in adulthood the effects become more obvious. Fluid intelligence, based upon this, thus shows a decline as soon as the development of CNS structures is exceeded by the rate of CNS breakdown. Experience and learning accumulate throughout development. The influence of these is felt in the development of crystallized intelligence, which increases throughout adulthood. It, too, will decline after the rate of loss of structure supporting intelligent behavior exceeds the rate of acquisition of new aids to compensate for limited anlage functions [Horn, 1970, p.466].

Many recent writers, however, have doubted the wisdom of postulating such a one-to-one correspondence between certain types of tasks and distinct causal factors. Many fluid tasks of abstract reasoning, for example, are profoundly influenced by sociostructural variables (see Buck–Morss, 1975; Labouvie-Vief & Chandler, 1978). It is true that purported age differences often result from a mixture, in a typical cross-sectional study, of subjects of vastly different experimental histories, but it is similarly evident that failures to demonstrate high-level cognitive performance are often quite readily remediated if the proper specialized training or motivational conditions are provided (see Labouvie-Vief, 1977 for review). As a result, a second major view, a distinction between *competence* and *performance*, has tended to influence research. This view argues that deficits are not necessarily a part of aging, but are often the result of cohort-related differences in education, and age-graded systems that discourage competence in the older adult.

The writer identified with this second interpretation for several years. As elaborated elsewhere (Baltes & Labouvie, 1973; Baltes, Reese, & Lippsitt, 1980; Baltes & Schaie, 1976; Labouvie-Vief, 1977; Labouvie-Vief & Chandler, 1978), the competence–performance posture, with its emphasis on plasticity and modifiability, has been able to integrate a considerable body of evidence. It has also suggested a more optimistic picture, as research aimed at providing proper supports for intellectual competence has usually shown rapid, often generalizable, and sometimes stable performance improvements.

Still, this second interpretation has not been completely satisfactory; it has provided a relaxed variant rather than a qualitative transformation of models of the first type. It has retained an implicit and invidious assumption—namely, that the standards of competence used to assess purported deficits were valid in the first place, and that to train elderly people on tasks derived from these standards helped to establish a point of wider than academic interest.

The present writer was forced by research participants themselves into an altogether different approach, and a few anecdotal observations are in order because of a powerful interaction between researcher and participants. Whereas my research approach appeared to make good academic sense, it produced a variety of disturbing reactions in many of my elderly subjects. Although they felt the approach was valid in *spirit*, they thought it was wrong in *strategy*; and they voiced this opinion in a variety of equally forceful ways. Many lost interest and dropped out of research; others felt upset and misused; the more assertive and opinionated ones told me that my battery of tasks was altogether unrelated to what they felt should define intelligent behavior. "I know what you *want* me to do in this problem," one subject said recently, "but it just isn't true!"

What was truly astounding about this observation was that is was practically undocumented in the literature. I set out, therefore, to reread several key studies between the lines. And, indeed, in one I learned that older people had simply refused to learn a task that required the pairing of numbers and nonsense syllables and forced the researchers (Hulicka & Grossman, 1967) to redesign their task to deal with more meaningful material. I was reminded of an episode when, as an undergraduate, I had lacked the courage to refuse the stressful task of learning nonsense syllables presented on a memory drum and it appeared that these older adults had intelligently refused to do what many college students will let themselves be subjected to. And similarly, it appeared that my "own" elderly subjects had demonstrated a kind of intelligent pragmatism in their reaction to the tasks they were asked to do.

At this point, a third general hypothesis started to take shape. Namely, whether biological or sociocultural, our available views of aging still talked about regressive change. Might it not be possible that part of what we called regression reflects a failure to account for the specific modes in which knowledge is reorganized and represented in adulthood? It is significant to emphasize in this context, that most current measures of intellectual performance have been validated against criteria of academic success of young people in educational settings. Demming and Pressey (1957) have voiced the resulting interpretive ambiguity:

> Most investigations of adult traits appear to involve this problem. For instance, the July 1956 issue of the *Journal of Gerontology* contains two excellent reports indicating decrease in problem solving in older years, as shown by an alphabet maze and a puzzle board. But should not problems and matter usual in adult life, rather than in childhood and school, be employed in such investigations? Might some of these adults have then be found decidedly competent in dealing

with problems in their world and of concern to them? Wechsler seems to have
gone even further when he urged the probability that not only human abilities
change with age, but that the significances of the abilities themselves are altered
at different ages . . . and with different levels of functions at the same
level. . . . It would seem that we ought to have special tests of intelligence for
older individuals just as we now have for young children [p. 147].

Intellectual Transitions in Later Life

It is possible, then, that adulthood brings new and adaptive forms of
cognitive change, and that many demonstrations of deficit must be seen as
a result of our failure thus far to point out such adult-specific change
dimensions. This notion that regressive changes in adulthood are only apparent and a conceptual artifact resulting from misapplied standards of
maturity is, on the surface, and enticing proposition. At a deeper conceptual level, it faces a set of awesome tasks. First, it must provide a link with
current notions of developmental processes in earlier life, showing how
adult intellectual capacities emerge from earlier ones through continuous
qualitative transformations. Second, it must provide a theoretical rationale
for the apparent deficits in cognitive performance in later life.

Both of these problems appear forbidding. Yet, they are so only from
the viewpoint of traditional developmental models that have (a) seen
developmental change as cumulative; (b) explicated standards of developmental maturity through models of formal logic; and (c) defined adaptation at the level of the individual. In contrast, such cumulative, individual-
level models are inherently limited in life-span analysis. A developmental
perspective on adulthood and aging demands a threefold reformulation of
the assumptions inherent in most models. First, developmental change may
not be cumulative in the sense usually understood, but it may demand a
reintegrative dissolution of earlier levels. Second, mature cognition
demands an integration of "pure" logic with pragmatic constraints. And
third, intellectual adaptation cannot be measured only at the individual
level, but results from the pooled resources of a population. In this section,
we will discuss these three issue; in the next section, we will attempt to
utilize them to build the scaffold of a life-span view of aging and cognition.

LINEAR CUMULATION AND NONLINEAR INTEGRATION

Developmental psychologists are apt to think of developmental stages
as a hierarchical arrangement in which one stage builds upon another. To
argue for continued development after young adulthood may be
similar,therefore, to arguing that a pyramid can continue to grow on top

while its bottom erodes away. The pyramid metaphor is not the only possible or even the most reasonable view of developmental orders, however. Instead, it is necessary to introduce a second prototypical view of development that may be called a nonlinear one, in contradistinction to the linear view of pyramid construction.

By far the most pervasive assumption underlying the interpretation of aging changes is the linear view. It is based on a principle which, following Piaget (1971), may be called linear cumulation. This principle has been inherited from the conceptual traditions of logical positivism and elementarism; it holds that complex, abstract cognitions are built of more basic, direct, or veridical sensory and perceptual data. This linear view is best represented by the familiar symbol of a tree structure, in which communalities between lower-level nodes give rise to higher-level nodes and so on, resulting in a none-upon-none construction of concepts. This is a bottom–up view in which each layer becomes more and more removed from contact with a sensory world.

Development is pictured as a cumulative series in which lower-level responses are retained, and must be retained, as higher ones are added. Methodologically, this assumption is reflected in the use of Guttman scales in developmental research (see Wohlwill, 1973). But such cumulative orders constrain the interpretation of what is to follow some stage indicated by a hypothetical "most mature" attribute. The only patterns permitted are further additions or deletions of stages on the top (Coombs & Smith, 1973). The only way in which one can represent aging then, is by what Coombs has called a "first in–last out" sequence (or, alternatively, a "last in–first out" sequence). Thus aging is in effect pictured as a mirror image of growth and development.

Many models of intellectual changes in adulthood and aging reflect this prototype interpretation. It is sometimes captured by the phrase that aging brings a return to a childlike state. It is a view Rubinstein (1968) has traced to Ribot's law of the regression of intellectual functioning in pathology and aging:

> Regression first affects more complex organizations. In mnemonic organization, the "new" dies prior to the old, the complex before the simple. Thus in old age one will often remember events long past while forgetting recent ones. . . . Volitional control is lost first, the control of automatic action later. In this way cognitive disorganization follows the reverse order of its development through sequential stages [p. 409; author's translation].

Thus mnemonic aging has been said to reflect a failure to utilize more abstract codes and a return to more shallow modes of processing (e.g., Craik, 1977); psychometric investigations have similarly claimed that aging brings a regression of abstract functions (e.g., Horn, 1978); and extensions of Piaget's theory also have claimed that aging may bring a disintegration of abstract, formal-logical thinking (e.g., Hooper, Fitzgerald, & Papalia, 1971).

This "first in-last out" concept of regression raises several important objections. Not only does it fail to account for the common-sense fact that older adults are profoundly different from young children, but more importantly, it is at variance with what we know are the most important and pervasive aging changes. Virtually all of the evidence available indicates that the earliest and most dramatic losses throughout the adult life span occur in sensory and psychomotor functioning. In fact, many of these losses appear to start as early as adolescence, when the individual has barely mastered complex cognitive skills (for review, see Botwinick, 1978; Horn, 1978).

An alternative view of the sequencing of skills in development might be indicated by the following example taken from a study by Piaget in which children, aged 5 and 12, and adults were given a perceptual line-estimation task such as two lines displaced by an angle (see Figure 1.1a). In this task, the youngest group was the most accurate, although accuracy of estimation *de*creased as the subjects' age *in*creased. How does one account for such

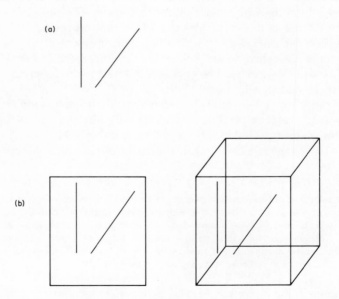

Figure 1.1. (a) Line estimation task used by Piaget. (From Piaget, 1972.) (b) Different interpretations of the line lengths result from two- and three-dimensional frames.

results? On the one hand, there is a negative correlation between age and response accuracy. Unless one refers to other criteria, one would have to conclude that this is an example of regression. On the other hand, Piaget argues that this example reflects a case of *progression*. In particular, it results from a developmental restructuring of visual space: The mature adult possesses a projective concept of visual space. As a result, the task completely changes its qualitative nature. The child perceives a two-dimensional array, the adult a projection of three-dimensional array in two dimensions. And note now that the adult's gain in maturity introduces a degree of ambiguity, as the line lengths are completely undetermined unless the particular two-dimensional array in which they are to be located is specified (see Figure 1.1b). In other words, we are dealing here with a disordinal relationship between developmental level and response accuracy.

The view suggested by this example is in contrast with the usual view of cumulative development. It still assumes that one stage builds upon the preceding one. But there is a significant difference: Progression entails both a gain and a loss. A gain, because it involves a hierarchical progression, and a loss because it may imply a reintegrative dissolution of lower levels. Thus efficiency at lower levels may be given up in favor of efficiency at a next higher level (for a more detailed explication of such nonlinear structures, see Labouvie-Vief & Schell, in press). In this way, development may take on a "first in–first out" structure (Coombs & Smith, 1973).

The linear view of development is an idealistic one, visualizing a perfected, mature endstate. The nonlinear view does not argue for perfection. It is a trade-off view of development—in order to gain a new integration, one must give up an earlier one. And it follows from this view, that if we want to understand adulthood and aging we need to ask, not "What is the universally adaptive value of the intellectual skills elaborated in adolescence?" but rather "What, if any, are the limits or failures of these skills from the perspective of adult adaptation?"

Note, also, that this nonlinear, trade-off view makes explicit another assumption contained in the linear cumulative view. If life-span development, rather than exposing a simple linear progression, is a matter of an interweaving of losses and gains, one needs an explicit criterion by which local losses can be said to be in the service of long term gains. We are dealing with a problem that no longer can be solved with the hopeful though naive foresight of the logical positivist. We see that only by positing an outcome, a developmental endstage, can development take on the simple linear structure (see Toulmin, 1971), and aging by implication, the simple downhill slide. It is through hindsight, in other words, that the "first in–last out" view of development and aging has been constructed. It is not an objective, bottom–up view at all, but the consequence of having utilized a specific endpoint: It is thus truly a top–down view, in Popper and Eccles' (1978) terminology. And to that extent, it is particularly germane to reexamine the standards of intellectual competence that have directed current notions of adulthood cognitive change.

A CRITIQUE OF "PURE" LOGIC

What are these standards of cognitive maturity? In general, in the era of logical positivism of the early twentieth century, psychologists emphasized the criteria of formal logic. Piaget (1972), in particular, stressed the adaptive value of formal logic in both individual and scientific development. In his view, adolescence brings a movement from the concrete to the hypothetical, a move that opens a world of possibility rather than concrete reality to the youth. The result is a high degree of flexibility; rather than being embedded in their own concrete viewpoint, youth can approach any subject matter from multiple perspectives. New possibilities and viewpoints alien to their background can be comprehended; problems generated by permutation can be examined in a purely abstract, formal way for logical cohesiveness, while personal likes and dislikes, and even pragmatic utility do not distract their judgments.

Now it is possible that this ability to engage in abstraction, out of the context of pragmatic considerations, is particularly adaptive in youth who are involved in exercising these newly acquired skills, and in carving out a sense of personal and professional identity (Erikson, 1968). Here the ability to maintain flexibility and to avoid foreclosure through a premature channeling of energies and interests may be highly adaptive. Youth is a time of examining options and alternative viewpoints, and in a complex society this moratorium (Erikson, 1968) may be a precondition for the formation of later mature commitments.

While the theme of youth is flexibility, the hallmark of adulthood is commitment and responsibility. Careers must be started, intimacy bonds formed, children raised. In short, in a world of a multitude of logical possibilities, *one* course of action must be adopted. This conscious commitment to one pathway and the deliberate disregard of other logical choices may mark the onset of adult cognitive maturity (Perry, 1970; Riegel, 1973). At the same time, commitment may bring a return to pragmatic necessities. Playful exercise of cognitive schemes, endless generation of "ifs" and "whens," no longer may be adaptive; the task becomes instead an attempt to best utilize one's knowledge toward the management of concrete life situations. Cognition becomes constrained by necessities: strategic control of one's life, managing time, conserving energy (Birren, 1969; Schaie, 1977). This phase may bring a relinquishment of the earlier emphasis on resolving contradictions: Contradiction must be accepted as part of adult life (Clayton, 1975), which accepts and even thrives on imperfection, compromise, and the necessity to fumble.

If the interpretation suggested here is correct, then the "pure" logic of adolescence or youth might represent a budding but not yet equilibrated mode of thinking, a preparatory mode of adult thought. And indeed this is just what Piaget (1967) suggests:

> With the advent of formal intelligence, thinking takes wings and it is not surprising that at first this unexpected power is both used and abused . . . each new mental ability starts off by incorporating the world in a process of egocentric assimilation. Adolescent egocentricity is manifested by a belief in the omnipotence of reflection, as though the world should submit itself to idealistic schemes rather than to systems of reality [pp. 63–64].

And, Piaget proposes further, it is only after the youth has negotiated a realistic fit between logical schemes and concrete limitations of everyday life that we can talk of mature cognitive adaptation:

> True adaptation to society comes automatically when the adolescent reformer attempts to put his ideas to work. Just as experience reconciles formal thought with the reality of things, so does effective and enduring work, undertaken in concrete and well-defined situations, cure dreams [pp. 68–69].

The pure logic of youth may, of course, serve a local or temporary adaptive value, and therefore its importance should not be denigrated. It permits a circulatory exercise of operatory schemes that are to be put to pragmatic use later on. It thus helps guarantee the flexibility demanded of mature adult adaptation. This is our first proposed conclusion: Adulthood brings structural change, not just in the perfection of logic, but in its reintegration with pragmatic necessities.

Erikson's (1978) view is particularly important in this context, as it suggests that the resulting integration is of just the sort discussed by Piaget: namely a realization that logic is merely a *necessary* condition and becomes a *sufficient* element of adult life only if subordinated to a hierarchically higher goal—generative social-system maintenance. It is important, then, to distinguish between logic as a *goal* and logic as a *tool* (see also Leontiev, 1977). As a tool, logic is embedded in a social context with all the constraints society brings, and it is the major task of adulthood to achieve this cognitive subordination of logic to social-system needs. Indeed, it is exactly because of this that Erikson (1978) has emphasized the adult concerns with commitment, generativity, and social responsibility.

INDIVIDUAL VERSUS POPULATION-LEVEL ANALYSIS

The limits of "pure" logic imply that logic is itself an open system (i.e., one that becomes a component of a superordinate system within which it is validated; see Labouvie-Vief, 1980). We have argued that adulthood may bring a subordination of logic *qua* logic to the needs of the social system and indeed, this argument makes good adaptive sense. As Piaget (1971) argues, the individual, through his constructions, contributes toward adaptation in an important sense; yet ultimately, the individual is also embedded in a social system that serves to select those constructions that are to be incorporated into the adaptive repertoire of the individual. In Piaget's (1971) words:

> . . . the social group plays the same role that the population does in genetics and consequently in instinct. In this sense, society is the supreme unit, and the individual can only achieve his inventions and intellectual constructions insofar as he is the seat of collective interactions that are naturally dependent, in level and value, on society as a whole [p. 368].

Now just as it is possible to view the adaptive capacities of the individual organism from the perspective of their differentiation and hierarchic integration so we may view the social system itself as a highly differentiated organism or collective, which channels individuals into diverse specialized roles. And indeed, as Piaget has repeatedly argued, it is at this "transindividual" level that criteria of adaptive competence are usually located.

This view of the social system as a more integrative, stable level of analysis immediately suggests an important principle in the formulation of dimensions of life-span change. This principle relies on a distinction between dimensions of development as a progressive series of more and more stable intergrations on the one hand, and the individual's specialized and possibly temporary role in this social system on the other. Once adaptation is defined at the population or social-system level rather than at the individual level, it is no longer necessary to insist on a single set of standards by which maturity is to be gauged. Rather, it becomes altogether consistent with a life-span view of adaptive change, to allow for a degree of slippage or variability at the individual level. Indeed, such variation may be a prerequisite for the flexible and differentiated functioning of the population as a whole.

This argument may be clarified by discussing briefly how it bears on the interpretation of purported deficits in formal logical ability. It has long been a bothersome observation to developmental psychologists and cognitive anthropologists that tasks of formal reasoning display systematic variability as a function of social class, educational level, ethnicity, cultural background, and professional specialization (for review, see Buck-Morss, 1975). Some have opted for a hierarchical interpretation of this finding (e.g., Luria, 1976; Niemark, 1975) and thus subsumed both sociocultural and age-correlated variance within *one* hierarchy. Others, conversely, have argued that the resulting implications of lower and higher levels of cognitive maturity are less compelling if one allows for *heterarchical* models (e.g., Buck-Morss, 1975; Cole & Scribner, 1974), which relate particular modes of thought to the specialized niche the individual occupies in society.

Piaget (1972) has been quite aware of the theoretical importance of this problem of specialization and conceded that his model of adulthood may represent a somewhat specialized case in need of further elaboration and differentiation. As Greenfield (1976) has phrased it:

> The Western scientist is in theory no longer the only possibility. Piaget leaves it as an open question whether this developmental diversification means that formal operation thinking, the highest stage in his developmental theory, will appear in different domains for different people, according to occupational role (e.g., law students will reason at the formal level about juridicial but not physical concepts) or 'whether there will appear new and special structures that still remain to be discovered and studied' (p.11). The latter alternative supports, by extension, a position of extreme cultural relativism, something very new in Piagetian theory. Piaget's question concerning the possibility of cognitive structures still to be discovered poses an important challenge for comparative study both within and between cultures [p. 331].

By implication, developmental researchers would have to draw a careful distinction between those age-related differences that are actually due to the different educational and professional specialization of different cohorts and a more pervasive change dimension that transcends those profession-related differences. The argument for cohort specialization has, of course, been most forcefully led by Schaie and his associates (e.g., Baltes & Schaie, 1976; Schaie & Gribbin, 1975; Schaie & Labouvie-Vief, 1974). Yet such factors do not preclude attention to broader developmental dimensions of cognitive change.

The combined importance of dimensions of specialization and developmental change was underscored in a recent study (Sabatini & Labouvie-Vief, 1979) in which scientists and teachers, approximately matched in terms of years of education, were assessed with a battery of Piagetian tasks. Here, training in science was found to have an overriding effect; no clear age effect whatever was obtained. Yet at the same time, there was evidence that the older subjects found the problems simplistically dimensionalized, and reported that they experienced interference of their more complex real-world knowledge. And indeed, when the tasks were redesigned to allow for a free expression of the way in which subjects might naturally dimensionalize the problems, a strong age effect emerged: Older subjects produced more complex structures (as determined by Greenfield & Schneider's [1977] tree structure scoring procedure) than younger ones. Specifically, the younger adults produced more asymmetries and more empty nodes than older ones, and although they produced more categories than the retirees, those of the retirees were *more* hierarchically interrelated.

Implications and Reinterpretations

Much of the foregoing has established the point that many of the criteria of cognitive competence may be too specialized to permit a fair evaluation of potential progressions in cognitive functioning in middle and later adulthood. Thus a "loss" in formal logical ability may not represent a disintegration, but a move toward a more stable integration in which the pragmatic constraints of social life create pressures towards pragmatic syntheses—those in which experience is put in the service of systems that reach wider and wider spatiotemporal extension. Also we have argued that in forming such further superordinations a trade-off may be called for. In this way, demonstrated losses in certain cognitive modes may not be at all contradictory to the assertion that new developmental integrations continue to be formed. Rather, the critical point to be examined is whether or not such losses are made up, at some more stable level of analysis, by new cognitive modes. In this section of the chapter, we will point out three general areas of such continued change. In so doing, the trade-off nature of such a nonlinear developmental view will be emphasized.

THE SOCIAL INTEGRATION OF COGNITION

The view expressed here is, of course, one that rejects the bifurcation so often found in models of development: that between informal, social thinking and formal logical thinking. Indeed, one of the structural transitions of adulthood should be to achieve a new integration in which logic, initially decontextualized, is reembedded in its social context. As Piaget (1967) put it, "reason which expresses the highest form of equilibrium reunites intelligence and affectivity."

Only a few studies have yet addressed this hypothesized structural feature. One is Perry's (1968) analysis of the conflicts and their eventual resolution experienced by college students as they move from the relatively closed, sheltered "logic"of their home environment to the pluralistic environment of a college community. Here, conflicts are created exactly by that feature of logic which Piaget calls the egocentricity of youth—a belief in the omnipotence of reflection. And this feature also creates, according to Perry, specific social and cognitive vulnerabilities: a search for absolute values, for authoritative statements, for ideological certainty. College life, however, may induce a slow erosion of this absolutism of adolescent logic:

> Reason reveals relations within any given context; it can also compare one context with another on the basis of metacontexts established for this purpose. But there is a limit. In the end, reasons itself remains reflexively relativistic, a property which turns reason back upon reason's own findings. In even its farthest reaches then reason will leave the thinker with several legitimate contexts and no way of choosing among them—no way at least that he can justify through reason alone. If he is still to honor reason he must now also transcend it; he must affirm his own position from within himself in full awareness that reason can never completely justify him or assure him [pp. 135–136].

Thus, for Perry, youth will eventually accept the inherent relativity of multiple intellectual perspectives. At the same time this cognitive realization signals a new integration: One needs to discontinue one's search for logical certainty and to accept the pragmatic constraints of adulthood. One needs to give up absolutism and idealism for commitment and specialization.

More recently, Gilligan and Murphy (1980) have applied a similar analysis to the domain of moral development. In this research area, maturity has been defined primarily by formal universalistic criteria that are claimed to reflect universal "justice structures" (Kohlberg, 1976)—and from this perspective, adult concerns with social convention have signaled a possible regression of moral development (e.g., Papalia & Bielby, 1974).

Now the universalistic, idealistic thinking about moral issues is, of course, exactly what one would expect in youth who are apt to believe in the "omnipotence of reflection." From this perspective, the occasional observation that adulthood may bring a return to a more conventional level of morality (see Gilligan & Murphy, 1980) is not bothersome, either. Yet we would predict profound structural differences between the conventionality of the concrete operational child and that of the mature adult—that of the adult should be based not on an assertion of authority *qua* authority but on an understanding of the genuine complex constraints of the social system.

This is just the interpretation advanced in Gilligan and Murphy's (1979) study. These authors concluded:

> In our attempt to reconnect a cognitive stage theory of development with data on late adolescent and adult thinking about real problems of moral conflict and choice, we found it necessary to posit a different notion of maturity to account

for the transformation in thinking that we observed. These transformations arise
out of recognition of the paradoxical interdependence of self and society, which
overrides the false simplicty of formal reason and replaces it with a more encompassing form of judgment [p. 33].

This transformation is particularly well demonstrated by the response
of one subject who recalls, after about 7 years, his earlier response to the
moral dilemma of whether Heinz, a husband, should steal a drug to save
his dying wife:

This is a very crisp little dilemma and you can latch onto that principle pretty
fast, and in that situation you can say that life is more important than money.
But then, when you reflect back on how you really act in your own life, you
don't use that principle, or I haven't yet used that principle to operate on. And
none of the people who answer the dilemma that way use that principle to
operate on because they were blowing $7,000 a year for their education at Har-
vard instead of giving it the Children's Fund to give porridge to the kids in
Botswana, and to that extent, answering the dilemma with that principle is not
hypocritical, it's just that *you don't recognize it.* I hadn't recognized it at the
time, and I am sure they didn't recognize it either [p. 24].

We may propose, then, two modes of cognition in adulthood that
define the endpoints of a developmental continuum. At one end, we see an
individualized, relatively egocentric, formal–logical mode characteristic of
youth. It is a mode which may be given to idealization and to a separation
of thinking and affect (Neisser, 1976). At the other end, we may discern an
awareness of the complexity of social-system embeddedness that creates
new pressures towards syntheses. This hypothetical polarity is particularly
well demonstrated in Birren's (1969) analysis of the decision making of successful career men and women of different ages. First, problems were defined differently by the two age groups. The younger ones defined them
from the narrow individualistic (but, of course, stage-appropriate) perspective of their own career advancement. Thus they tended to seize upon an
opportunity to demonstrate their competence to do a job single-handedly
at the cost of intellectual and work overload (and, no doubt, occasional
blunders). The older ones, in contrast, defined the problem as one of max-
imizing benefits and minimizing risks for the system within which they
operated. They had come to realize and admit their individual restriction in
that endeavor, and instead relied on the intercoordination of experts and
advisors whose pooled resources might guarantee more stable payoffs.

It is important, at this juncture, to stress that each of those modes may
have its own adaptive value. The younger adult, with his or her tendency
to demonstrate independence, may be able to develop highly specialized,
often novel skills. The older adults, conversely, may feel overwhelmed by
the demands of specialization; they may also according to Birren, have

developed a sharp awareness of their own limitations in dealing with information overload. Yet in so doing, they also have come to view decisions as
embedded in a complex social matrix, and they have learned to utilize that
matrix to optimize decisions. The critical issue is thus not whether one or
the other mode is better in any absolute sense, but rather that effective
social action may require the collaboration of both sets of resources. Brent
(1978) has put forward this notion:

> The younger cohorts in any collective at any given time—i.e., those which most
> recently came into existence—seem to be specialized for providing the flexibility
> necessary for adapting to changes in existing environmental conditions and for
> expansion into new environmental niches, while the older cohorts appear to be
> specialized for maintaining the existing organismic collective within the en-
> vironmental niches to which they have already adapted—thus providing a se-
> cure base of operations from which the younger cohorts can venture out [p. 25].

RIGIDITY VERSUS STABILITY

The movement we have described in the foregoing section is one we
have elsewhere (Labouvie-Vief, in press) called the adult's concern with
social-system stability, and in the current population-dynamic framework
this movement can be said to represent a structural advancement over the
cognitive modes of youth. Such a concern with social-system maintenance
may, of course, bring a certain coventionalism—a conventionalism that
is sometimes captured by the notion that advanced age brings
a greater degree of "rigidity." Yet in many cases, the term *rigidity* may have
been too readily applied to behaviors that are structurally coherent and
functionally adaptive.

The argument for the potentially adaptive value of adult resistance to
change thus far has been established most forcefully in ethological studies
of intercohort regulations. In many species, for example, the younger individuals are found to be more attracted to transitory change, whereas the
older ones impose controls on the innovation of new habits. The adaptive
significance of such differential attraction to innovation is often attributed
to the fact that the exploratory curiosity of the young can be detrimental to
the troop as it may embrace adaptive and maladaptive techniques with un-
differentiated, naive enthusiasm: Thus the more "rigid" behavior of the
older animals serves to select those innovations that are more likely to be
adaptive. Rather than being "rigid," therefore, it may reflect a degree of accumulated wisdom that increases adaptive advantages for the troop. As
Kummer (1971) suggests:

> there is little doubt that conservatism, too is adaptive. The inflexible adults of
> the troop form a safety reservoir of the previous behavioral variant, which will
> survive the invention for at least ten years. If the new behavior should turn out

> to be harmful, say because of parasitic infection, they would survive. In
> spreading new behaviors, adult rigidity has the same function as low mutation
> rates in evolution [p. 129].

Significantly, such accrued wisdom is a highly valued trait in many primate species. Kummer and Kurt (1971), for example, report on the ecological and dominance relationship of Hamdryas baboons, in which the youngest and strongest males occupy more marginal positions. They are thereby excluded from reproductive participation, though they also serve to protect the troop from predators. Conversely the older members are more likely to be reproductively active; even postreproductively, however, their accumulated experience provides a privileged position in scouting for and locating food sources. Thus, even though they may experience physical decline, older individuals often serve as leaders (see also Hinde, 1974; Kummer, 1971; Rowell, 1966).

PROCESSES OF MEMORIZATION AND LANGUAGE COMPREHENSION

From the perspective of its research implications, the most specific advantage of the trade-off view proposed here may lie in its ability to predict a somewhat altered view of research in the processing and retention of units of information. Such deficits now appear to be quite pronounced at the level of fairly low-order information. But if the reasoning here is right, we must ask whether the generalizations of deficit deriving from this research continue to hold if we studied encoding processes occuring at higher levels with stimuli that have a higher degree of structure; for example, sentences or texts. If the "first in–last out" sequence holds, one would predict a failure of processing and retention mechanisms at higher levels of complexity; if the "first in–first out" sequence holds, the opposite should be true.

Research on relatively complex encoding processes in adults past college is very sketchy at present. What little evidence is available on such processes is entirely inconsistent with the notion that such processing is deficient in adulthood. Two studies, for example, dealt with the processing of sentence meaning rather than memorization of exact verbatim detail. One was a dissertation by Hurlbut (1976), and the second a study by Walsh and Baldwin (1977). Both used Bransford and Frank's (1971) paradigm, and no differences were found between young and old subjects in the integration of information across unit sentences. Yet younger (mean age 21.5) adults recalled more verbatim information than the elderly (mean age 71.9) (Hurlbut, 1976).

It is possible to speculate then that adulthood brings qualitative changes in the processing of information. Could it be, for example, that the loss of specific, low-structure detail is a trade-off one has to accept when attending to higher units of meaning? And is it possible that this process continues throughout adulthood and becomes particularly pronounced at even higher levels of encoding—for example, the level of amalgamations of propositions in text material? The Soviet researcher Istomina (1967, in Loewe, 1977, pp. 119–120) advanced such an interpretation. Her study used isolated words and integrated texts as test items. When recall was in terms of isolated words, young subjects did much better than the old; but when recall was scored for higher-order propositions and inferences, the old were more efficient. Istomina suggested on this basis that "with increasing age different aspects of memory change in different ways. While memory for immediate detail shows marked decline in later life, memory for logical relationships which are mediated by a process of active abstraction, not only fails to show any deficit, but does in fact improve [c.f. Loewe, 1977, p. 120; author's translation]." More recently, Zelinski, Gilewski, and Thompson (1979) also have reported that elderly subjects tend to focus on such higher-order propositions.

Following up on this suggestion, we started pilot research on the processing of discourse. Our materials were short stories, and the age-related differences were striking: Younger subjects produced detailed, quite faithful summaries of the story; elderly subjects produced highly general summaries. Moreover, these summaries were often in a normative form such as a moral or a metaphor.

We have since followed up this finding by breaking down text structure into a number of hierarchical levels and are finding that older adults attend to higher-order propositions, younger adults to detail. At the same time, it appears that the elderly subjects' attention to detail is *qualitatively* different from that of the younger subjects. First, they report they are uninterested in detail. Second, this lack of attention shows in their performance: When we built in foils at the level of detail (say, the story mentions a white crane lying on its side), detail recall is systematically distorted in the direction of real-world inferences (say many elderly may recall a pink crane standing on one leg).

We have started from this and similar evidence to develop a working model that we are testing in a series of studies. We believe that in the study of aging and cognition, one must look simultaneously at the integration of information at several levels. Thus one may find evidence of deficit when focusing on one level, only to find that deficit is made up at another level. We might say that it is possible, and certainly testable, to propose the following hypothesis. When we are dealing with stimuli of low structure, deficits in aging may appear pronounced. When one shifts to stimuli of higher structure, a kind of trade-off situation in which lack of detail processing is made up by meaning processing emerges. It is not too improbable to conclude that this is an altogether useful strategy for adaptation: The mature and older adult has experienced the limitations of his or her memory, and learned to attend to those codes that are less likely to be transitory, thus more permanent and stable.

This adaptive interpretation of the adult's attention to higher-order units of meaning, captured by Birren (personal communication) by the notion of an age-related "race between the bit and the chunk," receives support from several further empirical sources. First, it is known that, if recall is followed for a prolonged period of time, lower-order information tends to decay rapidly, whereas recall of meaning-preserving kernel transformations displays greater temporal stability (e.g., Bartlett, 1932; Dooley & Christiaansen, 1977). Second, a few studies also have demonstrated that the elderly may have acquired more accurate knowledge of the functioning of their mnemonic system (Lachman & Lachman, 1979; Zelinski *et al.*, 1979). Thus it is possible that they have learned selectively to attend to more informative units of meaning.

It must be emphasized that this move toward stability, if supported by further research, involves both a gain and a loss. On the one hand, the lack of attention to lower-order, transitory units of meaning may imply that adult learning becomes relatively closed to new information intake. On the other hand, the adult may utilize structures already highly developed and specialized toward a continued structural recombination and stable reduction of experience—a process that may capture the wisdom of the older organism (Seitelberger, 1978). Thus different periods of the life span will display specialized but different modes of processing as captured in this statement by Schopenhauer:

> Life could be compared to an embroidery of which we see the right side during the first half of life, but the back in the latter half. This back side is less scintillating but more instructive: it reveals the interpatterning of the threads [p. 215; author's translation].

Conclusions and Caveats

The present chapter has argued that many of the purported cognitive deficits of adulthood and later life must be reevaluated within the framework of a more general developmental model. In this model, adulthood cognitive structures are a direct and logical extention of those youth-centered ones that currently are emphasized predominantly in both theory and research on developmental processes. In an era of biophysical reductionism of the past, changes in physiological adaptability have been equated by fiat with a general deficit in adaptability. Yet, as I have argued here, adaptability can be examined from many levels of analysis and by many standards; and by the more population-dynamic standards here proposed, we can suggest that aging may serve to increase adaptability of the social collective as a whole, hence form a progressive stage of a general developmental program.

To some readers, the view proposed here may appear overly optimistic. Thus, several caveats are in order. A first objection that might be raised is that it is absurd to claim, given the preponderance of biophysiological losses to the aging individual, that the older person realizes some ultimate "best" end stage of development. We must be careful, however, to delimit the sense in which one is to call postmaturational changes progessive. Here, they are not called progressive in the sense that they imply a cumulative, additive integration of all earlier developmental achievements (as suggested in the use of Guttman scales). Rather, they are called progressive in the sense that the individual moves, in a fashion that follows the logical sequence of, for example, Piaget's theory, to integrations and equilibria that are of a higher order of spatiotemporal extension and permanence. It is important to distinguish, therefore, between a logical progression and the notion of adaptability. And it is exactly a failure to enforce this distinction that has created our current inability to deal with adulthood, and especially aging, in a developmental model.

In fact, it is part of the argument developed here that adaptation by its very nature is a trade-off process: Specialized adaptation to one context implies a failure to be adapted to another. And, as Piaget has argued in the context of child development, each stage can be understood only if this trade-off is fully accepted. Thus it is not sufficient, according to Piaget, to view the child as a quantitatively diminished adult; children develop highly adapted structures to process information within their range of spatiotemporal extension. Similarly, although adults in some contexts will be deficient if compared to youth, in other contexts they will display new structures that are uniquely adapted to the tasks of adulthood.

Further, due to the value of this trade-off, I am not claiming that youth is to be understood merely as a way station to adulthood. The specialized adaptations of youth may be particularly significant in accommodations to new environmental change. Yet the specialized adaptations of adulthood and aging may be to create a counterforce, a pressure to integrate change with behavioral components that have proven their adaptive value over many generations.

Adaptability and cognition, from this perspective, are utimately judged at a social level, the level of the pooled resources of the total population.

Each life stage, at best, achieves a temporary or local adaptation. Even biophysiological decrements, in this view, are not unambiguously maladaptive. Sensory and psychomotor losses may create a sensual abstraction that permits a transcendence of youthful egocentrism and a greater ease with suprapersonal issues, and investment of one's self in culture's heritage. And ultimately, they may well prepare the elderly person to face that last developmental task: dying.

References

Baltes, P.B., & Labouvie, G.V. Adult development of intellectual performance: Description, explanation, and modification. In C. Eisdorfer & M.P. Lawton (Eds.), *The psychology of adult development and aging.* Washington, D.C.: American Psychological Association, 1973.

Baltes, P.B., Reese, H.W., & Lippsitt, L.P. Life-span developmental psychology. *Annual Review of Psychology,* 1980, *31,* in press.

Baltes, P.B., & Schaie, K.W. On the plasticity of adult and gerontological intelligence: Where Horn and Donaldson fail. *American Psychologist,* 1976, *31,* 720–725.

Bartlett, F.C. *Remembering.* Cambridge, England: University Press, 1932.

Birren, J.E. Age and decision strategies. In A.T. Welford and S.E. Birren (Eds.), *Interdisciplinary topics in gerontology* (Vol. 4). Basel: S. Karger, 1969.

Botwinick, J. *Aging and behavior.* New York: Springer, 1973.

Botwinick, J. Aging and behavior (2nd ed.). New York: Springer, 1978.

Bransford, J.D., & Franks, J.J. The abstraction of linguistic ideas. *Cognitive Psychology,* 1971, *2,* 331–350.

Brent, S.B. Individual specialization, collective adaptation and rate of environmental change. *Human Development,* 1978, *2,* 21–33.

Buck-Morss, S. Socioeconomic bias in Piaget's theory and its implication for cross-culture studies. *Human Development,* 1975, *18,* 35–49.

Cattell, R.B. Theory of fluid and crystallized intelligence: A critical experiment. *Journal of Educational Psychology,* 1963, *54,* 1–22.

Clayton, V. Erikson's theory of human development as it applies in the aged: Wisdom as contradictive cognition. *Human Development,* 1975, *18,* 119–128.

Coombs, C.H., & Smith, J.E.K. Detection of structure in attitudes and developmental process. *Psychological Review,* 1973, *80,* 337–351.

Craik, F.I.M. Age differences in human memory. In J.E. Birren & K.W. Schaie (Eds.), *Handbook of the psychology of aging.* New York: Van Nostrand Reinhold, 1977.

Demming, J.A., & Pressey, S.L. Test "indigenous" to the adult and older years. *Journal of Counseling Psychology,* 1957, *4,* 144–148.

Dooling, D.J., & Christiaansen, R.E. Levels of encoding and retention of prose. In G.H. Bower (Ed.), *The Psychology of learning and memory* (Vol. 11). New York: Academic Press, 1977.

Erikson, E.H. *Identity, youth, and crisis.* New York: W.W. Norton, 1968.

Erikson, E.H. *Adulthood.* New York: W.W. Norton, 1978.

Gilligan, C., & Murphy, J.M. Development from adolescence to adulthood: The philosopher and the dilemma of fact. In D. Kuhn (Ed.), *Intellectual development beyond childhood.* San Francisco: Jossey–Bass, in press.

Greenfield, P.M. Cross-cultural research and Piagetian theory: Paradox and progress. In K.F. Riegel & J.A. Meacham (Eds.), *The developing individual in a changing world.* (Vol. 1), *Historical and cultural issues.* Chicago: Aldine, 1976.

Greenfield, P.M., & Schneider, L. Building a tree structure: The development of hierarchical complexity and interrupted strategies in children's construction activity. *Developmental Psychology,* 1977, *13,* 299–313.

Hinde, R.A. *Biological bases of human social behavior.* New York: McGraw–Hill, 1974.

Hooper, F., Fitzgerald, J., & Papalia, D. Piagetian theory and the aging process: Extensions and speculations. *Aging and Human Development,* 1971, *2,* 3–20.

Horn, J.L. Organization of data on life-span development of human abilities. In L.R. Goulet & P.B. Baltes (Eds.), *Life-span developmental psychology.* New York: Academic Press, 1970.

Horn, J.L. Human abilities: A review of research and theory in the early 1970's. *Annual Review of psychology,* 1976, *27,* 437–485.

Hulicka, I.M., & Grossman, J.L. Age-group comparisons or use of mediators in paired-associate learning. *Journal of Gerontology,* 1967, *22,* 46–51.

Hurlbut, N.L. *Adult age differences in sentence memory.* Unpublished doctoral dissertation, University of Wisconsin, 1976.

Jones, H.E. Intelligence and problem solving. In J.E. Birren (Ed.), *Handbook of aging and the individual.* Chicago: University of Chicago Press, 1959.

Kohlberg, L. Moral stages and moralization: The cognitive–developmental approach. In T. Lickona (Ed.), *Moral development and behavior.* New York: Holt, Rinehart & Winston, 1976.

Kummer, H. *Primate societies: Group techniques of ecological adaptation.* Chicago, Illinois: Aldine Publishing Co., 1971.

Kummer, H., & Kurt, F. Social units of a free living population of Hamadryas baboons. *Folia primatology,* 1971, *1,* 4–9.

Labouvie-Vief, G. Adult cognitive development: In search of alternative interpretations. *Merrill–Palmer Quarterly,* 1977, *23,* 227–263.

Labouvie-Vief, G., & Chandler, M.J. Cognitive development and life-span developmental theory: Idealistic versus contextual perspectives. In P.B. Baltes (Ed.), *Life-span development and behavior.* New York: Academic Press, 1978.

Labouvie-Vief, G., & Schell, D. Information processing in aging: A developmental view. In B. Wolman & G. Stricker (Eds.), *Handbook of developmental psychology.* Englewood Cliffs, N J.: Prentice-Hall, in press.

Lachman, J.L., & Lachman, R. Age and the actualization of world knowledge. In L.W. Poon, J.L. Fozard, L. Cermak, D. Arenberg, & L. Thompson (Eds.), *New Directions in memory and aging: Proceedings of the George Talland Memorial Conference.* New Jersey: Lawrence Erlbaum Associates, 1979.

Leontiev, A.N. *Probleme der Entwicklung des Psychischen.* Stuttgart: Fischer, 1977.

Loewe, H. *Lernpsychologie: Einfuehrung in die Lernpsychologie des Erwachsenenalters.* Berlin: Deutscher Verlag der Wissenschaften, 1977.

Luria, A.R., *Cognitive development: Its cultural and social foundations.* Cambridge, Mass.: Harvard University Press, 1976.

Neimark, E.D. Intellectual development during adolescence. In F.D. Horowitz (Ed.), *Review of child development research.* Chicago, Illinois: University of Chicago Press, 1975.

Neisser, V. *Cognition and reality.* San Francisco: W.A. Freeman, 1976.

Papalia, D.E., & Del Vanto Bielby, D. Cognitive functioning in middle and old adults: A review of research based on Piaget's theory. *Human Development,* 1974, *17,* 424–443.

Perry, W.I. *Forms of intellectual and ethical development in the college years.* New York: Holt, Rinehart & Winston, 1968.

Piaget, J. *Six psychological studies.* Random House, New York, 1967.

Piaget, J. *Biology and knowledge.* Chicago: University of Chicago Press, 1971.

Piaget, J. Intellectual evolution from adolescence to adulthood. *Human Development,* 1972, *15,* 1–12.

Popper, C., & Eccles, J. *The self and its brain.* New York: Springer, 1978.

Riegel, K.F. Dialectic operations: The final period of cognitive development. *Human Development,* 1973, *16,* 346–370.

Riegel, K.F. History of psychological gerontology. In J.E. Birren & K.W. Schaie (Eds.), *Handbook of the psychology of aging.* New York: Van Nostrand Reinhold, 1977.

Rowell, T. Forest living baboons in Uganda. *Journal of Zoology,* 1966, *147,* 344–364.

Rubinstein, S.L. *Grundlagen der allgemeinen psychologie.* Berlin: Volkseigener Verlag Berlin, 1968.

Sabatini, P., & Labouvie-Vief, G. Age and professional specialization in formal reasoning. Paper presented at the 1979 Meeting of the Gerontological Society, Washington, D.C., November 1979.

Schaie, K.W. Toward a stage theory of adult development. *International Journal of Aging and Human Development,* 1977, *8,* 129–138.

Schaie, K.W.,& Gribbin, K. Adult development and aging. *Annual Review of Psychology,* 1975, *26,* 65–96.

Schaie, K.W.,& Labouvie-Vief, G. Generational versus ontogenetic components of change in adult cognitive behavior. A fourteen-year cross-sequential study. *Developmental Psychology,* 1974, *10,* 305–320.

Seitelberger, F. Lebensstadien des Gehirns—Strukturelle und funktionale Aspekte. In L. Rosenmayr (Ed.), *Die menschlichen lebensalter.* Munich: R. Piper & Co. Verlag, 1978.

Toulmin, S. The concept of "stages" in psychological development. In T. Mischel (Ed.), *Cognitive development and epistemology.* New York: Academic Press, 1971.

Walsh, D.A., & Baldwin, M. Age differences in integrated semantic memory. *Developmental Psychology,* 1977, *13,* 509–514.

Wohlwill, J.F. *The study of behavioral development.* New York: Academic Press, 1973.

Zelinski, E.H., Gilewski, M.J., & Thompson, L.W. Do laboratory tests relate to self-assessment of memory ability in the young and the old? In L.W. Poon, J.L. Fozard, L. Cermak, D. Arenberg, & L. Thompson (Eds.), *New directions in memory and aging: Proceedings of the George Talland Memorial Conference.* New Jersey: Lawrence Erlbaum Associates, 1979.

Chapter 2

Life Satisfaction Research in Aging: Implications for Policy Development

NANCY LOHMANN

When one examines the results of the past 40 years of academic focus on gerontology, one finds an abundance of studies reporting the relationship between the dependent variable of life satisfaction[1] (or the two related constructs of morale and adjustment) and various independent variables that include demographic differences among the aged. A newcomer to the field of gerontology could raise an "emperor's new clothes" question about the centrality of this paradigm: Why is it that life satisfaction (or morale or adjustment) is so important in gerontological research? What benefits have been realized from the past 40 years study of these concepts?

This chapter examines the utility of the gerontological focus on these three constructs as well as some of the empirical findings of the relationships between them and certain demographic variables. It also examines a few of the methodological problems that have kept the empirical findings from being of greater social utility.

Before undertaking this examination, however, preliminary comments about the relationship of the constructs of "life satisfaction," "morale," and "adjustment" to one another are in order. Social scientists typically define

---

[1] Life satisfaction has been the object of study for over 40 years. Cavan, Burgess, Havighurst and Goldhammer (1949) report three studies of "adjustment" and "happiness" that preceded their own pioneering one.

TRANSITIONS OF AGING

the constructs they examine in two ways: through the use of a nominal, or dictionary-type, definition, and through the use of an operational definition, which specifies certain procedures that are to be performed. The empirical studies reported in the gerontological literature typically use both definitional approaches to distinguish the construct being examined from other related constructs. With regard to these three constructs, such definitions often maintain that each of the constructs measures some conceptual area that is separate and unique from the area measured by the other constructs. For example, the definitions of life satisfaction often explicitly indicate that this characteristic can be distinguished from the characteristics of morale and adjustment and that there is no conceptual overlap among these three constructs. However, this author's previous work suggests that the definitions of these three constructs do indeed overlap one another. This work involved an examination of the construct validity of each of them (see Lohmann, 1977a, 1980). It was found that the nominal definitions of the three constructs were typically similar to the point of being indistinguishable. The range of definitions used for each construct was no greater than the range of definitions among each of the three constructs. In addition, the most common operational definitions of the constructs (Cavan Attitude Scale, Kutner Morale Scale, Dean Morale Scale, Philadelphia Geriatric Center Morale Scale, Life Satisfaction Index A, Life Satisfaction Index B, a global question) when applied to the same population, were found to share a common underlying construct. Thus, although there may be some aspect of the current operational definitions of these constructs which is unique to one of the three constructs, there is also a major aspect common to all three. Given this finding, the term *life satisfaction* will generally be used henceforth and will refer to the common element shared by all three constructs.

Why Examine Life Satisfaction?

What might explain the plethora of gerontological studies examining the life satisfaction of the aged? What benefits have occurred because of this examination? Has, in fact, the emperor been outfitted with new clothes? At least three explanations could be advanced as to why so much gerontological literature has focused on this dependent variable.

One of the explanations deals with the contribution to knowledge-building represented by studies of life satisfaction; another deals with the tendency of developing disciplines to focus on a few paradigms. The third possible explanation deals with the uses of such research in the development of public policy. Whereas it is likely that all three explanations operating together explain the focus of gerontological research on the construct of life satisfaction, this examination will deal with all three as if they could and did operate independently of each other.

One could argue that the focus on life satisfaction simply reflects our wish to know: knowledge for the sake of knowledge, if you will. If this were the case, one could assume that the accumulated efforts of 40 years of research on this topic would have brought us closer to the truth than we were at the start of the research. We should be more certain of what life satisfaction is and how it relates to other aspects of life than we were 40 years ago. However, when one examines the product of all this knowledge seeking, as will be done in more detail later, one finds that there is no discernably greater certainty about what life satisfaction is and what it is related to than there was at the start of this intellectual journey. In fact, there are so many contradictory findings with regard to the relationships concerning life satisfaction that few general statements of "truth" or "fact" can be safely made.

One could also argue that the focus on life satisfaction represents not as much the pursuit of knowledge as it does the pursuit of peer approval, given the adoption by those in the growing discipline of gerontology of a paradigm that emphasizes this concept. In fact, most research reports on life satisfaction start not with a philosophical discussion of how the research contributes to knowledge but with an acknowledgment of the work of others. It is almost as if such research has meaning, not because of what it contributes to our search for knowledge, but because of the tacit approval it represents of the research focus others have taken. Thus we become involved in an act of mutual affirmation where my research is important because you also engaged in research on this topic and your research is important because of my research on this topic.

A final argument that could be used to explain the focus on life satisfaction is the potential impact such research could have on the development of public policy. Thus, research on the life satisfaction of the aged could be justified not only as a search for knowledge for its own sake, nor as a disciplinary activity, but also because of the impact that could result from such research on the lives of the older people who are the objects of study. Such research could further the "pursuit of happiness" the Constitution indicates is an inalienable right by suggesting activities that could be undertaken on behalf of older people that would assist them in finding happiness and satisfaction.

The role of gerontological research on life satisfaction, given this latter justification, would be to identify those variables that influence the level of satisfaction and are subject to public policy manipulation. Such policy manipulations could result in increased life satisfaction among older people. These manipulations could, in turn, contribute to the further development of knowledge, since they would represent a form of experimental manipulation rarely possible at present.

It is this last statement that could be used most persuasively to argue that the emperor does, in fact, have new clothes. The importance of life satisfaction research to the field of gerontology could be found in the utility of such research in improving the lives of the aged; it is the potential utility of such research that makes a compelling argument for the continuation of this research thrust. The applicability of current research toward this end will be examined later in this chapter. Before this examination, however, a summary of some of the findings of the past 40 years with regard to life satisfaction is in order.

Findings with Regard to Life Satisfaction

As was suggested earlier, in spite of the wealth of studies reporting on the relationship between life satisfaction and various demographic variables, few definite statements may be made about the "true nature" of this relationship. The findings with regard to any one of the many variables that have been studied are often contradictory. Some of the possible explanations for these contradictory findings will be explored later; at present, the discussion will be limited to a summary of findings on five variables: marital status, retirement, health, housing, and social activity. These five variables have been selected in preference to the other variables[2] that have also been the object of research because they illustrate the varying possibilities for social policy manipulations.

MARITAL STATUS

Several studies report a positive relationship between marital status and life satisfaction. For example, Cavan et al. (1949); Maddox and Eisdorfer (1962); Martin (1973); and Messer (1967) all report that married older people are more satisfied with their lives than are unmarried older people. However, not all studies have found this positive relationship to be statistically significant. Spreitzer and Snyder (1974), for example, found a

---

[2] For a discussion of the other variables that have been studied, the reader is referred to Adams (1971), Larson (1978), and Lohmann (1977a).

positive relationship in their study of a national probability sample but found the relationship was not significant at the $p = .05$ level or greater.

Zibbell (1972) found a positive relationship that was significant only for the males in his sample; not for the females. Both Kutner, Fanshel, Togo, and Langer (1956) and Morgan (1976) found that after a period of widowhood, the widoweds' satisfaction equaled that of their married peers and, in the Morgan study, even surpassed the morale of the married. Both Edwards and Klemmack (1973) and Morgan found an important control variable that affected the relationship of marital status to life satisfaction. They both found a positive relationship between satisfaction and marital status but the relationship was eliminated when the effects of income were controlled. Morgan also found that when employment status was held constant, the effects of widowhood were eliminated. Reichard, Livson, and Peterson (1962) found that marital status and adjustment were not related for their sample of males.

Thus, although many studies have found a positive relationship between marital status and life satisfaction, the findings have not been uniformly positive nor have they always found the relationship to be a strong one. The explanatory power of this variable when compared with that of other variables such as income is also questionable. Our ability to subject this variable to manipulations through public policy, should it be found to be one with great explanatory power is also uncertain. The non-susceptibility of this variable to policy manipulation will be dealt with later.

RETIREMENT

The studies that have examined the relationship between retirement and life satisfaction and found the nonretired to be more satisfied than retirees include those of Edwards and Klemmack (1973), Harris (1975), and Strieb and Schneider (1971). Similar findings also have been found in studies that have examined only female retirees. Both Fox (1977) and Jaslow (1976) found that female retirees had lower morale than those not retired. Jaslow, however, found that this relationship did not hold among those retirees who had an income over $5000. Strieb and Schneider (1971) also found that both work and income affect satisfaction; they found that both work and socioeconomic status affected morale independently and equally. Chatfield (1977) found that when income was held constant, there was no difference between the morale of the recently retired and nonretired except for those having an income of less than $4999.

There are some exceptions to these findings on retirement. The most

significant are those of Thompson (1973), who examined a national probability sample of 1589 males. She found that:

> The retired exhibited lower morale than the employed principally because they
> had more negative evaluations of their health, were more functionally disabled,
> were poorer and were older and not simply because they were retired [p. 344].

Chatfield (1977) found that although retirees had lower satisfaction
scores, the effect of retirement was apparently time-related; the scores of
those retired for over 1 year were not significantly lower than the scores of
those not retired. George (1978) found those who were unemployed, which
included the retired, were more satisfied than those employed.

Thus, as with marital status, one could conclude that a numerical preponderance of the studies indicate a positive relationship between being
employed and having high morale. However, significant questions may be
raised about whether it is the act of retirement that, in itself, reduces
satisfaction or whether other factors, including health and income, may be
more related to satisfaction than employment status. Unlike marital status,
however, employment and retirement are more easily manipulated through
public policy interventions and have, in fact, been subject to such manipulations.

HEALTH

Several studies have found a strong positive relationship between health
status and satisfaction, with those in good health being more satisfied than
those in poor health. Among those studies is that of Thompson (1973),
referred to earlier. Other studies finding this relationship include Cutler
(1972), Cavan et al. (1949), Edwards and Klemmack (1973), George (1978),
Maddox and Eisdorfer (1962), Messer (1967), Palmore and Kivett (1977),
Sauer (1977), and Sprietzer and Snyder (1974). Medley (1976) found that
health satisfaction was the second best predictor for females. Markides and
Martin (1979) found that self-reported health was the second greatest
predictor of satisfaction for males but the greatest predictor of satisfaction
for females. As an illustration of the sometimes contradictory findings in
this area, Seymour (1972) found health to be most closely related to the life
satisfaction of females but not of males. Zibbell (1972) found health to be
most closely related to the life satisfaction of males but not of females.

There are few studies that have examined health that have found it did
not predict some part of life satisfaction. This differentiates it as a variable
from the two previously discussed variables—marital status and retirement
—about which some findings indicate that a relationship exists and others

that there is no relationship. With regard to health, the primary disagreement is about the strength of the relationship between it and satisfaction; some studies find it the most important variable and others find it to be of less importance. The degree to which this variable can be influenced and manipulated in old age is also uncertain.

HOUSING AND THE PHYSICAL ENVIRONMENT

Another variable of interest is that of the physical environment, including housing, and the impact it may have on life satisfaction. Carp (1966, 1967) and Lawton and Cohen (1974) have compared older people who moved to better quality housing with those who did not, and found the satisfaction levels of the "movers" significantly higher than that of the "nonmovers." Schooler (1970) examined the effects of housing and the physical environment on a national probability sample and hypothesized that the effects of environment were mediated through the effects of social relationships. He found, however, that his hypothesis was disallowed and that environmental effects had both greater and more direct explanatory power than did social relationships.

Another aspect of the physical environment that has been examined is the impact an age segregated or integrated environment has on satisfaction. Rosow (1967) found that a certain type of older person, whom he termed the "insatiable," did have higher morale when they lived in areas densely populated by other old people. Teaff, Lawton, Nahemow, and Carlson (1978) also found that those in an age-segregated environment had higher morale. Gubrium (1970), however, found that age concentration had a minimal effect on the satisfaction of the Detroit population he studied. Poorkaj (1967) found that an age-segregated environment did not necessarily result in higher morale. Woodard (1969) found that those living in their own homes had higher morale than those living in a retirement community. Thus the effects of age segregation are not clearcut.

A final aspect of the housing environment that has been studied is the effect of constraint within that environment on satisfaction. Both Smith and Lipman (1972) and Wolk and Telleen (1976) found that those in less constraining environments, that is, environments that provided greater individual choice, had higher levels of satisfaction than those in more constraining environments.

It would appear, then, that housing is a variable that is capable of influencing life satisfaction as well as a variable that we have manipulated historically through public policy. As yet, too few studies have been done for us to conclude that this variable could exert a greater influence over the level of life satisfaction than could other variables, such as income and health.

The final variable to be examined, and the variable that has been the object of the most heated debate among gerontologists, is the relationship between social activity and life satisfaction. Among those finding a positive relationship between a high degree of social activity and a high level of life satisfaction are these 17 studies: Burgess (1954); Cavan *et al.* (1949); Erlich (1972); Graney (1975); Haven (1968); Havighurst and Albrecht (1953); Havighurst, Neugarten, and Tobin (1968); Kutner *et al.* (1956); Lawton (1972); Lowenthal and Haven (1968); Maddox (1963); Markides and Martin (1979); Palmore and Luikart (1972); Pihlblad and Adams (1972); Seymour (1972); Tobin and Neugarten (1961); and Wylie (1970).

Others have reported positive relationships but have indicated that those relationships disappear when other variables are controlled. For example, Lemon, Bengston, and Peterson (1972) indicated that when controls were introduced, a strong positive relationship between activity and satisfaction existed only for married females. Edwards and Klemmack (1973) reported the relationship between activity and satisfaction disappeared when controls for health and socioeconomic status were introduced. Bull and Aucoin (1975) also found that the relationship disappeared when controls for health and socioeconomic status were introduced.

Still others have reported finding no relationship between activity and satisfaction. Cumming and Henry (1961) are among the most prominent in this category. In addition, Thompson (1973) in her study of a national probability sample of males found activity to be a weak predictor of life satisfaction. Connor, Powers, and Bultena (1979), although finding some measures of activity related to life satisfaction, found that the number of people interacted with and the frequency of interaction were of little importance for adjustment. They argue that the time has come to stop examining easily quantifiable aspects of activity, such as role counts, or interaction counts, and to begin examining some of the more qualitative aspects of activity. It may be that some of the lack of congruence with regard to findings of the role of activity is due to measurement error, rather than to real differences.

Given the contradictory findings in this area, the nature of the relationship between social activity and life satisfaction is uncertain. Social activity, however, like employment status and housing, is subject to influence by public policies. A wide variety of social programs including senior centers, group dining programs, and senior companionship programs reflect policy efforts to influence social activity.

SUMMARY OF RESEARCH FINDINGS

As this review has suggested, 40 years of research on the relationship between life satisfaction and these five variables has not resulted in any clearcut answers with regard to the causes or correlates of satisfaction. The significance of some variables in explaining life satisfaction levels is obviously greater than that of others; health, for example, could more persuasively be argued to be related to life satisfaction based upon the research to date than could marital status. In addition to differing with regard to the apparent relationship between any variable and satisfaction, the variables differ from each other with regard to the extent that they may be influenced by public policy. The remainder of this chapter will focus upon those areas we might attempt to influence through policy and those areas in need of additional attention, if our influencing efforts are to be successful.

Life Satisfaction Research and Policy

Although the correlates and causes of life satisfaction have been the object of gerontological research for an extended period of time, the results of that research have exerted very little impact on the development of aging policy. In part, this is merely an extension of what we know to be the case in other fields; social science research rarely informs public policy in the direct way those of us in the academy may wish. However, the failure of this research to have a more significant impact in the development of policy is also due to some limitations of the research.

In part, the research findings are less influential than might be desired because they have dealt with variables subject to minimal manipulation through policy. Thus we have sometimes examined things that cannot be influenced. The findings also have been less relevant because they have often focused upon reporting correlational data rather than on developing causal models; the correlational data provide little guidance as to which variables have the greatest explanatory power or which are intervening in their effects. A final reason for the failure of this research to more fully inform policy is the sometimes contradictory findings that make translation into policy difficult. These contradictions may have their roots in measurement and other methodological errors, rather than in true differences within populations. The remainder of this chapter will suggest some changes that might be made in the nature of the life satisfaction research that would serve to make future research more policy relevant.

VARIABLE MANIPULATION

One of the factors limiting the utility of life satisfaction research for public policy development has been the tendency to focus upon variables that are not easily manipulated through policy. For example, the variable of marital satisfaction is subject to very little acceptable manipulation, as are the variables of age, surviving children, or siblings, often the object of study. Even if marital happiness should prove to be very important in explaining life satisfaction, there is very little we can do to increase the happiness of those who are already married and even less that we can do for those who are unmarried, given sex ratios in old age and the normative value placed on dyadic relationships.

Health status, although subject to some influence in old age, cannot be wholly influenced by public policy. Given the nature of physical decrements in aging and the high incidence of chronic conditions, our best chance to influence health is in concentration on the young, who are the future aged. By introducing them to preventive health care, we may produce future generations of older people whose health status contributes to their life satisfaction. Our chances, however, of reversing older persons' heart conditions, chronic brain syndromes, or arthritis, and thus increasing their life satisfaction are relatively remote. Although health appears to be an important factor in influencing life satisfaction; it does not appear to be one that we can hope to affect greatly for the present generation of older people through public policy manipulations. At best, we can hope that the provision of health care will ameliorate health conditions and thus reduce further declines in life satisfaction.

The remaining three variables discussed, retirement, housing, and social activity, are all subject to manipulation through public policy. In addition, we have a past history of influencing all three of these areas through the passage of social legislation and creation of social programs. However, this legislation has rarely been passed in response to research findings suggesting its importance in increasing the life satisfactions of older people. Future research on life satisfaction, if we are concerned about its social utility, should perhaps focus upon substantive areas like these three, where the potential for policy manipulation exists. With such a focus, the likelihood of the research results having a positive impact upon the lives of those we study will be increased.

CAUSAL RELATIONSHIPS

An additional change that is needed if life satisfaction research is to be of greater utility is an increased focus of that research on causal relationships rather than on merely correlational ones. Such a change may be taking place already, since several recent articles on life satisfaction have focused on causal relationships and the development of causal models of life satisfaction. (See Markides & Martin, 1979, and Medley, 1976.) As scientists, we are aware that correlation is merely an indication of relationship, and that causality is often more difficult to establish. In spite of the increased difficulty, however, we need to be focusing to a greater degree upon the development of causal models to explain life satisfaction. Such a focus will enable us to separate those variables that are most critical in producing life satisfaction from those that are less important.

METHODOLOGICAL SOPHISTICATION

The final area that requires our attention, if future studies of life satisfaction are to be of greater utility, is that of further refining our methodological sophistication, especially in the area of measurement. Part of the explanation for the sometimes contradictory findings with regard to the correlates and causes of life satisfaction lies in the measurements we have used and the measurement error that may be represented by them. As this author has observed earlier (Lohmann, 1977a), there appears to be almost a "new car" mentality with regard to the measurement of life satisfaction with the belief that "new is better." Thus as new measurements are published, they tend to be adopted by others, regardless of the methods of validating those new measures or of their reliability. Those new measures often have been developed using only criterion validity, rather than the preferred construct validation techniques. They are often of moderate reliability at best. They often have been developed on samples that have systematically excluded major portions of the aged populations, as is the case with The Philadelphia Geriatric Center Morale Scale (Lawton, 1972), which Lawton indicates is appropriate for very old populations. They often are used by others on very different populations where their appropriateness is questionable. Thus the approach to measuring the dependent variable of life satisfaction has not always reflected what we know to be the best scientific approach. Using measures that are less valid or reliable than they should be has produced a mass of contradictory findings with regard to life satisfaction which defies translation into policy prescriptions.

There are efforts to remedy this problem. Conner, Powers, and Bultena (1979), for example, call attention to the measurement problem as a possible explanation for the contradictory findings on the relationship of social activity and life satisfaction and attempt to deal with that problem by developing a multiple measure of activity. My own research has represented an effort to increase the validity and reliability of the measurement of life satisfaction and, using the methods of construct validity, has resulted in a measure of life satisfaction having a higher degree of reliability than existing measures (Lohmann, 1977a, 1980). Additional attention must be paid to the problem of measurement, however, with the goal of developing measures that have construct validity and that have been developed on samples that reflect all segments of the aged population. While working on such measures, it should be remembered that the ultimate goal is the development of measures that will yield policy-relevant research.

Conclusion

The principal argument of this chapter has been that one of the justifications for the focus of so much gerontological research on life satisfaction is that this focus could result in the development of public policy that contributes to improved lives for older people. However, the potential of this research as a source of more informed policy has rarely been met during the past 40 years, in part because the research findings are often contradictory. These contradictions may be due to measurement error and suggest the need for greater attention within the field to the development of more valid measures. An increased emphasis upon causal research and upon those variables capable of being manipulated through policy would also increase the benefits produced by life satisfaction research.

References

Adams, D. Correlates of satisfaction among the elderly. *The Gerontologist*, 1971, *11*(4), 64–68.

Bull, C., & Aucoin, J. Voluntary association participation and life satisfaction: a replication note. *Journal of Gerontology*, 1975, *30*(1), 73–76.

Carp, F. *A future for the aged.* Austin: University of Texas Press, 1966.

Carp, F. The impact of environment on old people. *The Gerontologist*, 1967, *7*(1), 106–108.

Cavan, R., Burgess, E., Havighurst, R., & Goldhamer, H. *Personal adjustment in old age.* Chicago: Science Research Associates, 1949.

Chatfield, W. Economic and sociological factors influencing life satisfaction of the aged. *Journal of Gerontology*, 1977, *32*(5), 593–599.

Conner, K., Powers, E., & Bultena, G. Social interaction and life satisfaction: An empirical assessment of late-life patterns. *Journal of Gerontology*, 1979, *34*(1), 116–121.

Cumming, E., & Henry, W. *Growing old.* New York: Basic Books, 1961.

Cutler, S. The availability of personal transportation, residential location, and life satisfaction among the aged. *Journal of Gerontology,* 1972, *27*(3), 383–389.

Edwards, J., & Klemmack, D. Correlates of life satisfaction: a re-examination. *Journal of Gerontology,* 1973, *28*(4), 497–502.

Fox, J. Effects of retirement and former work life on womens' adaptation in old age. *Journal of Gerontology,* 1977, *32*(2), 196–202.

George, L. The impact of personality and social status factors upon levels of activity and psychological well-being. *Journal of Gerontology,* 1978, *33*(6), 840–847.

Graney, M. Happiness and social participation in aging. *Journal of Gerontology,* 1975, *30*(6), 701–706.

Gubrium, J. Environmental effects on morale in old age and the resources of health and solvency. *The Gerontologist,* 1970, *10*(4), 294–297.

Harris, L. and Associates. *The myth and reality of aging in America.* Washington: National Council on Aging, 1975.

Haven, B. An investigation of activity patterns and adjustment in an aging population. *The Gerontologist,* 1968, *8*(3), 201–206.

Havighurst, R., & Albrecht, R. *Older people.* New York: Longmans, Green, 1953.

Jaslow, P. Employment, retirement and morale among older women. *Journal of Gerontology.* 1976, *31*(2), 212–218.

Kutner, B., Fanshel, D., Togo, A., & Langner, T. *Five hundred over sixty.* New York: Russell Sage Foundation, 1956.

Larson, R. Thirty years of research on the subjective well-being of older Americans. *Journal of Gerontology,* 1978, *33*(1), 109–125.

Lawton, M. Assessment, integration and environments for older people. *The Gerontologist,* 1970, *10*(1), 38–46.

Lawton, M. The dimensions of morale. In D. Kent, R. Kastenbaum, & S. Sherwood. *Research, planning and action for the elderly.* New York: Behavioral Publications, 1972.

Lawton, M., & Cohen, J. The generality of housing impact on the well-being of older people. *Journal of Gerontology,* 1974, *29*(2), 194–204.

Lemon, B., Bengston, V., & Peterson, J. An exploration of the activity theory of aging: Activity types and life satisfaction among inmovers to a retirement community. *Journal of Gerontology,* 1972, *27*(4), 511–523.

Lohmann, N. Comparison of life satisfaction, morale and adjustment scales on an elderly population. (Doctoral dissertation, Brandeis University), *Dissertation Abstracts International,* 1977, *38*(1B), 418–419. (a)

Lohmann, N. Correlations of life satisfaction, morale and adjustment measures. *Journal of Gerontology,* 1977, *32*(1), 73–75. (b).

Lohmann, N. A construct validation of seven measures of life satisfaction, adjustment and morale. *International Journal of Aging and Human Development,* 1980, *11*(1), 1–9.

Maddox, G., & Eisdorfer, C. Some correlations of activity and morale among the elderly. *Social Forces,* 1962, *40*(3), 254–260.

Markides, K., & Martin, H. A causal model of life satisfaction among the elderly. *Journal of Gerontology,* 1979, *34*(1), 86–93.

Martin, W. Activity and disengagement: Life satisfaction in inmovers into a retirement community. *The Gerontologist,* 1973, *13*(2), 224–227.

Medley, M. Satisfaction with life among persons sixty-five years and older. *Journal of Gerontology,* 1976, *31*(4), 448–455.

Messer, M. The possibility of an age-concentrated environment becoming a normative system. *The Gerontologist,* 1967, *7*(4), 247–251.

Morgan, L. A reexamination of widowhood and morale. *Journal of Gerontology*, 1976, *31*(6), 687–695.

Neugarten, B., Havighurst, R., & Tobin, S. The measurement of life satisfaction. *Journal of Gerontology*, 1961, *16*, 134–143.

Palmore, E., & Kivett, V. Change in life satisfaction: A longitudinal study of persons aged 46–70. *Journal of Gerontology*, 1977, *32*(3), 311–316.

Pihlblad, C., & Adams, D. Widowhood, social participation, and life satisfaction. *Aging and Human Development*, 1972, *3*(4), 323–330.

Poorkaj, H. Social psychological factors and "successful aging". Doctoral dissertation, University of Southern California, *Dissertation Abstracts International*, 1967, 28(1A). (No. 306)

Reichard, S., Livson, F., & Peterson, P. *Aging and personality*. New York: John Wiley and Sons, 1962.

Rosow, I. *Social integration of the aged*. New York: The Free Press, 1967.

Sauer, W. Morale of the urban aged: a regression analysis by race. *Journal of Gerontology*, 1977, *32*(5), 600–608.

Schooler, K. Effect of environment on morale. *The Gerontologist*, 1970, *10*(3), 194–197.

Seymour, G. Activity level, the sense of personal autonomy and life satisfaction in old age. Doctoral dissertation, Boston University Graduate School, *Dissertation Abstracts International*, 1972, 33(5B), 2331–2332.

Smith, K., & Lipman, A. Constraint and life satisfaction. *Journal of Gerontology*, 1972, *27*(1), 77–82.

Spreitzer, E., & Snyder, E. Correlates of life satisfaction. *Journal of Gerontology*, 1974, *29*(4), 454–458.

Streib, G., & Schneider, C. *Retirement in American society*. Ithaca: Cornell University Press, 1971.

Teaff, J., Lawton, M., Nahemow, L., & Carlson, D. Impact of age integration on the well-being of elderly tenants in public housing. *Journal of Gerontology*, 1978, *33*(1), 126–133.

Thompson, G. Work versus leisure roles: An investigation of morale among employed and retired men. *Journal of Gerontology*, 1973, *18*(3), 339–344.

Wolk, S., & Telleen, S. Psychological and social correlates of life satisfaction as a function of residential constraint. *Journal of Gerontology*, 1976, *31*(1), 89–98.

Woodard, R. Selected aspects of personal adjustments of aged persons among an older population of Greely, Colorado. Doctoral dissertation, Colorado State College, *Dissertation Abstracts International*, 1891, 1969, 30(4B).

Zibbell, R. Activity level, future time perspective and life satisfaction in old age. Doctoral dissertation, Boston University Graduate School, *Dissertation Abstracts International*, 1972, 32(7B), 4198–4199.

Chapter 3

Physical Activity as It Relates to the Health of the Aged

ANDREW C. OSTROW

Based on testimonies presented by experts in the fields of cardiology, psychiatry, geriatrics, and exercise physiology before the United States Senate Subcommittee on Aging in April of 1975, Congress amended the definition of social services provided by the Older American Act to include services designed to enable older persons to attain and maintain physical and mental well-being through programs of regular physical activity and exercise (Clarke, 1977). Subsequently, the Alliance Committee on Aging was formed under the auspices of the American Alliance for Health, Physical Education, and Recreation to promote scientific information as it relates to gerontology, and to coordinate and promote programs of physical activity and exercise for the elderly. The committee has worked closely with the National Association for Human Development, which has developed the "Active People Over 60" program in cooperation with the President's Council on Physical Fitness and Sports, under a grant sponsored by the Administration on Aging. Under this grant, workshops have been organized to train physical fitness leaders (including older persons themselves) to promote and encourage physical fitness standards among the elderly.

The thrust of these programmatic and legislative efforts rests on the assumption that participation in physical activity and programs of exercise

41

is beneficial to the physical and mental health of the individual over the life cycle. It has been stated by deVries (1979) that "ideally, physical fitness is a condition which should be achieved in youth, pursued through middle age, and never relinquished insofar as that is humanly possible [p. 8]." Clearly, there is a need to identify and explain the level of current involvement in physical activity among older persons, as well as to examine the potential values inherent in engaging in programs of regular physical activity for the elderly.

Therefore, the purposes of this chapter are (a) to examine and to account for what is known about the level of involvement in physical activity among the elderly; and (b) to explore the role that physical activity plays (or could play) in maintaining and improving the health of the elderly, with particular emphasis on examining the effects of engaging in programs of physical activity on the psychological well-being of the elderly. It is apparent that the term *physical activity* can refer to an array of movement activities evident in the life experiences of the elderly. For the purposes of this paper, physical activity is defined and delimited to structured, nonutilitarian gross human movement primarily manifested in such activities as sports, games, dance, and calisthenics (Kenyon, 1968a).

Declining Involvement in Physical Activity as a Function of Age

In 1972, the Opinion Research Corporation of Princeton, New Jersey conducted a National Adult Fitness Survey for the President's Council on Physical Fitness and Sports in which 3875 men and women aged 22 and over were interviewed (Clarke, 1973). Data presented (see Table 3.1) indicated that only 39% of Americans aged 60 or older ($N = 979$) participated in any systematic exercise. The favorite form of exercise for this age group was walking. The most frequent reason given for not exercising was "I'm too old." Few older persons engaged in more vigorous forms of physical activity such as swimming or bicycling. The percentage of individuals engaged in vigorous physical activity appeared to decline with increasing age.

These findings were supported by Nielsen (1974) who interviewed 51 older persons from three senior centers. These individuals reported a decrease in organized, vigorous physical activity participation relative to their reported youth and middle age activity levels. The most popular forms of physical activity for these individuals were walking and working around the house (gardening, etc.).

Table 3.1
Present Adult Participation in Exercise for Age Groups by Percentages[a]

Exercise forms	Age groups				
	22–29	30–39	40–49	50–59	60-over
	Men				
	(N = 381)	(N = 319)	(N = 338)	(N = 384)	(N = 517)
Walking	36	27	39	39	46
Bicycling	28	17	18	13	4
Swimming	25	23	15	14	4
Calisthenics	23	13	10	10	5
Jogging	19	8	8	6	2
Weight training	16	6	3	2	1
	Women				
	(N = 427)	(N = 363)	(N = 338)	(N = 346)	(N = 462)
Walking	51	45	41	38	33
Bicycling	28	31	20	10	2
Calisthenics	22	17	16	9	6
Swimming	17	16	13	5	4
Jogging	7	5	2	2	0
Weight training	1	1	0	1	0

[a] Adapted from Clarke (1974).

In a review of eight research studies, McPherson (Note 1) concluded that involvement in physical activity declines with age, and that the decline occurs earlier and more frequently among women and in those individuals with lower levels of educational attainment. Illustrative of the data reviewed by McPherson (Note 1) is a national survey of over 40,000 Canadians, in which it was found that regular sport activity involvement is inversely related to age, with females less active than males at all ages.

Based on these research data, it may be fallacious to assume that the need for involvement in physical activity diminishes with increasing age. The cohorts examined in these cross-sectional surveys vary considerably on a number of mediating variables that may interact with the noted decline in involvement in physical activity across age. For example, data reported in the National Adult Fitness Survey clearly indicate that the better educated and more affluent segments of the population are more inclined to engage in physical activity. Fitness awareness was lowest among the elderly, the poor, and the poorly educated—all of whom exercised the least. Previous experience in school sports appears to serve as a precursor for subsequent involvement in physical activity across the life span. The percentage of subjects reporting that they had taken a physical education class while in school showed a drastic decline at the age of 60 or older (Clarke, 1973, 1974).

Clearly, previous opportunity, interest, and involvement in a variety of physical activities promote continued participation and persistence in physical activity as the individual ages (Bultena & Wood, 1970; Espenschade, 1969; Nielsen, 1974). Individuals who are provided with reinforcement for participation, with appropriate social role models who encourage participation, and who are socialized to believe that society sanctions involvement, will participate in physical activity. There are a number of research studies (e.g., see the excellent review by Lewko & Greendorfer, 1978) that suggest that boys and girls are differentially socialized into (or out of) sport, and that the differentially perceived sex appropriateness of sport activities (Promoli, McCabe, & Shaw, 1977) accounts for part of the variance attributable to the involvement by boys and girls in sport. Have we also fostered age related normative sanctions and expectancies for participating in physical activities?

While sanctions against women's involvement in sport appear to be lessening and are not as severe as for previous female cohorts, it is suggested by this writer that age-related norms and barriers for involvement in physical activity, particularly vigorous physical activity, blatantly exist. One only has to read the newspaper or watch television to observe agism through the practice of depicting adolescents or young adults selling the products of sporting good companies and other leisure activity sponsors. Appropriate role models are needed across the life span if involvement in physical activity is to be promoted throughout life.

Research studies exist suggesting that even as children we begin to form stereotypes about older people (Hickey, Hickey, & Kalish, 1975), and that we continue to form and maintain stereotypes and establish role expectancies that are highly age related (Ahammai & Baltes, 1972). Often, and sometimes unfortunately, age functions as a socially constructed category that defines appropriate role behaviors at specific points in the life cycle. This resultant age grading of behavior results in the establishment of normative age criteria for entering and relinquishing select roles, such as involvement in physical activity (McPherson, Note 1). It is apparent that inappropriate age-related sanctions, founded more on myth than on empirical evidence, may lead to the discrimination of the older segment of our population, particularly regarding their participation in vigorous physical activity. Research in progress by this author is attempting to identify to what extent stereotypes exist among college-age students in how they view the appropriateness of participation by males and females who vary in age in selected sport activities. Clearly, this issue needs also to be addressed among individuals who vary in age across the life cycle.

Attitudes toward Participating in Physical Activity
among the Elderly

Of current research interest to this author, are the attitudes of older persons toward participating in physical activity. When subjects in the National Adult Fitness Survey (Clarke, 1973) were asked if they felt they were getting enough exercise, interestingly, the data suggested that the percentage of subjects responding in the affirmative linearly increased with age. Conrad (1976) suggested that older Americans: (a) believe their need for exercise diminishes and eventually disappears as they grow older; (b) tend to vastly exaggerate the risks involved in vigorous exercise after middle age; (c) overrate the benefits of light, sporadic exercise; and (d) underrate their own physical abilities and capacities. Nielsen (1974) reported that the majority of senior citizens he investigated felt they engaged in enough physical activity for people their age. It is apparent that the elderly place a low priority on their need for vigorous physical activity. These attitudes, combined with diminished risk-taking behaviors evident during motor performances (Welford, 1958), obviously limit the motivation and interests older people have toward engaging in physical activity.

A review of literature reveals a paucity of research on attitudes held by the elderly toward participating in physical activity. In an extensive review of literature by Albinson (1975) on attitude measurement in physical education, only one reported study dealt with an elderly population. Swanson (1976), utilizing a semantic differential approach, found that senior citizens held the most negative attitudes toward physical activity among the age-classified samples investigated. Harris (1970) compared highly active and sedentary groups of middle-aged males and reported that the active group (unlike the sedentary group) had always participated in vigorous sports, were more interested in participating than in watching sports on television, and were more aware of the values that regular exercise held for them.

This author (Ostrow, Note 2) has presented a preliminary set of data designed to examine the construct validity of a proposed conceptual model (Figure 3.1) characterizing attitudes of the elderly toward participating in lifetime sports. The model represents a modification of Kenyon's (1968a, 1968b) conceptual model characterizing attitudes held toward physical activity. Kenyon's model has been extensively examined in the research literature (see excellent reviews by Albinson, 1975; Loy, Note 3), including research on children's attitudes toward physical activity (Simon & Smoll, 1974).

Kenyon's model is based on the premise that physical activity can be reduced to logical subsets or factors that are based on the perceived instrumental (or satisfaction) values held for physical activity. Subsequent

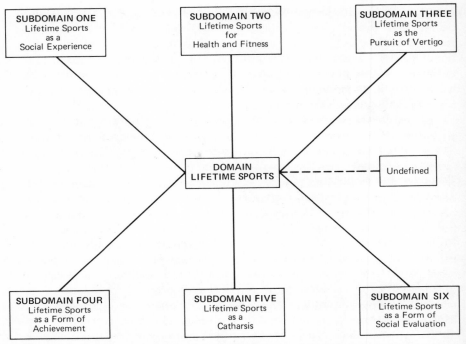

Figure 3.1. A conceptual model characterizing attitudes of the elderly toward engaging in lifetime sports.

factor analytic studies supported the existence of six instrumental factors—physical activity as a social experience, physical activity for health and fitness, physical activity as the pursuit of vertigo, physical activity as an aesthetic experience, physical activity as a catharsis, and physical activity as an ascetic experience (Kenyon, 1968a). Sidney and Shephard (1976), using a semantic differential approach based on Kenyon's model, found that (a) elderly males and females placed greater value upon physical activity as a form of health and fitness than did high school students; (b) elderly females were less attracted to the sensation of vertigo than the high school females; and (c) elderly males placed greater value on physical activity as an aesthetic experience than did the high school males.

This author's conceptual model focuses on lifetime sports as the attitudinal target, rather than the broader multidimensional concept of physical activity. Four factors were adopted from Kenyon's original model —participation in lifetime sports as (a) a social experience; (b) a form of health and fitness; (c) the pursuit of vertigo; and (d) a form of catharsis. However, unlike Kenyon's interpretation of catharsis as both tension reduction and hostility expression and reduction, catharsis was defined and delimited to the value of participation in lifetime sports as a means of reducing anxiety and tension. Research by Loy (Note 3) suggests that additional values for engaging in physical activity should be postulated and examined. Consequently, two additional factors were proposed in the model—participation in lifetime sports as a means of achievement, and as a form of social evaluation.

Extensive research studies exist (e.g., Alderman, 1974; Maehr, 1974) supporting the inherent value of participation in lifetime sports as a means of expressing the achievement needs of the individual. Of interest to this author was whether, and to what extent, elderly subjects would value participation in lifetime sports as a means of expressing their acheivement needs. In addition, Martens (1976) and Scanlan (1978) have suggested that participation in competitive sport serves as a form of social evaluation (i.e., as a means of evaluating one's ability based on information received from other persons vicariously or directly involved in the same competitive process). Much of their theoretical work on social evaluation stems from Festinger's (1954) social comparison theory, and Veroff's (1969) developmental theory of achievement motivation. Of interest to this author was whether, and to what extent, elderly subjects would value participation in lifetime sports as a form of social evaluation.

To establish the construct validity of the proposed conceptual model characterizing attitudes of the elderly toward participating in lifetime sports, a 60-item Likert format attitudinal inventory was constructed, containing 10 items per postulated factor based on a 4-point ordinal scale. Figure 3.2 presents a schema depicting the criteria used in selecting items for incorporation in the inventory. An intuituve-rational strategy (Goldberg, 1972) was adopted in the development of items for each scale; items

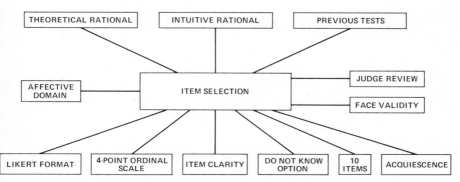

Figure 3.2. Item selection schema for assessing attitudes of the elderly toward participating in lifetime sports.

were written and accepted if they appeared to be theoretically and intuitively consistent with the scale for which they were intended. Items were reviewed by three judges for content validity. Some items within each scale were counterbalanced to minimize the response set of acquiescence.

Copies of the 60-item inventory were distributed to 800 male and female subjects residing in a retirement community in New Jersey during the fall of 1978. These subjects also received a questionnaire designed to assess their levels of primary (actual) and secondary (vicarious) involvement in physical activity (Kenyon, Note 4), so as to correlate their attitudes toward lifetime sports participation with their actual involvement in physical activity (including lifetime sports).

Criteria were established (Figure 3.3) to retain items based on the internal item pool structure of subjects' responses to the inventory. Unfortunately, the initial return rate was extremely low ($N = 72$), a result somewhat consistent with Shephard's (1978) contention that volunteerism is inversely proportional to age.

Table 3.2 presents the results of a preliminary factor analysis conducted on subjects' ($N = 62$ usable data sets) responses to the 60-item inventory. A principal component analysis was conducted, followed by Kaiser's varimax rotation method. Although the data suggest that catharsis, social evaluation, and social experience may be viable factors in the model, these conclusions may be fallacious in view of the fact that the number of variables entered into the data matrix almost exceeds the number of subjects examined.

It is suggested that the value of this pilot research lies in the effort to bridge theory with empiricism in an attempt to understand the attitudes older persons have toward participating in physical activity. Clearly, the validation of a conceptual model of this nature requires extensive and con-

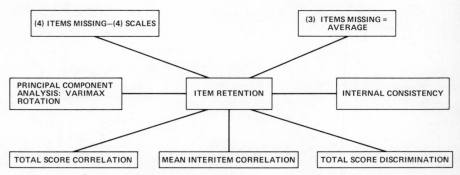

Figure 3.3. Item retention schema for assessing attitudes of the elderly toward participating in lifetime sports.

Table 3.2
Varimax Orthogonally Rotated Single Factor Weightings for Elderly Subjects' ($N = 62$)
Responses to the Lifetime Sports Attitude Inventory[a]

	Factor 1	Factor 2	Factor 3	Factor 4	Factor 5	Factor 6
ACH1	−0.00747	0.50594	0.10488	0.18569	0.12284	0.29228
ACH7	−0.03997	0.07611	0.22283	0.08958	0.02988	0.01274
ACH13	0.39789	0.08424	0.12135	−0.21911	0.04440	0.18331
ACH25	−0.06411	0.35438	0.20572	0.10071	0.09107	0.14055
ACH31	0.09590	0.11202	0.27331	−0.00820	0.87735	−0.07729
ACH37	−0.00215	0.26153	0.56146	0.10952	0.17317	0.09981
ACH43	0.44923	0.29662	0.26463	0.08732	0.29092	−0.30626
ACH55	−0.36017	0.42239	0.45064	0.01799	0.15913	0.18379
CATH2	0.15194	−0.04977	0.69081	−0.05158	0.09835	0.10290
CATH8	0.26749	0.08889	0.10333	0.17320	−0.21416	−0.07225
CATH14	0.32366	0.04505	0.57279	0.03366	−0.09689	0.00106
CATH20	0.41856	−0.11380	0.55477	0.13180	−0.02780	0.27923
CATH26	0.12091	−0.17262	0.38414	0.29043	−0.10929	−0.42486
CATH32	0.09441	0.28750	0.58875	0.31276	0.17232	−0.01420
CATH38	0.15732	−0.11352	0.38178	0.05138	−0.04390	−0.01385
CATH44	0.71796	0.10666	0.02860	0.03613	0.13301	−0.03482
CATH50	0.09133	−0.03687	0.66891	−0.01539	0.06661	−0.27122
CATH56	−0.01109	0.08078	0.84449	−0.01387	0.04143	0.07619
HF3	0.14088	0.08295	0.11941	0.72812	−0.00519	0.11153
HF9	0.13412	0.31368	0.21337	0.45942	−0.02128	0.07953
HF15	0.26363	0.12848	0.37186	0.63070	0.24217	0.02270
HF21	0.37138	0.17721	0.13071	0.03438	0.12800	−0.02234
HF27	−0.02909	−0.18172	0.52765	0.56114	0.19366	0.03037
HF33	0.02993	0.01558	0.78056	0.18191	0.11765	−0.09440
HF45	0.14078	0.88878	0.02158	0.08561	0.10587	−0.01764
HF57	0.33121	0.24457	0.50787	0.08499	0.17597	−0.06528
SEVAL4	0.26427	0.03131	0.05127	−0.01893	−0.10946	0.82233
SEVAL10	0.09858	0.27568	0.01527	0.01232	0.00814	−0.03949
SEVAL16	0.02268	0.21922	0.09519	0.03286	0.08413	0.01417
SEVAL22	−0.05133	0.07861	0.15227	0.18074	−0.17046	0.07150
SEVAL28	0.23210	0.08598	0.15658	0.11247	0.17291	0.06271
SEVAL34	0.37202	0.15850	−0.27679	0.05641	0.25888	0.03331
SEVAL40	0.75016	0.03280	−0.03801	0.17546	−0.01258	0.07109
SEVAL46	−0.09152	0.21557	0.29460	−0.06449	−0.01807	−0.16783
SEVAL52	0.70498	−0.12066	0.31356	0.13317	0.05418	0.10093
SEVAL58	0.86660	0.07520	0.03447	0.10900	0.01693	0.13425
SEXP5	−0.09282	−0.05063	−0.04751	0.39239	0.23695	0.21273
SEXP11	−0.12674	−0.25538	−0.00328	0.40627	0.28552	−0.03723
SEXP17	0.06718	−0.08108	0.27512	0.48531	−0.07769	−0.02625
SEXP23	0.03364	0.01300	0.73971	0.32458	0.01540	0.02579
SEXP29	0.26034	−0.04311	0.08325	0.08293	0.04846	−0.01945
SEXP41	0.09060	0.10872	0.12580	0.04957	−0.01780	0.08299
SEXP47	−0.01025	0.62855	−0.03477	0.17366	−0.11713	−0.06768
SEXP53	0.31554	0.14448	0.16159	0.52070	0.03467	−0.20786

(continued)

Table 3.2 (continued)

	Factor 1	Factor 2	Factor 3	Factor 4	Factor 5	Factor 6
SEXP59	0.20998	−0.19926	0.16253	0.49756	0.12374	−0.07541
V6	0.42517	−0.31331	0.24184	−0.32093	−0.06538	−0.05639
V12	0.12556	0.17642	0.04970	0.82568	−0.14210	−0.10932
V18	−0.05690	0.50729	0.30046	−0.01966	−0.03932	0.33975
V24	0.40264	−0.06691	0.13551	0.22340	−0.11599	0.26397
V30	0.18356	0.19690	−0.10628	0.08957	−0.07504	0.05996
V36	0.01667	−0.01097	−0.13863	0.09093	−0.37986	0.16937
V42	−0.27340	0.09007	0.03360	−0.03887	−0.44492	0.04071
V48	0.26316	0.04002	0.10098	0.01950	0.16965	−0.04514
V54	0.62774	0.06359	0.06722	0.09456	0.04909	−0.01601
V60	0.07219	0.26922	−0.02051	−0.04763	0.02282	−0.07657
Eigen Values	11.939798	6.600187	4.328339	2.928014	2.652204	2.447246
Portion	0.217	0.120	0.079	0.053	0.048	0.044
Cum Portion	0.217	0.337	0.416	0.469	0.517	0.562

[a] ACH = achievement; CATH = catharsis; HF = health and fitness; SEVAL = social evaluation; SEXP = social experience; V = vertigo.

tinuous testing of elderly subjects. Cross-cultural variations among the elderly in language and experience may preclude utilizing a structured behavioral inventory of this nature in assessing the construct validity of the proposed attitude model. Structured interviews or semantic differential assessments may be more viable assessment strategies for understanding the attitudes of the elderly toward participating in physical activity. It is suggested, however, that understanding the attitudes that the elderly segment of our population has toward participating in physical activity is a paramount concern, particularly if successful programs of physical activity are to be implemented for the elderly.

Role of Physical Activity in the Mental Health of the Elderly

Much of the impetus for presenting research to this point on what is known about the elderly's involvement in and attitudes toward physical activity has been based on the premise that physical activity is beneficial to the health of the older person. There are an extensive number of research investigations to support the contention that the values of physical fitness and activity are not circumscribed by age. Exercise physiology research investigations (e. g., see excellent reviews by Clarke, 1977; Nielsen, 1974;

Shephard, 1978) clearly document evidence supporting the trainability of older people through exercise—even among individuals who have been inactive for many years. Through programs of regular exercise such as calisthenics, jogging, and swimming, improvements have been found among the elderly on systolic and diastolic blood pressure, percentage of body fat, vital capacity, oxygen pulse, blood volume, working heart rate, and blood lactate concentration. In general, exercise can significantly improve the physical working capacity and efficiency of the older person. In fact, in one of the few research investigations on elderly women, Adams and deVries (1973) reported that the trainability of these subjects was of similar magnitude to those commonly reported for young females.

This is not to suggest that physical activity, particularly vigorous physical activity, can inhibit physiological change due to aging or the infliction of disease. However, it is suggested that many physiological changes, particularly the loss of aerobic capacity or vigor (deVries, 1979), occur because of habitual inactivity, a deconditioning that appears to occur from our increasingly sedentary life style as we age. It is a serious mistake to believe that our need for exercise diminishes and eventually disappears as we grow older. It is clear that any intelligent choice of life style cannot operate to the exclusion of participation in vigorous physical activity.

Of particular interest to this author is the role that physical activity plays in the mental health of the aged. A review of the literature reveals a shocking scarcity of research that addresses this issue. Buccola and Stone (1975) investigated the psychological effects of participation in a 14-week (3 days per week) jogging or cycling program on men aged 60–79 years. Psychological assessment was limited to scores on Cattell's 16 PF. Posttest analyses of data revealed statistically significant improvements on the traits of surgency and self-sufficiency among those who *elected* the jogging treatment. The cycling group did not evidence any personality change. A 16% subject mortality rate, and the theoretical question of whether personality trait change can be expected to occur when the time spent at a treatment by each subject averaged 114 minutes per week, may limit the ecological validity of this investigation.

Young and Ismail (1976) studied the effects of a physical fitness program on personality change among young and middle-aged high and low physically fit men. The program consisted of calisthenics, progressive running, and recreational activities for a duration of three 90-minute sessions per week for 4 months. The Cattell 16 PF, Eysenck's Personality Inventory, and the anxiety scale of the Multiple Effect Adjective list were used to assess personality change. Initially, the highly fit young group was more dominant and aggressive than the highly fit middle-aged group. Both high-fit groups were more unconventional, composed, secure, easy going, emotionally stable, adventurous, and intellectually inclined than the two low-fit groups. At the end of the 4-month program, the high-fit men were more self-sufficient, and all subjects were more socially precise, persistent, and controlled. What was not clear to this author was the hypothesized rationale for expecting multiple personality trait change as a result of this program. One also cannot rule out the attention provided by these investigators as effecting some of the personality change noted.

Olson (1975) examined the effect of a 15-session, 8-week training program of slow stretch, rhythmic breathing, and special upright exercises on the body image scores of elderly nursing home residents. A control group met during the same time frame for 15 group discussions. Significant improvements in body image were reported for the exercise treatment group.

In a study by deVries and Adams (1972), the tranquilizing effect of exercise was contrasted to the ingestion of meprobamate among 10 subjects aged 52–70 years of age. The investigators found that 15 minutes of walking at a heart rate of 100 beats per minute was sufficient to effect muscular relaxation that lasted for at least 1 hour following exercise. In fact, these investigators claimed that in a single dose, exercise had a significantly greater tranquilizing effect on the musculature, without any undesirable effects, than did meprobamate.

Sidney and Shephard (1976) examined the psychological effects of a 14-week (1 hour, 4 days per week) physical training program of fast walking, jogging, and other forms of endurance work on elderly males and females. Subjects were classified as high- or low-frequency participants, and high- or low-intensity participants based on their observed frequency of attending the program, and on their reported heart rates and observed vigor of participation, respectively. The majority of these subjects had maintained a sedentary life style. The investigators reported a statistically significant, but modest overall decline in manifest anxiety (using Taylor's Manifest Anxiety Scale) among these subjects; most of the decline was attributed to subjects classified as high-frequency but low-intensity participants. No changes were found, however, on a life satisfaction index administered to these subjects. In reference to body image, initially, the female subjects had a more negative concept of their bodies than the male subjects, and a larger discrepancy between their perceived and ideal body image. Whereas the training program was not specifically designed to affect body image, the investigators reported a posttest improvement in body image scores among subjects classified as high-frequency–high-intensity participants. Interestingly, the investigators found that on Kenyon's semantic differential assessment of attitudes toward physical activity, the subjects' attitudes toward physical activity as a means of tension relief improved significantly as a result of the training program.

Stamford, Hambacker, and Fallica (1974) examined the effects of a

12-week treadmill training program on the mental functioning of nine geriatric mental patients. Eight patients served as controls and received similar social stimulation. Whereas improvements in working heart rate and systolic blood pressure were reported in the experimental group, no significant changes in self-concept, sensitivity to others, and impulse regulation (as assessed by the Draw-A-Person Test) were found among these subjects. It is not clear to this author why changes in these psychological parameters should be expected to occur via treadmill exercise.

While the number of investigations examining the psychological effects of participation in physical activity is limited, the majority of studies reported clearly support the positive role that physical activity plays (or could play) in the mental health of the aged. Of particular interest is the suggestion that participation in physical activity serves as a means of reducing anxiety and tension in the elderly. An early report by Cureton (1963) indicated that in his extensive assessment of 2500 adults who had participated in physical conditioning programs at the University of Illinois, decrements in nervous tension were found. And studies reported previously by deVries and Adams (1972), and Sidney and Shephard (1976) support Cureton's (1963) earlier findings. In an extensive review of the literature examining the effects of physical activity on anxiety, Orth (Note 5) concluded that: (a) there is an inverse relationship between physical fitness levels and manifest anxiety; (b) short-term exercise can reduce state anxiety, particularly among subjects who are initially highly anxious; and (c) the prescribed usage of physical exertion can reduce clinical anxiety symptoms and/or phobic reactions. The majority of studies reviewed by Orth (Note 5) focused on younger populations. Nevertheless, there is no theoretical justification for maintaining that the results of these studies cannot be extrapolated to the aged. Studies by deVries and Adams (1972) and Sidney and Shephard (1976) would seem to support this contention. One must recognize, however, that the findings of this limited number of studies may not be generalizable to elderly subjects who do not manifest a great deal of anxiety, who are extremely inactive, and/or who would not be willing to volunteer for participation in physical activity programs of this nature. Clearly, extensive and replicative research investigations are warranted.

Summary and Recommendations

This chapter sought to examine the involvement in and attitudes toward physical activity by the elderly. In addition, the role that physical activity plays in the mental health of the elderly was explored. Evidence presented suggested a declining involvement in physical activity with increasing age. Although no definitive explanation for this pattern is available, it was suggested that cultural expectations in the form of age-related normative sanctions and barriers may be, in part, responsible for the increasingly sedentary life style we pursue as we grow older. A conceptual model was presented that is designed to explore the instrumental values older persons place on participation in physical activity. Finally, evidence was presented supporting the physiological trainability of the elderly, and the potential positive role that physical activity participation could play in the mental health of the older person.

It is clear that social change must occur if physical activity throughout the life cycle is to become an integral part of each individual's life style. Socialization into physical activity must occur during youth and must be continually enculturated and reinforced throughout the life cycle of each individual. Stereotypes and other barriers for participation by the elderly in physical activity must be eliminated.

Programs are needed to train adult fitness leaders (particularly among the elderly) who are sensitive to the physiological constraints and psychological needs of the older person. Exercise prescription must be carefully monitored and adapted to each individual's exercise tolerance level. Exercise prescription must be progressive and must advance the older person's psychological tolerance limits as well (Clarke, 1977). Transportation assistance, improved facilities, and increased government and private foundation support are essential if these objectives are to come to fruition. Guidelines have been developed (e. g., Clarke, 1977; Shephard, 1978) to ensure that every effort will be made to protect the dignity and welfare of each participating individual. The challenge lies in our willingness to be an advocate for a life style initiated, saturated, and sustained in physical activity.

Reference Notes

1. McPherson, B. D. Aging, and involvement in physical activity: A sociological perspective. Paper presented at the International Congress of Physical Activity Sciences, Quebec City, July, 1976.
2. Ostrow, A. C. Validation of a conceptual model characterizing attitudes of the elderly toward lifetime sports: A preliminary report. Paper presented at the Midwest American Alliance for Health, Physical Education, and Recreation Convention, Madison, Wisconsin, April, 1979.
3. Loy, J. W. The professionalization of attitudes toward play as a function of selected social identities and level of sport participation. Paper presented at the International Seminar on Play in Physical Education and Sport, Tel Aviv, Israel, April, 1975.
4. Kenyon, G. S. Values held for physical activity by selected urban secondary school

students in Canada, Australia, England, and the United States (Contract OEC-6-10-179). Washington, D.C.: United States Office of Education, 1968.
5. Orth, D. The effects of physical activity on anxiety: A review of the literature. Unpublished paper, West Virginia University, Morgantown, 1978.

References

Adams, G. M., & deVries, H. A. Physiological effects of an exercise training regimen upon women aged 52 to 79. *Journal of Gerontology*, 1973, *28*, 50–55.

Ahammai, I., & Baltes, P. Objective vs. perceived age differences in personality: How do adolescents, adults, and older people view themselves and each other? *Journal of Gerontology*, 1972, *27*, 46–51.

Albinson, J. G. Attitude measurement in physical education: A review and discussion. In B. S. Rushall (Ed.), *The status of psychomotor learning and sport psychology research*. Nova Scotia: Sport Science Associates, 1975.

Alderman, R. B. *Psychological behavior in sport*. Philadelphia: W. B. Saunders, 1974.

Buccola, V. A., & Stone, W. J. Effects of jogging and cycling programs on physiological and personality variables in aged men. *Research Quarterly*, 1975, *46*, 134–138.

Bultena, G., & Wood, V. Leisure orientation and recreational activities of retirement community residents. *Journal of Leisure Research*, Winter, 1970, 3–15.

Clarke, H. H. (Ed.). National adult physical fitness survey. *President's Council on Physical Fitness and Sports Newsletter*, 1973, 1–27.

Clarke, H. H. (Ed.). National adult physical fitness survey. *Physical Fitness Research Digest*, 1974, *4*, 1–27.

Clarke, H. H. (Ed.). Exercise and aging. *Physical Fitness Research Digest*, 1977, *7*, 1–27.

Conrad, C. C. When you're young at heart. *Aging*, 1976, *258*, 11–13.

Cureton, T. H. Improvement of psychological states by means of exercise fitness programs. *Journal of Association of Physical and Mental Rehabilitation*, 1963, *17*, 14–17.

deVries, H. A. Role of exercise in aging. *American Alliance for Health, Physical Education, and Recreation News Kit on Programs for the Aging*, March, 1979, 1–8.

deVries, H. A., & Adams, G. M. Electromyographic comparison of single doses of exercise and meprobamate as to effects on muscular relaxation. *American Journal of Physical Medicine*, 1972, *3*, 130–141.

Espenschade, A. S. Role of exercise in the well-being of women 35–80 years of age. *Journal of Gerontology*, 1969, *24*, 86–89.

Festinger, L. A. A theory of social comparison processes. *Human Relations*, 1954, *17*, 117–140.

Goldberg, L. R. Some recent trends in personality assessment. *Journal of Personality Assessment*, 1972, *36*, 547–560.

Harris, D. V. Physical activity attitudes of middle-aged males. In G. S. Kenyon (Ed.), *Contemporary psychology of sport*. Chicago: The Athletic Institute, 1970.

Hickey, T., Hickey, L., & Kalish, R. Children's perceptions of the elderly. *Journal of Genetic Psychology*, 1968, *112*, 227–235.

Kenyon, G. S. A conceptual model for characterizing physical activity. *Research Quarterly*, 1968, *39*, 96–105. (a)

Kenyon, G. S. Six scales for assessing attitude toward physical activity. *Research Quarterly*, 1968, *39*, 566–574. (b)

Lewko, J. H., & Greendorfer, S. L. Family influence and sex differences in children's socialization into sport: A review. In D. M. Landers & R. W. Christina (Eds.), *Psychology of motor behavior and sport-1977*. Champaign, Ill.: Human Kinetics Publishers, 1978.

Maehr, M. L. Toward a framework for the cross-cultural study of achievement motivation: McClelland reconsidered and redirected. In M. G. Wade & R. Martens (Eds.), *Psychology of motor behavior and sport.* Champaign, Ill.: Human Kinetics Publishers, 1974.

Martens, R. Competition: In need of a theory. In D. M. Landers (Ed.), *Social problems in athletics.* Urbana: University of Illinois Press, 1976.

Nielsen, A. B. Physical activity patterns of senior citizens. Unpublished master's thesis, University of Alberta, 1974.

Olson, M. I. The effects of physical activity on the body image of nursing home residents. Unpublished master's thesis, Springfield College, 1975.

Promoli, F., McCabe, J., & Shaw, S. Attitudes toward individuals participating in sex stereotyped sports. *Proceedings of the Ninth Canadian Psycho-Motor Learning and Sports Psychology Symposium,* Banff, Alberta, 1977.

Scanlan, T. K. Social evaluation: A key developmental element in the competitive process. In R. A. Magill, M. J. Ash, & F. L. Smoll (Eds.), *Children in sport: A contemporary anthology.* Champaign, Ill.: Human Kinetics Publishers, 1978.

Shephard, R. J. *Physical activity and aging.* Chicago: Year Book Medical Publishers, Inc., 1978.

Sidney, K. H., & Shephard, R. J. Attitudes toward health and physical activity in the elderly: Effects of a physical training program. *Medicine and Science in Sports,* 1976, *8,* 246–252.

Simon, J. A., & Smoll, F. L. An instrument for assessing children's attitudes toward physical activity. *Research Quarterly,* 1974, *45,* 407–415.

Stamford, B. A., Hambacker, W., & Fallica, A. Effects of daily physical exercise on the psychiatric state of institutionalized geriatric mental patients. *Research Quarterly,* 1974, *45,* 34–41.

Veroff, J. Social comparison and the development of achievement motivation. In C. P. Smith (Ed.), *Achievement-related motives in children.* New York: Russell Sage Foundation, 1969.

Welford, A. T. *Aging and human skill.* London: Oxford University Press, 1958.

Young, J. R., & Ismail, A. H. Personality differences of adult men before and after a physical fitness program. *Research Quarterly,* 1976, *47,* 513–519.

Chapter **4**

The Competent Older Woman

CAROL BOELLHOFF GIESEN
NANCY DATAN

Among the most common stereotypes associated with aging is the image of the old as dependent, passive, incompetent, and generally unable to deal with the problems and crises of life. The consequences of this belief may be both positive and negative. Its positive consequences can be seen, for example, in the thoughtful efforts of many individuals and groups who seek to eliminate or alleviate the problems and stresses encountered by the elderly as well as in the concern expressed by adult children toward the happiness and welfare of their elderly parents. These positive gestures, however, are countered by the many negative attributes associated with aging and the patronizing attitudes sometimes surrounding helpful efforts. Although the patronization of the elderly may include elements of protective concern, on the whole it reflects a view of older individuals as victims unable to help themselves. As David Gutmann (Chapter 7, this volume) has pointed out, this view is not confined to the nonprofessional. Despite cross-cultural and research evidence suggesting that executive capacities may develop in adulthood, psychiatrists and psychologists continue to view their older patients as the victims of irremediable loss.

Aging in general is often perceived in a negative manner; furthermore, this is compounded by a double standard: Increasing age for women is perceived more negatively than increasing age for men (Bell, 1979). The

57

presence of a double standard of aging is not surprising in a society where double standards for the sexes have long been the rule. However, we shall suggest that the negative qualities associated with aging women are inaccurate reflections of their actual capabilities. In addition, we will propose that the stereotype of the older woman as dependent, passive, and lacking competence is based upon two misconceptions. The first of these misconceptions is that the older woman of today has not had to acquire a level of competence similar to that required of older men. The second misconception is that with increasing age, the ability to exhibit competence in the resolution of everyday problems decreases. Thus, our paper rediscovers the obvious: That life brings change, change brings growth—and with growth, competence. We will argue that the double standard of aging is an inaccurate reflection of personal and interpersonal competence in older women and that the stereotype of older women as passive, dependent, and lacking in instrumentality is based upon a misconception.

A review of research on perception of old age (McTavish, 1971) has shown that older people in general are seen as ill, tired, mentally slower, forgetful, less able to learn new things, grouchy, withdrawn, unproductive, defensive, less likely to participate in activities, and more likely to feel sorry for themselves—an image of aging that is negative for both sexes. Unfortunately, egalitarianism in stereotyping the aged is not the rule. The negative stereotypes of age hit women harder than men: A double standard can be seen in jokes about aging, in the perceived need for age concealment, and in the norms and images associated with the sexuality of later life (Bell, 1979; Datan & Rodeheaver, 1977, 1979; Palmore, 1971). In the language of our culture, the phrase "you old woman" is more insulting than the term "you son-of-a-bitch."

In 1930, Carl Jung included in an essay on the stages of life a discussion of the awakening to social responsibility and social consciousness of women after their fortieth birthdays. According to Jung, these women who "donned the trousers and opened up a shop" (Jung, 1930) could be observed to possess a "masculine" tough-mindedness and sharpness. In his discussion, he compared masculinity and femininity and their psychic components to a "definite store of substances of which, in the first half of life, unequal use is made." In the earlier part of their lives, Jung said, women use much of their store of feminine substance and in the latter part a "hitherto unused supply of masculinity" becomes available. While he did not address the issue of competence and instrumentality directly, his view of aging women contradicts the stereotyped view of older women in our culture; in Jung's view dependency and passivity are replaced by tough-mindedness, sharpness, and a decline in sentimentality. Unfortunately, this transformation was considered by Jung to represent a "loss" of "feminity," not a gain in humanity.

A family developmental perspective has been employed by David Gutmann (1975) in his discussion of parenthood as a key to a comparative study of the life cycle. In the early phases of life, both sexes are involved in the acquisition of those qualities essential to parenthood, that is, the inculcation of trust in others, the joy of competence, the attainment of reliable inner controls, and the training of executive ego capacities. In early parenthood, the narcissism of childhood is transformed into the nurturance of parenthood and, during these early years, women nurture their husbands and children. These changes follow as a natural outcome of the fulfillment of adult developmental potentials; potentials which will not be realized if parenthood is not experienced. According to Gutmann (Chapter 7, this volume) parenthood is vital to maturation for women. As a pivotal period of life, maternity initiates the decisive separation from their mothers and the introduction to, and acceptance of, a finite life cycle. A lack of the parental experience predisposes women to developmental pathology in later life; thus, parenting assumes an essential role in the development of women.

As the responsibilities of parenting diminish, women tend to become more aggressive, domineering, and authoritarian. Gutmann suggests that these changes in women are accompanied by changes in men toward dependency and affiliation; together these changes represent a trend toward a "normal androgyny" of later life (Chapter 7, this volume). The implications of Gutmann's work, as with those of Jung, contradict the prevailing stereotype of the older woman. Indeed, Gutmann suggests that increased instrumentality and decreased dependency are among the age-related changes seen in women, changes that lead to the maturation of new executive capacities.

In a world where both sexes daily encounter the experiences that shape their lives, the acquisition and expression of competence and instrumentality cannot be assumed to be limited to a particular age or sex. Chiriboga and Thurnher (1976) reported that the older women in an urban sample perceived themselves as becoming more assertive, less dependent, capable of resolving their problems, and as shifting from a subordinate role within the family to one of authority. They describe the women in this age group as having "hit their stride" in their older years and as resembling middle-aged males with respect to competence; their subjects tended to attribute to themselves the qualities of confidence, self-control, and versatility. Their findings are consonant with those of Huerta and Horton (1978) who reported that elderly victims, both female and male, of flood disasters were better able to cope with the emotional impact and material losses than were younger victims. The competence of both sexes in dealing with large-scale disaster was so striking that the authors suggested that a support network of elderly females and males be organized to cope with future incidences such as floods and other natural disasters.

To sum up, theory and research suggest that the stereotypical views of older women are misconceptions shared by many who have not yet realized that the accumulation of time does not erode the accumulation of experience and the learned ability to cope effectively with life. Unfortunately, the misconceptions persist. Evidence of these misconceptions was found in a recent small-scale projective study investigating younger and older respondents' perceptions of the types of problems experienced by young people and old people (Giesen, 1979). Respondents were shown stimulus pictures of women and men of various ages and were asked to describe the types of problems the pictured individuals might be encountering, to recommend feasible solutions, and to describe the probable outcomes for older persons experiencing such problems. Although young and old respondents recommended similar solutions, young respondents were likely to forecast the efforts of older individuals at problem solving as doomed, while older respondents foresaw effective coping.

In general, younger respondents saw negative outcomes as a consequence of the increasing inability of older people to implement solutions to problems, particularly older women. The perceived problems and the anticipated negative or doubtful outcomes associated with older women were seen by younger subjects as primarily stemming from increased dependency needs, decreased instrumentality, and a taskless future. In short, younger respondents seemed to suggest that older women had completed their life tasks and nothing further remained. Younger subjects' perceptions of older men, though also negative, were more favorable. They were seen as having fewer problems than older females, as being relatively more capable of implementing problem solutions, and as acting in their later years as advisors and mentors of younger people. It is interesting to note that, in some instances, a problem shared by both older women and men was attributed to different causes. Loneliness, for example, was perceived as occurring in older women because life had passed them by, whereas loneliness in older males was seen as due to their own decision to reduce social participation.

In order to further examine the characteristics attributed to older women and men, a list of 32 terms (e.g., dependent, generous, traditional, lonely), which had been used by the younger respondents as descriptors for the stimulus pictures of older persons, was presented to 150 undergraduate psychology students. They were asked to check the sex and age category most applicable to each term. The results from this brief survey showed that young students perceived old age for women as characterized by negative affect (e.g., fearful, grieving, suspicious) and by passivity and decreased instrumentality (e.g., dependent, incompetent, accepting). For males, old age was also characterized by negative affect (e.g., bitter, angry, rigid); however, decreased instrumentality was less evident and autonomy more obvious (e.g., independent, refuses advice, wise, experienced).

The consistency of these findings with those of other studies demonstrating negative perceptions of the old, and particularly the older women, is not surpising. It is, however, disappointing. A large majority (80%) of the 150 undergraduate respondents were students in an introductory life-span developmental psychology course; their curriculum had not taught them optimism. If, as Philibert (1977) has suggested, we create our own old age as we teach our children, we must begin by recognizing the remarkable pervasiveness of negative stereotypes of the old.

The Concept of Competence

Competence has been defined by White (1959) as the "capacity to interact effectively with the environment," whereas interpersonal competence has been defined as a "set of abilities allowing individuals to shape the responses they get from others [Weinstein, 1969]." The notion of competence in popular usage, however, is often confined to individuals' skills in a limited occupational context, for example, with reference to a specific set of occupational abilities. The competent mechanic, for instance, understands the complexities of engines and is capable of diagnosing their malfunctions and restoring them to good working order, while a competent physician may be able to perform a somewhat similar service for human beings. The competent business manager supervises finances, employee relationships, and productivity, and directs these concerns to maintain a satisfactory level of profit. Though "housewife" is an occupation (Lopata, 1971), it is seldom seen as such; housewives are rarely described as "competent."

The competence of professional men is generally seen as the natural outcome of a combination of individual ability, prolonged effort, and experience. If, however, these professionals are women, their professional competence may be viewed as somewhat unusual and their personal lives may be regard with some suspicion (Datan & Rodeheaver, 1979; Horner, 1970). In addition, while competence is a prerequisite for success in any occupation, the term *competent* is not usually applied to the normative tasks and role responsibilities of women who are homemakers. Success in the completion of these normative tasks and responsibilities, however, may require competence at a level at least equal to, and in some circumstances, greater than the level of competence required for occupational success. The fact that competence in women is and always has been a necessary ingredient in the survival of families appears to have been overlooked.

Although narrow research perspectives and a concept of bipolar sex role behaviors (Rebecca, Hefner, & Oleshansky, 1976) may have led to this oversight, more than 25 years ago, White (1952) predicted that researchers would fail in their efforts to describe human growth, including the growth of competence, unless a thorough investigation of the nature of individual reality was made. White included the many external factors contributing to personal change, the inner motivations and inhibitions directing an individual's responses to external factors, and the ability of the individual to change the environment. His model would not exclude the competent housewife.

The Growth of Competence

One model of human development that encompasses both external and internal determinants of growth and change is the dialectical model, a model in which contradiction and the negation of contradiction constitute the basis for continuing development. Riegel's dialectical interpretation suggests that all growth or development occurs as a result of the pressures applied by the interactions of four interdependent dimensions: the outer-physical, inner-biological, sociological-cultural, and the individual-psychological. Asynchronous interactions among one or more of these four dimensions creates crises or disequilibrium for individuals, thereby posing problems in adjustment and producing the impetus for developmental change (Riegel, 1975).

The concept of crisis, however, although defined as "situations which place high demands on individuals to adjust their behavior to new circumstances [Lieberman, 1975]," gains meaning as disequilibrium only when viewed as either a long-term condition or a sudden impact that throws an individual off balance (Riegel, 1975). The terms *crisis* or *disequilibrium* then may be applied to situations that place high demands on individuals either to adjust their behavior to new long-term circumstances or to react adaptively to sudden impacts in such a way that equilibrium may be eventually regained.

We suggest that adaptive reactions to crises or periods of disequilibrium imply the use of behavioral competence: That is, an intentional change in behavior, such that an individual surmounts or survives a life crisis or period of imbalance, is an expression of competence. In the remainder of this chapter, we shall apply a dialectical interpretation of development to the retrospective accounts of older women describing their perceptions of their growth in competence and the crises or periods of disequilibrium they perceived as causing their change. The exploratory interviews reported here were gathered over a period of 1½ years as part of two studies in stress and coping and problems and coping strategies (Giesen, 1978 a, b). Most of the women in these studies were the wives of underground miners; all were residents of Morgantown or the immediate area. Their demographic characteristics are described in detail in Table 4.1.

Contrary to our students' beliefs, most of the women in this investigation believed that they had gained in competence over the years and that they were now more able to deal effectively with their lives than previously. The changes they had undergone were attributed to learning, and learning was attributed to their experiences over time. As a result of these experiences, the women believed they had increased their abilities to cope with and solve problems, and in addition, had acquired other qualities such as patience, consideration, and reflectiveness. Their perceptions of themselves as more effective individuals were described as increased self-confidence and as being "stronger in a lot of ways," "more independent," and as "better at solving problems." One woman, for example, said, "A lot of things that I used to couldn't cope with, I'm more apt to able to cope with," and another woman reported, "I think I solve [problems] quicker . . . . I seem to be faster . . . you become more mature because of problems . . . . I think I can solve problems better by being exposed . . . it makes you learn how to be more independent." A third woman considered herself better able to solve problems because "I generally *know* what there is to do, what can be done . . . it's experience, I guess, really . . . having

Table 4.1
Demographic Characteristics of Respondents

Respondent number	Age	Number of children	Marital status	Education	Husband's occupation
1	62	4	Married	9	Miner (retired)
2	57	4	Married	10	Miner
3	49	5	Married	8	Miner
4	68	3	Widow	8	Laborer (deceased)
5	67	3	Widow	8	Laborer (deceased)
6	65	2	Married	10	Miner (retired)
7	51	7	Married	8	Miner
8	43	3	Married	12	Miner
9	47	6	Married	10	Miner

had to cope with trials before. You know what you *can* do . . . and what
other people might have done . . . and you decide on the right one, or
what you think is the right one and do it . . . you just can't wait for
someone to tell you."

Other changes mentioned by these women were the gradual acquistion
of a greater understanding of life and its problems and the ability to reflect
on problems. One woman reported that "I can understand a lot of things
better now than I could when I was younger . . . life in general is easier to
see" while another woman said, "I think you learn to think things through,
you know, before you jump to a conclusion," and still another woman
stated that, "after you get a few years older, you get a few years wiser . . .
I mean I stop and think more . . . where years back I might just fly to
pieces . . . . I think after you get a little older you get more sense."

Competence in Childhood: Women's Interpretations

These women's perceptions of their increased ability to deal effectively
with the problems of life cannot be assumed to have been acquired only in
adulthood and, in fact, their memories of the tasks of childhood suggest
that competent performance in those tasks was both required and ap-
proved. A miner's wife, recalling the tasks of her childhood said, "when we
were children everybody had to work . . . we milked cows, fed chickens,
fed pigs, helped with the dishes, learned to cook . . . we learned to do all
those things and we *wanted* to do them . . . back in those days you *had* to
work." Another older woman recalling the need for each family member to
share the family chores said, "we depended on each other . . . they didn't
have [running] water then and if you didn't get spring water, you didn't
have any . . . so you got water from the water that was dripping
underground in the mines . . . we marched like little soldiers inside the
mine . . . everybody had to or you didn't get your clothes washed or
anything."

For some of the women, the responsibilities of youth and adolescence
included the rearing of younger siblings, caring for aging grandparents, or
making a financial contribution to the family. One woman, for example,
said "I didn't get to go to [high] school . . . my father got hit in the head in
the mine and they didn't have [health benefits] like they've got now . . .
but you had to pay your bills . . . so . . . I walked on into town and got a
job."

These women's recollections of their early tasks are colored by the sense
of necessity; children, whether female or male, carried a share of responsibility for the family's welfare. Their contributions were not less because

they were female, and they entered young adulthood confident of their ability to learn and perform the tasks of marriage, parenting, and occasional wage earning.

Competence in Adulthood

For most older women today, the transition from childhood to adulthood was marked by marriage and parenthood. The women in this study underwent just such a transition. The tasks they had formerly performed in their parents' homes they now performed in their own homes; and for some, the crises of their parents' lives were encountered again in their own lives. Most of the women felt that becoming a parent was a major source of change in their lives and they described themselves as having "grown up" because of parenthood. One woman said that "I think I grew up more . . . you know, once you have one baby and then another; it just seems like it changes you . . . you know you've got to do more and all," while another woman said, "It's necessary that you change when you have children and you need to change really rapidly sometimes . . . I've changed and I think I'm a better person now."

In addition to learning new skills as parents, the skills that were learned as children and adolescents were expanded through necessity: If a husband was injured, unemployed, or exhausted, there was no question raised over the appropriateness or inappropriateness of taking on new tasks, but only the urgency of family needs. One woman recalled, "When he couldn't work, then I went to work . . . I've worked at a shirt factory, for doctors, in a laundry, in stores . . . a lot of different places." Another woman said, "I even delivered papers, then I'd come home and get ready and get my ride because I worked in a factory . . . *then* I'd come home and cook supper and go to the ball park because I worked in a concession stand . . . and then on other nights I'd do my housework."

Learning to be competent as a wage earner was not the outer limit of their new learning, however, and most of these women also found it necessary to learn home skills traditionally associated with masculine roles. The various tasks they learned throughout adulthood included shearing sheep, making hay, putting up siding, repairing home appliances, doing plumbing, driving trucks, managing a small business, and last but not least, becoming politically effective. One woman, for example, said, "I've worked on machines and dryers and irons and sweepers and fans . . . and sometimes even on the television," while another woman spoke with pride of obtaining needed school supplies for her own and other children by successfully working for election to the local school board.

While none of the women considered themselves to have led easy lives, they did not feel their lives had been any more difficult than those of other women they knew. The wide range of skills they had acquired and their competence and effectiveness in utilizing those skills were not viewed as deviating from the normal role responsibilities of wives and mothers, and in fact, they believed that doing what needed to be done for their families, and doing it well, was their primary role responsibility.

The Competent Older Woman

The competence and capability of women who have spent 40 or more years coping with a harsh environment and economy, we have found, is not relinquished in late adulthood. The executive processes of middle age—mastery, selectivity, self-awareness, and a wide use of cognitive strategies (Neugarten, 1968)—are carried on into the later years as a matter of course. There is no retirement for most of the older women interviewed; one does not retire from the occupation of homemaker at 62 or 65, and for many women, as the responsibilities of parenthood become fewer, they are replaced by increased instrumental activity in other areas of their lives.

Neugarten (1968) has said that "middle age marks the beginning of a period in which latent talents and capacities can be put to use in new directions," a statement that is strongly supported by the widening range of activities in which the women in this study participate. One older woman, for example, became interested in ceramics in late middle age and as her parental responsibilities decreased over time a hobby became a full-time business, including production, retailing and conducting classes. Another woman pursued her early interest in politics. She taught herself the intricacies of political affairs by active participation at the local level, by reading about and observing legislative business, and by eventually organizing a working political group of women whose efforts are now sought at every local election campaign. Still another woman found full time employment when her husband retired, worked until her own forced retirement, and then replaced this activity with full-time voluntary services including the recruitment and organizing of a small group to expand these services.

The Varieties of Competence

The experiences which led to learning and development were described by the women as "everyday living," "having to take care of things," and as "having to go on anyway even when things don't go the way you want." In short, these women told us that the tasks of women's lives require and engender competence, and indeed, endurance and tenacity.

We have noted that most of the women felt that becoming a parent was a major source of change in their lives and that they felt they had matured and become more effective individuals as a result. Their reports support Gutmann's statement (Chapter 7, this volume) that parenthood represents a pivotal developmental period in the life cycle for women. One aspect of parenting that several women perceived as producing individual growth was their desire to supplement their husband's income as a means of providing for their children the "things in life you want your children to have." Rearing children while simultaneously earning a supplemental income was specifically mentioned as contributing to their growth in self-confidence and competence. One woman who reported that she felt she had to work to "give to" her children, also felt that "when you do that you have to give up something and it boils down to what's important . . . regardless of what you can find to do." The sacrifice of their leisure time or the addition of outside part-time or full-time employment to an already busy working day constituted one of the responsibilities of parenthood and one that a conscientious parent did not shirk.

In addition to child rearing and supplemental wage earning, for one woman a growth in self-confidence and competence was brought about as the result of having to overcome a physical handicap. She had injured her leg and hip as a child and, as a result, had spent many years in a wheelchair or on crutches. The injury continued to handicap her movements throughout adolescence and into adulthood, even though the condition had improved so that she could walk with a cane. As she learned to carry out her responsibilities for her husband and children despite the handicap of limited movement, she learned that not only was she capable of accomplishing routine household duties, but that she also could manage quite well as a wage earner. She recalled that, "I think I was afraid of the public because I was crippled . . . . I had an inferiority complex which I know now wasn't good for me . . . . I overcame it after a certain length of time . . . worked it out, I guess." For this woman, the desire to become a mother and a wife and the necessity to earn a salary provided additional impetus for overcoming her physical limitations and, as a result, she learned that "there's hardly anything I couldn't do."

Without exception, all of the women believed that their personal development would continue as they grew older. They perceived these future changes to be the inevitable result of continuing to learn through day to day experiences, the resolution of new problems, and their own desires to become better persons. One woman described her anticipated change in the future as due to the fact that "we never cease learning and maturing

. . . we learn from other people's mistakes one way or another . . . there's always change, there's always something you have to do and you *do* it." Another woman said, "You can always improve . . . but it's more or less up to the person if you want to improve . . . then you just keep working at it," and a third woman said, "I think we change every day . . . it's necessary that you change." In general, their attitudes toward their future selves are best described by one woman who reported that, "I hope to be a better person . . . I don't *want* to stay the same when there's things to learn . . . you know, you can always get to be better if you try."

Discussion

We have proposed that a double standard of aging forms the basis for the stereotypical view of the older woman, and that this view is based upon misconceptions that disregard the competence needed for the normative life tasks of women and assume the loss of competence with increasing age. The women in this study have had to become competent and effective individuals in order to insure the survival of their families. The basis for this competence was laid down in childhood, not only as they learned to perform routine household chores, but also as they acquired a sense of pride in their performance and individual responsibility for the welfare of their family. These qualities were carried into adulthood at a time when economic conditions were harsh and marriage and parenthood meant the sacrifice of more than leisure time. Whatever their adolescent dreams of marriage and childrearing had been, the reality of adulthood imposed upon them the additional burden of wage earning, of learning to acquire a variety of new skills, and of learning to accept and adapt to the problems and crises of life.

That they were in fact competent and effective in dealing with their lives cannot be doubted. There is no hint of passivity or dependence in the behavior of women who willingly take on two jobs in order to spare their husbands complete exhaustion. Neither is there any lack of instrumentality shown in decisions to seek employment so that they could provide for their own children the benefits they had not had as children

It might be argued that some portion of their competence and instrumentality is due to the influence of their particular subculture. All of these women were reared in the often harsh and stringent conditions of rural Appalachia where tradition emphasizes independence, endurance, and the acceptance of a difficult and labor-filled life. This argument fails when these West Virginia women are compared to the metropolitan sample of Chiriboga and Thurnher (1976). The women of their study live and work in a large city, about one-third were educated beyond high school, and the authors suggest their social position is more likely the result of social mobility than of self-motivated advance. The women in our sample, however, live and work in a mountainous rural and semirural area at a considerable distance from any metropolitan influence. All have been undereducated by today's standards, and their positions in society reflect a self-motivated desire to achieve security with their own environment rather than social mobility.

Notwithstanding demographic differences between the women in these two studies, city women (Chiriboga and Thurnher, 1976) see themselves in much the same way as our West Virginia women do. Both groups see themselves as competent and capable, able to be assertive when assertiveness is needed, capable of coping with the problems they encounter, and competent not only in caring for themselves but also in continuing to care for others when necessary. Their perceptions of themselves and the manner in which they continue to live out their lives denies the image of the older woman projected by our cultural stereotype.

Riegel's (1975) dialectical model offers a broad perspective under which the many modifying factors in the development of competence may be organized into separate, but not independent, categories. Many of the events in the lives of the women in our study, for example, may be described in terms of conflicts or contradictions between social–cultural pressures and individual–psychological desires. The resolution of these conflicts appear in some cases to have engendered new conflicts and resolutions such that the resolution of each succeeding conflict fostered the step-by-step growth of competent behaviors.

An example of this step-by-step progression may be seen in the recollection of one woman who described some of the events in her life as a series of trials to be overcome. One of the first of these was the necessity for her to overcome her fears concerning her husband's safety in the mine. She described this fear as "something that only a coal miner's wife could tell you . . . because you know he's going under there and you don't know when, or if he's coming out." Her desire to live a life free of this daily fear was in direct conflict with her own expectations concerning the appropriate behaviors of a miner's wife, with the occupational hazards of mining, and the social–cultural norms that directed her husband to seek the type of employment most likely to enable him to support his family.

Her conflict was resolved in part by devoting extra time and attention to childrearing and by assuming the major responsibility for household tasks in order to relieve her husband of this burden. In carrying out this resolution, however, she found it necessary to learn what her children were doing in school, how to help them advance, and how to carry out tasks such as home repairs and maintenance chores. As a result, she discovered that the education her children were receiving might not be sufficient to prepare them for a safer occupation, and that the materials they were given in school were inadequate. To aid in the resolution of this conflict, she found employment outside the home to insure that they would be able to attend college and, as she recalled, "I waited until January and then I got myself elected to the school board . . . I went and found out how much money we could use and went and got everything we needed."

The problems themselves were reflections of interactions between Riegel's (1975) social–cultural and individual–psychological dimensions: Initially, this woman wanted to be free of daily fear over her husband's safety, but the social–cultural and outer–physical environments were such that he could find employment only in mining. At the second step in the progression, she wanted her children to have a better education than the economy and the social organization composing the school board was providing. In her efforts to resolve these conflicts, she acquired new skills and new confidence in her ability to solve further problems. She carried these qualities onward, and now in late adulthood, anticipates that she will continue to be active in political and community affairs.

Although this woman is only a single example of how conflict and resolution may be a source of motivation for the acquisition of competent behaviors, her story is like those of most of the women in our West Virginia sample: In this way, they came to perceive themselves as capable individuals. Not all their accomplishments, of course, were as noteworthy as election to a school board. For some women, conflict and resolution centered about events as common in their lives as needing transportation and learning to drive a car, needing an income and learning to actively seek out employment, or needing to become efficient planners and learning to plan family affairs around two or more different working schedules. Although these problems may be considered common, they cannot be considered trivial when the need is urgent and the welfare of a family depends on a successful solution.

Conclusion

We have suggested that the stereotype of older women as passive, dependent, and lacking instrumentality is based upon two misconceptions: First, that older women have not had to acquire a level of competence similar to that of older men, and second, that competence in the resolution of everyday problems decreases with increasing age. The concept of competence, although often used to describe occupational performance, is

seldom applied to women carrying out their normative tasks and responsibilities. The successful completion of normative role tasks and responsibilities requires a level of competence similar to that required for occupational success, as we see clearly in the statements of the older women in our
sample. The recollections of the women concerning the tasks and responsibilities of their childhood and adulthood illustrate the need to acquire
competence in many areas including a variety of skills not usually
associated with "feminine" roles. They have told us that life brings change,
change brings growth, and with growth, competence emerges.

Moreover, we refuse to believe that the competence and capabilities acquired over a period of 40 years or so is suddenly relinquished in old age.
Our West Virginia women do not view themselves now as growing dependent and passive, nor do they anticipate becoming dependent and passive
as they grow old. On the contrary, they believe that, as they grow older,
they will continue to learn and develop and to become "better persons."
They believe the "everyday experiences" have taught them to cope with the
problems of life and that they will continue to cope.

Finally, we suggest that the double standard of aging, the myth that aging is swifter and harsher for women than for men, is in reality a double-
edged sword. If the older women in our sample are representative of older
women in general, then most women have acquired a wider variety of occupational skills than their husbands: They have encountered and resolved
a greater range of emotional and material problems, and they have not had
to leave their occupational world behind them as they aged. If prior skill,
experience, and a sense of usefulness are determinants of successful aging,
then the competent older woman, who we have failed to recognize, is advantaged over men in the transition to old age.

References

Bell, I. The double standard: age. In J. Freeman (Ed.), *Women: A feminist perspective*. Palo
   Alto, Calif.: Mayfield, 1979.
Chiriboga, D., & Thurnher, M. Concept of self. In M. Lowenthal, M. Thurnher, & D. Chiri-
   boga (Eds.), *Four stages of life*. San Francisco: Jossey–Bass, 1976.
Datan, N., & Rodeheaver, D. Dirty old women: The emergence of the sensuous grandmother.
   Invited contribution to symposium "Socialization to become an old woman." M.
   Seltzer, chairman. American Psychological Association, San Francisco, 1977.
Datan, N., & Rodeheaver, D. Beyond generativity: toward a sensuality of later life. In R.
   Weg (Ed.), *Aging: An international annual* (Vol. 1). Reading, Mass: Addison–Wesley,
   1979 (in press).
Giesen, C. Stress and coping among the wives of West Virginia coal miners. Unpublished
   master's thesis, West Virginia University, 1978.(a)

Giesen, C. Problems and coping strategies: A comparison between younger and older individuals. Unpublished manuscript, West Virginia University, 1978. (b)

Giesen, C. A brief survey on stereotypes of aging among college students. Unpublished manuscript, West Virginia University, 1979.

Gutmann, D. Parenthood: A key to the comparative study of the life cycle. In N. Datan & L.H. Ginsberg (Eds.), *Life-span developmental psychology: Normative life crises.* New York: Academic Press, 1975.

Horner, M.S. Femininity and successful achievement: A basic inconsistency. In J. Bardwick, E. Douvan, M.S. Horner, D. Gutmann, *Feminine personality and conflict.* Belmont, California: Brooks–Cole, 1970.

Huerta, R., & Horton, R. Coping behaviors of elderly flood victims. *The Gerontologist,* 1978, *18*(6), 541–546.

Jung, C.G. The stages of life. In J. Campbell (Ed.), *The portable Jung.* New York: Viking Press, 1971.

Lieberman, M. Adaptive processes in late life. In N. Datan & L.H. Ginsberg (Eds.), *Life-span developmental psychology: Normative life crises.* New York: Academic Press, 1975.

Lopata, H. *Occupation: housewife.* New York: Oxford University Press, 1971.

McTavish, D. Perceptions of old people: A review of research methodologies and findings. *The Gerontologist,* 1971 (Winter) Pt. *11,* 90–91.

Neugarten, B. *Middle age and aging.* Chicago: University of Chicago Press, 1968.

Palmore, E. Attitudes toward aging shown by humor. *The Gerontologist,* 1971 (autumn) Pt. *1,* 181–186.

Philibert, M. A philosophy of aging. Invited address, West Virginia University Gerontology Pro Seminar Series, November 1977.

Rebecca, M., Hefner, R., & Oleshansky, B. A model of sex-role transcendence. *Journal of Issues,* 1976, *32*(3), 197–206.

Riegel, K. Adult life crises: A dialectical interpretation of development. In N. Datan & L.H. Ginsberg (Eds.), *Life-span developmental psychology: Normative life crises.* New York: Academic Press, 1975.

Weinstein, E. The development of interpersonal competence. In D. Goslin (Ed.), *Handbook of socialization theory and research.* Chicago: Rand McNally, 1969.

White, R. *Lives in progress, a study of the natural growth of personality.* New York: Dryden Press, 1952.

White, R.W. Motivation reconsidered: The concept of competence. *Psychological Review, 66* (5), 1959, 297–333.

PART II

FAMILY TRANSITIONS OF AGING

Chapter 5

Intergenerational Relations in Later Life: A Family System Approach

LILLIAN E. TROLL

Most current thinking about intergenerational relations is from one of four perspectives: helping, influencing, interaction, and bonding. Welfare workers and policy makers are concerned with the amount and kind of aid exchanged by family members; occasionally they are interested in the way different generations feel about helping one another. Developmental and social psychologists are concerned with how much one generation affects another's values, beliefs, or behaviors. Family theorists and sociologists study how much members of each generation include members of other generations in their social interaction: how much they keep in contact or share family rituals. Only recently, a few developmental and personality psychologists have drawn attention to family bonding: how much members of one generation are attached to members of other generations. Very few theorists, researchers, policy makers, or professional workers have regarded the family as a system, particularly the family extended beyond the childrearing unit.

Helping studies usually focus on older or disabled individuals, either singly or as generalized categories that turn to sets of generalized others, such as children or kin, for goods and services. Variations in the family constellations or values of these old parents and their children or kin are ignored.

TRANSITIONS OF AGING

Socialization studies are often not too different. Again older people, in aggregate, are compared with younger generations, also in aggregate, to see similarities or differences in generation mean values or behaviors. Even where data have been collected by family, they are collapsed into generational groups so that only average generational differences can be observed: the generation of parents compared to the generation of children. Such a treatment loses any information about intrafamily processes. (See Troll & Bengtson, 1979; and Bengtson & Troll, 1978, for a more detailed discussion of this point.)

Social participation studies are usually like helping studies. In fact, visiting of older parents by their children is frequently counted as a kind of help.

The study of social bonding is the one perspective that, by concentrating on a person-to-person or dyadic relationship, keeps at least the measurement within the family. On the other hand, the attachment or bonding literature rarely examines dyadic relationships as part of larger interactional systems. Sociologists like Simmel (1950) have considered the differing structural properties of dyads and triads with reference to the impact of parenthood on a young couple (Aldous, 1978), or of an older mother-in-law upon a middle-aged couple but have not usually elaborated this hypothesis to larger systems. This is particularly true where older people are concerned, because the family members involved extend beyond the childrearing unit on which most family-system research has been based so far. Consideration of extended families as systems is just now, I think, emerging in theoretical and even to some extent empirical work. The recent volume edited by Lerner and Spanier (1978), although its topic is primarily reciprocal socialization, stimulated several heuristic attempts.

The primary focus of the present chapter is to draw attention to the value of a family system approach to intergenerational relations. In doing so, I will point to diversity of intergenerational relationships as a consequence of diversity in family boundaries and family themes. I will also look briefly—because that is all present evidence allows—at rural–urban variations. Finally, I consider the relation of developmental or period effects to intergeneration relationships.

Family Systems

In 1959 Hess and Handel brought forth *Family Worlds*, an examination of family themes and family cultures in childrearing family units. Their approach has not moved into the main stream of family literature. When I read *Family Worlds* in the middle 1060s, I was impressed. I tried to use the model for empirical research, but found this difficult. I could apply it only indirectly or peripherally, and for a while turned back to individuals and from there gradually into dyads. In the course of a two-generation study of personality similarites between Chicago-area college students and their parents (Troll, Neugarten, & Kraines, 1969), I developed a primitive measure of family integration, consisting of global ratings of all three interview protocols together (student, mother, father), which, to my surprise, contributed significantly to the parents' similarity with their child, even though it had been entered last into the multivariate stepwise regression analysis (Troll, 1967). Later, working with graduate students in a seminar on family dynamics, I developed a series of dyadic attachment scales also based on a model of the family as a system. Ratings by students and unrandomly selected other respondents were interesting enough to incorporate in a tentative chapter on attachment through the life span (Troll & Smith, 1976). Adaptations of these scales have been used in a study of family relationships of golden wedding couples (Parron, 1979). Parron found that her respondents, black and white husbands and their wives, rated their spouse first, their children next, siblings third, and friends last.

So far as theoretical adaptation is concerned, I considered the family system model in a speculative work entitled "Frameworks for the Study of Generations" (Troll, 1971b) and more recently developed this theme in collaboration with Vern Bengtson (Bengtson & Troll, 1978; Troll & Bengtson, 1979). In these two papers, we proposed that the construct of family themes could provide a possible explanation for diversity in intergenerational transmission: Why are certain characteristics transmitted in some families and other characteristics transmitted in other families? Why are youth of some lineages more susceptible to emergent "generation keynote themes" whereas youth in other families do not get caught up in them? We suggest that two major processes are at work (a) a family theme that pervades most members of an extended family and provides continuity in life outlook across generations; and (b) a partially emergent generation or cohort "keynote theme" that distinguishes each new cohort of youth from previous cohorts. Not all members of a cohort adopt the keynote theme—such as particular childrearing values, for example, or addiction to the Beatles. We think that only those youth who had grown up with general family themes that were synchronous with particular new keynotes would find them irresistible.

As a more general question, why are youth in some families more like their parents and other family members than are youth in other families? To look at family dynamics instead of at transmission of personality, why do families develop what Hagestad (1978) terms "demilitarized zones" in order to preserve what seems to be essential family integration and harmony? I made a similar point when I tried to explain my observation that college students and their parents fought about essentially trivial issues but not about important ones (Troll, 1972a).

In their preface, Hess and Handel (1959) refer to the efforts of clinical psychologists and psychiatrists to move beyond the two-person relationship of patient and therapist to a diagnosis of the entire family unit. They criticized these clinicians' approaches because although they pointed to the family as the operative unit, their concept remained those of a two-person or triangular relationship. On the other hand, Hess and Handel pointed out, those who study the famly as a group, sociologists and anthropologists, and who are interested in the forces that link family members to one another, do not include in their explanations of family cohesion any idea that the particular personalities of the individuals who comprise a family are essential elements of its structure.

Family Worlds presents case studies of five families. Perhaps because these families are seen as case studies and case studies are typically the method of the problem solver, this approach did not move as far away from that of the clinician as it might have. I liken this to the literature on coping, which derives from the psychotherapeutic perspective of ego defense mechanisms. Even though it stresses the positive instead of the pathological nature of such mechanisms, few studies of coping mechanisms (cf. Vaillant, 1974) have been able to shake off the mantle of the health–illness or medical model that shrouds behavior *cum* behavior in evaluations of efficacy. Nevertheless, it could be valuable to look at what Hess and Handel said, transposing parents and their young children to families of later life.

First, they define the family as a bounded universe. Its members

inhabit a world of their own making, a community of feeling and fantasy, action and precept . . . . In their mutual interaction, the family members develop more or less adequate understanding of one another, collaborating in the effort to establish consensus and to negotiate uncertainty. The family's life together is an endless process of movement in and around consensual understanding, from attachment to connectedness to withdrawal—and over again. Separateness and connectedness are the underlying conditions of a family's life, and its common task is to give form to both [p. 1] . . . . Within the family, events occur in far from random fashion; even uncertainty is given a customary place in a family's scheme of things . . . . There are tracks to which the interaction returns again and again. A family has discernible pattern and form [p. 2]. . . . The intrapsychic organization of each member is part of the psychosocial structure of his family. . . . . Neither the ties that bind the members to one another nor the barriers that separate them are adequately indicated by overt social behavior alone [p. 3].[1]

Congruence of images results from commonality of experience. There is a *family theme*, defined as a "pattern of feelings, motives, fantasies, and conventionalized understandings grouped about some locus of concern which has a particular form in the personalities of the individual members [p. 11]." Each individual's place in the family can be understood as the way in which he or she participates in this pattern. A theme could stand for some significant issue and the general direction of attempted solution, with each member playing a particular part in this solution.

There seem to be two main measures in such a family unit approach. One is the *family theme*, the other is a *family boundary*, which is an aspect of family integration. Let us now consider a family vis-a-vis an aging member. Suppose such a family values communication. Communicating is part of its theme. Members of such a family would tend toward self-disclosure and the sharing of confidences with other family members. If its boundary is strong—if it is strongly integrated, it would, perhaps, also exclude nonfamily members from the sharing of confidences, although there is no reason to believe that theme and boundary are correlated. Members of this family would feel badly if they were left out of the sharing, or if they left out some other family member. One of my students—a man in his middle twenties to judge by his appearance—reported, in the context of the study of grandparenting, that he always used to enjoy being with his grandmother and talking to her about all sorts of matters in his life. "But now when I talk to her, she doen't seem to get the point." He still visits her frequently and tells her about events in his life, but there is no more joy in the visits. They have become emptied rituals that bring pain because they remind him of what used to be and what should be. Many other class members did not understand why he felt so badly. Their families did not stress communication. Or, their boundaries were looser, they did not feel they had to communicate with all family members; they could easily substitute nonfamily members as communicants.

Here is another story. An old woman invites many members of her family for Thanksgiving. She has been important to all of them: sister, nieces and nephews, children and children-in-law, grandchildren, great grandchildren, and a few other collateral relatives. She prepares an ample and traditional Thanksgiving dinner, large turkey and all, and they come and enjoy her food and then sit down to enjoy once again her wit and warm conversation, and each other's company. But instead of the shared communication they expect, she launches into a bitter monologue about evils in the world and leaves them no room for participation. One by one, her guests and family members move off to talk among themselves, and she sits alone in the crowded room. From time to time, one or another takes a few steps toward her, but hesitates and then draws back. They are left feeling awkward, abused, and guilty. Their family rules have been violated.

These two stories, incidentally, are about people who are "middle-old." They are no longer "young-old" but have not yet become "old-old." They are not what they used to be but they do not require either money or nursing care. On the other hand, their signs of aging upset earlier family interaction patterns. If these particular families did not stress communication, they might not be sensitive to changes in communication. The fact that the one grandmother did not get the point of a conversation, and that the other grandmother thwarted conversation would not disturb families who stress a "strong, silent" theme, for example, or believe actions are more important than words. If so, since the grandmother was still there to be talked to and the old woman had brought her family together, no family readjustment would be necessary and the poignancy of these stories would not exist. Only where behavior change is related to family themes do changes reverberate throughout all members of the system.

Let us consider a different example. The family of one of my friends stresses physical vitality and exploration. My friend's mother, who used to be a brisk woman who went everywhere and saw everything, now move very slowly with a cane. My friend is still a brisk woman who goes everywhere and sees everything. On the other hand, as most family research shows, my friend feels responsible for her mother and wants to brighten her life—and in this family, brightening means going and seeing. But now, when the daughter arranges an outing for her mother, it cannot be spontaneous. It has to involve much forethought and preparation. Are there stairs her mother cannot climb? Will there be enough seats along the walks or aisles so her mother can sit down to rest frequently? When they walk, the daughter has to slow down her own rapid stride to match her mother's snail's pace. This is hard for both of them. Her mother tries to walk faster and then has to stop for breath. The daughter finds that she has gotten ahead and has to go back and wait. Instead of going to many places and seeing many things, they can go to only one place, and even that is exhausting. Both are frustrated. Her mother says, "It's no good. It's better if I stay home and not interfere with your pleasure." Her daughter thinks, "I wish I did not feel that I should include her," and then is angry at herself, and at her mother. In families with a different theme, this would not be the tragedy it is here. The mother would not value going and seeing and could enjoy her daughter's visits at home. The daughter would not feel she should help her mother look and see and would also not mind walking at a snail's pace and restricting her explorations.

Now consider family boundaries. My student continues to visit his grandmother even though he no longer gets reciprocation from her because his communication is geared to family members. Will he be able to turn to a wife or girl friend for such reciprocal review of life's events? Perhaps, but only if he is able to put them within the family boundary, to trust them the same way. The relatives in the Thanksgiving story turned to each other—all members of the extended family. Would they turn as readily to nonfamily members? Would a volunteer or hired companion serve the mother in the third story as well as the daughter, or would the interaction then be changed in quality? It may depend on the strength of the boundary in each family. Some families have more permeable boundaries and others tighter ones. Boundary strength varies widely within other species. Pig-tailed macaques are gregarious; they have weak family boundaries. If one family member is missing, others will do as substitutes, as will even non-family members who happen to be around. Some sea lions off the coast of California are described as so indiscriminately gregarious that they have as much fun playing with members of other species as with conspecifics (Bar-tholomew, 1952). Bonnet monkeys, although closely related to the pig-tailed macaques, are highly selective. While infant pig-tailed macaques whose mothers are removed (Rosenblum, 1979) will turn to wire sur-rogates, to other adults, male or female, or even to other infants, bonnet infants will become isolated and depressed. In naturally evolved settings, pig-tailed macaques form large troops, indiscriminate of age, sex, or family of origin. In naturally evolved settings, bonnet macaques form close-knit family groups, clustering within their family across generations but isolating themselves from other similarly bounded families. Elks are gregarious and the whole herd will participate even in births and childrear-ing (Altmann, 1963). Adult males, when they move off, remain in the general vicinity of their herd, apparently serving as scouts, and returning again to mingle gregariously at mating seasons. Moose, closely related to elks, are close-knit. Mothers and their children form secret and isolated units, the young clearly being trained not to let strangers near. Longitudi-nal studies of humans—at least American humans in Berkeley (Haan & Day, 1974)—show that indiscriminate gregariousness varies with age. It in-creases to a peak during adolescence and decreases during the adult years to greater selectively. In some human cultures, family units are more isolated than in others, even though few are as isolated as Parsons (1965) would have us believe. As Lopata (1971) has noted, members of some families are not encouraged to form friendships outside the family lest family secrets are dispersed—and almost everything would then be con-sidered a family secret. Other human cultures are more gregarious. Members of such families hardly recognize the difference between family and nonfamily, even for loyalty to spouse and children. It seems reasonable to hypothesize that aging people from tight-knit families are not likely to participate in indiscriminately gregarious senior centers or nutrition sites, nor to make new friends easily in nursing homes. They would feel comfortable only with members of their own family. Aging people from more gregarious families would enjoy community-provided group activities at least as much as family activities and find it easier to make new friends wherever they find themselves.

The kind of family older people belong to matters because most older people do have families. Surveys over the last 20 years (see Troll, Miller, & Atchley, 1978) have told us what we should have known from our own experience, that abandonment of older people by their families is a rare rather than a common occurrence. In present cohorts of older people, most who have no living children have never married. Only 20% of those over 65 have no children and most of those who do—more than 90% of them—are in close touch with their children. Not only that, most of those who have no living children do have nieces and nephews, brothers and sisters, and even cousins. It is true that there are some older people who are estranged from kin, and even some who have no kin at all—orphans, for example. These no-kin individuals also can be either gregarious or isolated. Since they are the ones most likely to come to the attention of people in the helping professions, and thus of social policy makers, it makes a difference even for them how gregarious they are in personality. Also, it is true that Americans have been socialized in a country formed by immigrants who left their relatives behind—at least for a while. We are prone, therefore, to extoll the virtues of isolated nuclear family units, and to believe that we indeed have isolated nuclear family units. It usually only takes a question, however, to establish the existence and importance for most of us of parents, sisters, brothers, aunts, uncles, cousins, all of whom we know, whom we see, and, sometimes even like.

Rural–Urban

Among the migrants of the last century are the rural to urban movers. Since it would be younger generations that would move to urban areas in search of employment or adventure and older generations that would remain behind or migrate back to the country, and also since rural people tend to hold traditional extended family values (Kerkhoff, 1965), we might expect not only greater isolation of older generations in rural areas than in urban areas, but also feelings of greater deprivation because their values lead them to expect loyalty and attention from children and other family members. There is no strong evidence for this, however. Recent studies of the effects of migration on kinship (see page 103, Troll, Miller, & Atchley, 1978) suggest strongly that disruptive effects are temporary at most. As Litwak (1960) stated, kin ties in the modified extended family may even assist exploration for occupational advancement. Furthermore, Britton and Britton (1967) found that older people in a rural area in Pennsylvania, although they missed their distant children, reported improved morale and pride from their success. Among most Americans, achievement values probably override familism values. There is also a tendency, after a period of time, for parents past retirement to move near their now settled middle-aged children—that is, if these middle-aged children have not already moved back near their parents. Eventually, more kin may be available to those who have moved to the new area than to those who stayed behind.

In rural Iowa, most social activity of older people is with kin (Powers & Bultena, 1976), at least among men. The same is true for golden wedding couples in semirural New Jersey (Parron, 1979). Two-fifths of the Iowa men and one-third of the women had no close friends outside of their immediate family. The older men interacted with their children and other kin, more often even than did the older women. We should keep in mind that not all rural areas of the United States are alike. The older people in rural Pennsylvania were fulfilled by the success of their children living far from home and did not mind their absence. In fact, those children who stayed near home might provide a constant reminder of their lack of success and thus lower their parents' morale. Children's success reflects on parents' success in rearing them. Geography did not affect family boundaries. In rural Iowa, family boundaries seemed relatively impervious and tight and kept social interaction within the family. In the southern Appalachian region, based on Youman's (1963; 1971) reports, the homogeneous folk character of the culture is associated with more permeable family boundaries. The extended family, like that of the pig-tailed macaques, includes the whole community. In Iowa, to overdo the same analogy, rural families may be more like the bonnet monkeys. Appallachian family boundaries may be much looser than those in rural Iowa and social interactions more generic: a niece or an aunt may be as close as a daughter, the man in the next house whom you have watched grow up as close as a son. Generational lines themselves could be blurred if childrearing continued throughout the fertile years and older people could have young children of their own about the same age as some of their grandchildren.

Measurement

In an earlier paper (Troll & Smith, 1976), I considered four implications of persisting family ties (a) the possible difference between dyadic and group bonds; (b) the distinction between a dyadic bond seen as a channel or track fixed at both ends (to both people involved) or seen as an attribute of one of the individuals concerned; (c) the nature of possible developmental changes in relationships, either transformations in the kind of attachment or in the object of attachment; and (d) the relation between affect and attachment. Relevant to the first point, dyadic attachment versus group solidarity, distinctions have been made between "attachment" defined as a two-person reciprocal relationship and "dependency" defined as a relationship with a set of (perhaps) interchangeable others (Gewirtz, 1972). Essentially, Gewirtz sees person-to-person bonds as different from person-to-group bonds. Bengtson and Black (1973) distinguish between "ties of sentiment between particular family members" and "feelings of solidarity" to the family as a whole. Adams (1968) differentiates between feelings of intimacy and obligation and relationships characterized by feelings of solidarity and loyalty.

How can we explain the persistence of parent–child relationships throughout life? They seem to override geographic and socioeconomic mobility as well as development changes in a way no other relationships seem to do. They even seem to override death, as Bowlby (1969) and Parkes (1972) point out in their discussion of grief. I (Troll, 1972b) found that parents were most often the persons mentioned spontaneously by adults of all ages (from 10 to 91) when they were asked to describe a man and a woman. Even people in the 70s and 80s chose their parents as referents, though the chances of those parents still being alive were small. Explanations like "imprinting" or "conditioning" do not explain why these ties seem to be even stronger or more durable on the part of parents than on the part of their children (Troll, 1971a). Is it because such bonds are archaic and precognitive in structure, as Mussen, Conger, and Kagan (1974, pp. 204–205) suggest, and different in kind from more cognitively determined love relationships? Are we back to something like Freud's "unconscious"? If so, would we explain parental love as a reawakening of an early infant form of relating with a substitution of child for parent as love object? Should we go even further and hypothesize that all later life passions are reawakenings of infantile love?

Evidence for qualitative differences between dyadic and group bonds comes from such disparate sources as the investigations of the mental health of older people and of the kinship relationships of younger adults. Lowenthal and Haven (1968) found that the existence of a confidante was the one significant difference between those old people who were able to live "normally" in the community and those who landed in the psychiatric ward. Adams (1968) found differences between the kinds of feelings and activities shared with parents, with siblings, and with friends. One shares basic values and feelings of duty and obligation with parents and children—all through life. One shares interests and recreation with friends.

Parron (1979) found similar distributions of interpersonal functions among the golden wedding couples she studied. Bengtson and Black (1973) suggest further that ties of sentiment are more likely to be felt for children and ties of obligation to be felt for parents. Siblings fall between these two.

The difference between dyadic bonds and group ties could be, on the other hand, as much quantitative as qualitative. The tight psychological space of a two-person system could foster more intense relationships than the wider space within which ties with nonparental relatives and friends exist. Intensity of relationship could be inversely related to the number of people involved. Whether this would hold true for old age, though, is debatable. There is no reason to believe that the loss of kin and friends in later life leads to more intense feelings for those still surviving, with the possible exception of the evidence for strong attachment to spouse among golden wedding couples.

In some families, individuals seem to be linked to the family as a whole rather than to any particular person or persons. Everybody is "kin" or "folks" or "relatives." Nieces are as close as sisters, as aunts, or perhaps even as mothers. The death of any one member in such a system would not affect the membership in the family of other relatives unless, perhaps, the close relative were a key linkage figure like a kin-keeper. Shanas, Townsend, Wedderburn, Friis, Milhhoj, and Stehouver (1968) refer to a "reservoir" of relatives available to old people. If an old woman, particularly an old widow, has a daughter, she is likely to live near her—and later, when incapacitated or poverty-stricken, to live with her. But if she has no daughter or loses her either because of moving or death, she lives near—and later with her niece, her granddaughter, her sister, or even a more distant woman relative. Such families we might now call the loose boundary type. But not all families are like this. In some, dyadic bonds are the only strong ones. The loss of a spouse or child or, to some extent, sibling would cause desolation.

When we talk about older generations, we should consider both person-to-person bonds, most likely to be parent–child, as well as person-to-group bonds, likely to be true of larger family networks or units. Hinde (1979), a British psychologist involved in the study of attachment between infant and parent, uses seven variables to describe interpersonal relationships. It may be heuristic to transpose these to later life.

1. *Content of Interaction.* What do family members of different generations actually do together? The anecdotes related earlier exemplified such activities. Family members may share ongoing experiences—the excitements and details of daily life. They may perpetuate family rituals on holidays, Friday night or Sunday noon gatherings, or birthday parties.

They may eat together, often special foods prepared in special ways (Grandpa Smith's Thanksgiving turkey or the Jones' birthday fruit cake). They may travel the world together, or they may talk to each other. Not all interactions are active or direct. In a way, the old woman in the Thanksgiving story who sat alone in the midst of the family gathering was herself inactive, but the others there were interactive. Her apparent exclusion intruded into and was an important part of the whole family scene. She was in it, not out of it. Reactions to her exclusion derived from and were in the idiom of that family's values of sharing. Some parents and children visit and talk; others visit but sit silently. Some visit and work together; they clean house, launder clothes, or drive to supermarket or clothing store.

Not only would the nature or content of interaction vary with family themes, but also the variety of activities. In some families, only one or two activities are shared; others share a much larger percentage of their lives. In a family where servicing activities are viewed as an important and major occupation of life, servicing of older or younger family members has a different meaning from what it has in families where it is considered unusual, perhaps even demeaning. Cleaning house or taking someone shopping can be seen as ordinary parts of daily life or as extraordinary, burdensome activities. If bathing is what a mother does only to an infant, an adult daughter who must bathe her old mother could be as upset as her helpless mother.

One effect of considering the whole family is to "raise our consciousness" about the number of people involved in any interaction or situation. When a daughter takes her mother shopping, it may seem superficially that only the daughter and mother are interacting or involved. The daughter's participation, however, can be determined by whether she feels that she is a favored child, or a good child, or an abused child relative to her siblings. The mother can be assessing the scene in terms of the rewards provided by all members of her family. Meanwhile, the daughter's siblings, husband, and children all have their own complexes of feelings about this event. They can each be keeping a balance sheet of reciprocal services and feel guilt, shame, denial, or gloating. Even the mother's sisters and brothers are involved, at least to the extent of weighing their own situations against that of their sister. Does the family as a whole believe that the daughter who takes her mother shopping once a week is performing as valuable a service as her brother who helps prepare their mother's income tax once a year or as her sister who takes their mother to the doctor every 6 weeks? Does the mother feel that she is being repaid for past services or that she is a shamefully dependent family member? Past family history and present shared family values are all prominent parts of any given interaction.

2. *Diversity of Interaction.* How many different things do family members do with each other? Is there just a shopping trip once a week, or is the once a week shopping trip just one of many shared activities? Are all the activities helping chores, or are there also fun outings? Do some family members get to do the chores and others the fun outings? Do intergenerational activities involving older members tend to evolve into chores like shopping and intergenerational activities involving younger members tend to be fun, like a picnic or amusement park trip?

3. *Quality of Interaction.* This could be measured in many ways: (a) intensity—are the interactions strong or weak, strong in affect (loving or hating) or weak in affect; stong in effort or weak in effort involved?; (b) nonverbal or verbal—is there a lot of talking, or mainly gestures; (c) coordination—are interactions initiated as much by one person as by others, participated in more by one person than by others?

4. *Patterning of Interactions.* Is there a pattern to the relative frequency of initiation or rejection of contact? Where neither older nor younger person either initiates or rejects contact, there would be no relationship; neither exists meaningfully for the other. Where both older and younger people initiate and reject contact, both are important to each other. Some intergenerational interactions could be like the "conflict-habituated" marriages described by Cuber and Harroff (1963), others like their "vital" or their "passive–congenial" types. Within a larger family group, there is likely to be an array of interaction patterns, with different children taking different positions with regard to initiating and rejecting contact with their parent while the parent shifts his or her mode from child to child, calling one child to complain about aches and pains and waiting for the call from another with delight over his or her triumphs.

5. *Reciprocity versus Complementarity.* Does each person return the same behavior as he or she gets? Do interacting partners support each other, or do they take opposite roles, some supporting, others asking for support?

6. *Intimacy.* This term has many definitions and many modes. There is physical intimacy, sharing of confidences, feeling of unity.

7. *Interpersonal Perception.* How does each family member perceive the others and also how do they all perceive the family situation? Often this perception is a shared "family theme." How are generation and sex differences perceived? Are younger men of most value and older women of least value? How is death treated or perceived? A family whose members tend to die at relatively young ages may share very different expectations of old age and death than one with many old members who are vigorous into their 90s.

Developmental Effects

I stated in the beginning of this chapter that one viewpoint on generational relations is to look at transmission of perceptions, of beliefs, values, and attitudes, both downward from parent to child and reciprocally, from child to parent. A review of family generational literature (Troll & Bengtson, 1979) concluded that political and religious beliefs and affiliations tend to be shared more by middle-aged parents and their young-adult children than by those middle-aged parents and their own parents. One exception is Bengtson's scale of individualism–collectivism, on which the two older generations in the California families he studied are more in agreement than the two younger. Grandparents in Hagestad's (1978) Chicago sample both influenced and were influenced by their children and their grand-children. The "sexual revolution" during the last 10 or 20 years affected the values of much of the American population—this is a period or historical effect. However, as demonstrated persuasively in recent findings by the University of Michigan investigators at the Social Research Institute (Antonucci & Bornstein, 1978), changes are usually more profound among younger people. Although there is little measurable similarity between parent–child dyads on sexual beliefs and practices, 60% of a sample of Chicago middle-aged mothers who had been reinterviewed by Angres (1975) said they had been influenced by their daughters' sexual behavior—toward adopting more of their daughters' values. In general, it seems that strong family bonds can either brake social change or accelerate it. Braking or acceleration may be a function of synchrony between a family theme and a generation keynote effect—which is usually the first step in the process of change. Again, so far as work and achievement values and general lifestyle characteristics are concerned, the correlations between young adults and their parents are usually greater than those between middle-aged people and their parents. The effect of developmental levels upon lineage transmission, however, is neither general nor obvious. It is a prime example of "selective continuity," which cannot at present be separated from period effects that influence the entire population. Grandparents and their grandchildren, incidentally, are usually less alike than parent–child dyads.

In our review of generations in the family mentioned above, Bengtson and I concluded that parent–child "attachments" are perceived as exceptionally strong interpersonal bonds throughout the life course. Where variations in perceived level of affect appear, they seem related to the ontogenetic status of the younger generation member—the "generation stake" effect hypothesized by Bengtson and Kuypers (1971). That is, at particular times of development, such as early youth or late adolescence, there may be less perception of closeness to family members than at other times of life. Older generations tend to exaggerate similarity between themselves and their children because they wish their values to persist. Younger generations, particularly at the time of establishing a unique identity, tend to minimize these similarities and exaggerate differences. Nevertheless, in Hill, Foote, Aldous, Carlson, and MacDonald's (1970) three-generation Minneapolis study, their youngest generation—young adult couples—endorsed kinship obligations and contacts the most and the oldest generation, their grandparents, endorsed them the least.

Studies of college students show repeatedly that whereas they and their parents may state there is a generation gap in society, they rarely say there is one in their own family. Most of the middle-aged respondents in Lowenthal, Thurnher, Chiriboga, and Associates (1975) San Francisco four-stage study felt good about their children. When adults of all ages were asked in my three-generation Detroit study to describe a man and a woman whom they knew, more than half of them referred to their parents (Troll, 1972b). Even the oldest respondents, in their 70s and 80s, were still using parents as reference persons.

Summary

To recapitulate, this chapter points out some advantages of applying a system approach to the study of families, even to extended families including aging members. It seems logical that families will react to the aging of their relatives in terms of their shared family theme or value system. All generations in a family share perceptions of how aging should go based upon models presented by earlier family members who grew old. If earlier old people in the family were hypochondriacal, it is more than likely that all will expect present aging members, as well as themselves when they get old, to be full of aches and pains—perhaps even the same aches and pains, although some will try the opposite and vow never to grow old like Aunt Sadie. If earlier old people in the family were stoical, it seems likely that present old people will keep a stiff upper lip and deny having any aging problems. Tightness or looseness of family boundaries also have been seen as affecting old people's interactions with kin and nonfamily members, including community organizations and social networks. Those accustomed to confining their interpersonal interaction to family members are less likely to join senior centers or to seek help from social agencies than those whose custom it has been to make little distinction between kin and nonkin.

References

Adams, B. *Kinship in an urban setting.* Chicago: Markham, 1968.

Aldous, J. *Family careers.* New York: Wiley, 1978.

Altmann, M. Naturalistic studies of maternal care in moose and elk. In H. Rheingold (Ed.), *Maternal behavior in mammals.* New York: Wiley, 1963. Pp. 223–253.

Angres, S. Intergenerational relations and value congruence between young adults and their mothers. Unpublished doctoral dissertation, University of Chicago, 1975.

Antonucci, T., & Bornstein, J. Changes in informal social support networks. Paper presented to American Psychological Association, 1978.

Bartholomew, G. A. *Reproductive and social behavior of the Northern elephant seal.* University of California Publication. *Zoology,* 1952, *47,* 369–472.

Bengtson, V.,& Black, D. Intergenerational relations and continuities in socialization. In P. Baltes & W. Schaie (Eds.), *Life-span developmental psychology: Personality and socialization.* New York: Academic Press, 1973.

Bengtson, V., & Kuypers, J. Generational difference and the developmental stake. *Aging and Human Development,* 1971, *2,* 249–260.

Bengtson, V., & Troll, L. Youth and their parents: Feedback and intergenerational influence in socialization. In R. Lerner, & G. Spanier (Eds.), *Child influences on marital and family interaction.* New York: Academic Press, 1978. Pp. 215–240.

Bowlby, J. *Attachment and loss.* New York: Basic Books, 1969.

Britton, J. H., & J. The middle-aged and older rural person and his family. In E. G. Youmans (Ed.), *Older rural Americans.* Lexington, Ky.: University of Kentucky, 1967.

Cuber, J., & Harroff, P. *The significant Americans.* New York: Appleton–Century–Crofts, 1963.

Gewirtz, J. L. *Attachment and dependency.* Washington, D.C.: Winston, 1972.

Haan, N., & Day, D. A longitudinal study of change and sameness in personality development, adolescence to later adulthood. *Aging and Human Development,* 1974, *5*(1), 11–39.

Hagestad, G. Patterns of communication and influence between grandparents and grandchildren in a changing society. Paper presented at the World Conference of Sociology, Upsala, Sweden, August, 1978.

Hess, R., & Handel, G. *Family worlds.* Chicago: University of Chicago Press, 1959.

Hill, R., Foote, N., Aldous, J., Carlson, R., & MacDonald, R. *Family development in three generations.* Cambridge, Mass.: Schenkman, 1970.

Hinde, R. Mother–young interaction: What primates can tell us. Paper presented at Parenting Conference, Rutgers University, April, 1979.

Kerckhoff, A. C. Nuclear and extended family relationships: A normative and behavioral analysis. In E. Shanas, & G. Streib (Eds.), *Social structure and the family: Generational relations.* Englewood Cliffs, N.J.: Prentice–Hall, 1965.

Lerner, R., & Spanier, G. *Child influences on marital and family interaction.* New York: Academic Press, 1978.

Litwak, E. Geographic mobility and extended family cohesion. *American Sociological Review,* 1960, *25,* 385–394.

Lopata, H. *Occupation: Housewife.* London: Oxford University Press, 1971.

Lowenthal, M., & Haven, C. Interaction and adaptation: Intimacy as a critical variable. *American Sociological Review,* 1968, *33,* 20–31.

Lowenthal, M., Thurnher, M., & Chiriboga, D. and Associates. *Four stages of life.* San Francisco: Jossey–Bass, 1975.

Mussen, P., Conger, J., & Kagan, J. *Child development and personality* (4th ed.). New York: Harper and Row, 1974.

Parkes, C. M. *Bereavement.* New York: International Universities Press, 1972.

Parron, E. Relationships in black and white golden wedding couples. Unpublished doctoral dissertation, Rutgers University, 1979.

Parsons, T. The normal American family. In S. Farber, S. P. Mustacchi, & R. H. Wilson (Eds.), *Man and civilization: The family's search for survival.* New York: McGraw-Hill, 1965.

Powers, E., & Bultena, G. Sex differences in intimate friendship of old age. *Journal of Marriage and the Family,* 1976, *38*(4), 739–747.

Rosenblum, L. Monkeys, mothers, peers, and others. Paper presented at Parenting Conference, Rutgers University, April, 1979.

Shanas, E., Townsend, P., Wedderburn, D., Friis, H., Milhhoj, P., & Stehouver, J. *Older people in three industrial societies.* New York: Atherton Press, 1968.

Simmel, G. The triad. In K. Wolff (Ed.), *The sociology of George Simmel.* New York: Free Press, 1950. Pp. 145–169.

Troll, L. Personality similarities between college students and their parents. Unpublished Ph.D. Dissertation, University of Chicago, 1967.

Troll, L. The family of later life: A decade review. *Journal of Marriage and the Family.* 1971, *33*, 263–290. (a)

Troll, L. Frameworks for the study of generations. Paper presented at National Council on Family Relations, Estes Park, 1971. (b)

Troll, L. In my opinion: Is parent–child conflict what we mean by the generation gap? *Family Coordinator,* July 1972, 347–349. (a)

Troll, L. The salience of members of three-generation families for one another. Paper presented to American Psychological Association, Honolulu, 1972. (b)

Troll, L., & Bengtson, V. Generations in the family. In W. Burr, R. Hill, G. Nye, & I. Reiss (Eds.), *Contemporary theories about the family.* New York: Free Press, 1979.

Troll, L., Miller, S., & Atchley, R. *Families in later life.* Belmont, Calif.: Wadsworth, 1978.

Troll, L., Neugarten, B., & Kraines, R. Similarities in values and other personality characteristics in college students and their parents. *Merrill–Palmer Quarterly,* 1969, *15*, 323–337.

Troll, L., & Smith, J. Attachment through the life span: Some questions about dyadic bonds among adults. *Human Development,* 1976, *19*, 156–170.

Vailliant, G. E. *Adaptation to life.* Boston: Little, Brown, 1974.

Youmans, E. G. Aging patterns in a rural and urban area of Kentucky. Lexington, Ky.: University of Kentucky Agricultural Experiment Station, 1963.

Youmans, E. G. Generations and perceptions of old age: An urban–rural comparison. *Gerontologist,* 1971, *11*, 284–288.

Chapter **6**

The Widowed Family Member[1]

HELENA ZNANIECKA LOPATA

Unless a human being never marries or parts from a spouse in divorce, one mate usually dies before the other or faces widowhood. *Role complexes, support systems,* and *life styles* of widowers, particularly of widows, in America have gone through enormous changes in recent decades.[2] These changes are a repercussive consequence of two sets of societal transitions, both in Europe and on this side of the Atlantic, which have taken place over three centuries. The first focused human attention on the economic institution, encouraged technological change and urbanization, developed mass education, and expanded the proportion of people who live long and healthy lives. The various social and scientific revolutions experienced by Europe and America since the seventeenth century produced yet another transformation in social structure by freeing many people from autocratic control by families, the class structure, the church, and governments demanding passivity from their citizens (see Aries, 1965; Laslett,

[1] "The Support Systems Involving Widows in Non-Agricultural Areas" study was funded with a contract from the Social Security Administration (SSA–71–3411) and Loyola University of Chicago. The final wave of interviewing was carried out the summer of 1974 through the Survey Research Laboratory of the University of Illinois. This chapter is based on materia originally prepared for a conference on the family, organized at Wayne University in 1975 by Constantina Safilios–Rothschild.

[2] This chapter is heavily influenced by the scarcity of data on widowers and the fact that the author has completed two major studies of widows.

1973; Shorter, 1975). The result is a conversion of social engagement in social roles and relations from an *ascribed* to a *volunteristic* manner for adult members, removing many traditional support systems but providing innumerable resources for the building of complex and multidimensional life spaces. That is, members can enter and exit a variety of social roles at different stages of their life courses. Increasing proportions of people are able, particularly in America, to develop flexible role clusters contained in extensive life spaces.

The full impact of these societal transitions was felt even in this society only relatively recently and did not affect all levels of the social structure uniformly; large numbers of Americans are in historical generations squeezed between past and present, socialized into dependence upon ascribed roles, and unable to function in an urban milieu demanding voluntaristic engagement. The traditional support systems upon which these people depended, the family, the village, or stable neighborhood, have been removed through various forms of social and geographic mobility, and they lack the personal resources needed to take full advantage of the social opportunities for engagement in society. These people fit the model of the aging American developed by Cumming and Henry (1961); they and the society are gradually disengaging as former roles drop away or lessen in importance. These individuals lack resources for reengagement in new roles or relationships. However, these people represent only one type of American. Another type of American is the traditional one still able to be engaged in an almost automatically involving family, neighborhood, or small town. These three types are not totally mutually exclusive; people can move to a certain extent from one to another. Generally speaking, however, these types of societal categories do not overlap much because different personal abilities and resources are required of each form of social engagement.

The changing relation between American society and its members from traditionally ascribed to volunteristic participation is particularly visible in the lives of widows and widowers. These people epitomize the three types of Americans; some people who lose a spouse find new ways of engaging in society, others go through a major step in disengagement, especially since this event is apt to occur after parents are no longer available for support, and children are already dispersed. Some of those who become widowed are already embedded in a stable set of relations that are not strongly disrupted by the death of the mate, and, although some change is necessitated, it does not require the creation of new roles (Berardo, 1968, 1970; Lopata, 1973a; Marris, 1958).

Three characteristics of the role complexes, support systems, and life styles of widows and widowers in this society will be examined in this chapter: the similarities and differences in how the manner of death of the spouse and succeeding events affect men versus women, the great hetero-geneity of the widowed population, and the emergence of a new type of widow.

Widowhood as a Neglected Aspect of Family Sociology

Berardo (1970) pointed out several years ago that the subject of widow-hood was really neglected by American sociologists. Since that time there has been some research on this subject, directly or through secondary analysis of data collected for other research purposes (Cohn, 1973; Harvey & Bahr, 1974). Much of social gerontology is actually dealing with the widowed, even when the elderly are being generalized about, but it is hard to separate what is specifically a consequence of widowhood and what emerges out of other role and life style changes. There are several rather obvious reasons for the neglect of this stage of the life course. Widowhood results from death, a subject about which there was only silence in the social science literature until Kubler-Ross (1969, 1975) and a few others recently opened it to intensive examination. Advances in medical knowledge and technology, the institutionalization of treatment and of housing the ill in hospitals rather than at home, and the idealization of youth, strength, and health have made dying and death "unnatural," a sub-ject so rejected as to lead Gorer (1965) to refer to it as a "pornography of death" (also see Aries, 1965; Fulton, 1965; Strauss & Glazer, 1965, 1968). The avoidance of the topic of death has been extended to avoidance of topics of grief, pain, and unhappiness. Our society wants people to be happy and satisfied; responses to a variety of adjustment or life and mar-riage satisfaction scales show that Americans follow this norm and do not admit disatisfaction, unhappiness, or loneliness.

Not only the topics of death and unhappiness have received societal and sociological neglect, but so also have the people who are associated with these events, the dying and their survivors. Recent studies report that widowers and widows feel shunned by their still married friends and other associates (Berado, 1967, 1968, 1970; Lopata, 1973a, 1973b, 1975a, 1979). They explain this avoidance as due to the fact that their presence reminds people of the death, sometimes even to the point of conscious or un-conscious assignment of blame for it, and also because friends fear that the widowed, particularly the recently bereaved, might display hurt or unhap-piness, or might cry and want to talk about their feelings. These fears are often founded in reality; most new widows and widowers do experience pain: pain over being deserted, of losing a love object, or at least a signifi-cant other, of grief and loneliness. Until recent dissemination of the findings of the importance of doing *grief work*, as Lindemann (1944) called the process of giving up the deceased and of reconstructing the self and social relations as a partnerless person, public display of grief was not encouraged. Even now the ideal reaction to death remains for most Americans to be stoic acceptance (Glick, Weiss, & Parkes, 1974; Gorer, 1965; Vernon, 1970). Relatives as well as friends try to prevent the bereaved from crying, even when they know that the process is necessary.

The societal attitude toward the widowed as objects of avoidance so that they can "work it out for themselves" and emphasis on widowhood as if it were a constantly grieving state is reflected in the research, sparse as it is, on this subject. Most of it has been restricted to the grief period and to the determination of "adjustment," to the death (Glick *et al.*, 1974; Maddison, 1968; Maddison & Walker, 1967). In fact, as Clayton, Halikes, and Maurice (1971) point out, much of the grief literature treats grief as a pathological condition, rather than as a normal process that people who lose a significant other must experience. This emphasis also neglects to examine the life styles of adult men and women who are no longer married because of the loss of the spouse but who are no longer in acute grief. The neglect reflects America's bias in favor of marital and familial life; the nonmarried or the no longer married are generally treated as a social problem. Widowhood is examined only through the prism of loss. This is particularly true of the widow in contrast to the widower, much in the same way that bachelorhood is idealized in contrast to spinsterhood. It is probable that the greater frequency of studying widows rather than widowers is based on the assumption that they face greater problems because they were so dependent upon the husband, whereas the man is seen as more independent of his marriage because of greater involvement in his occupation and in life outside the home. As we shall see, this assumption is actually wrong, but it certainly reflects the patriarchal bias of a society's view of women and men. As it is, except for the research now in progress or devoted to secondary analyses of data banks, there are not that many original studies even of widows (Barrett & Scheinweis, 1976; Baum, 1979; Chevan & Korson, 1972, 1975; Cohn, 1973; Harvey & Bahr, 1974; Lopata, 1973a, 1975c, 1979; Maddison & Agnes, 1968; Marris, 1958; Silverman *et al.*, 1974). Some of these analyses also deal with widowers, but the main emphasis is on widows.

Widows and Widowers: Similarities and Differences

In discussing widowhood, we are talking about a marital status that involves many people leading a variety of styles of life, for most of whom being a widow or widower is only one of the components. Few are still in the dramatic period of mourning. Of course, some people whose marriage ended in the death of the spouse grieve the rest of their lives, retain the social role of widow or widower as a set of relations, or keep such an identity as a pervasive one influencing all the roles they play. Generally, we find such a devotion to widowhood in only a few of America's ethnic subcultures, at least as far as modern urban women are concerned. For example, there is a definite role of widow among some Puerto Rican and Greek families in Chicago, although there seems to be an absence of a comparable role of widower. In other parts of the world and in other times in European and American history, the social role of widow has been of great family and community significance; its function was that of organizing ritual or serving as integrator, arbitrator, or match-maker. It involved not only the widow, but a definite social circle granting rights enabling her to carry out such functions (Lopata, 1972, 1973a; Znaniecki, 1965). There also have been many situations worldwide in which the status of widow was so pervasive as to influence all the roles a woman performed, often symbolized by special clothing, which assisted in labeling and depersonalizing the wearer (see Sarasvati's 1888 discussion of the child widow in traditional India). In going through anthropological literature, we fail to find any mention of special clothing worn by the widower once the period of mourning is over (Lopata, 1972). In fact, most references to the widower are to frequency and norms of remarriage, whereas the remarriage of widows traditionally has been either forbidden or guaranteed with little choice on their parts through the levirate or widow inheritance systems (Bernard, 1956; Bohannan, 1963; Lopata, 1972, 1973a). Of course, most societies of the world have been patriarchal and patrilineal, the wife leaving her family to join that of her husband and remaining there if it had *in genetricem* rights over the children she bore (Bernard, 1956; Bohannan, 1963).

There are over 10 million widows and 2 million widowers in American society, the gap increasing over the years. In 1956, for example, there were only 3 widows to 1 widower, and now the ratio is 5 to 1. At the turn of the century, the death rate (number of deaths, excluding fetal deaths, per 1000 population) was 17.7 for white males and 16.3 for white females. By 1956, the rates dropped for such males to 10.8, but the female rate dropped even further to 7.8, and by 1973 it went to 10.7 for males, and up to 8.2 for the females. The racial differences in life chances are apparent when we see that the nonwhite male rate was 28.7 and the nonwhite female rate was 27.1 in 1900. These dropped to 12.4 for the male and 9.5 for the female in 1956 and to 10.8 for the males and 7.6 for the females in 1973. The causes of death of the two sexes have varied over time and still do so. The life expectancy of women increased as soon as death in childbirth and from communicable disease decreased through improved health conditions and medical care.

Men tend to die more frequently at all ages and the increase is rapid after the age of 45. American society encourages the marriage of women to men older than themselves, thus increasing the probability of widowhood for them rather than for their husbands. The widows form 13.3% of the female population 13 years of age and over, and widowers form only 2.9% of the males in the same age group (U.S. Bureau of The Census, *Statistical Abstracts*, 1975, Table 46). The median age for widowers was 71.0 years in 1972, for widows it was 67.8 years. A woman between the ages of 65 and 74 has 43 chances out of a 100 to be widowed, whereas the man in that age cohort has only 9 chances out of 100. Of women 75 years of age and over, 68% are already widowed, whereas only 25% of the men are in that age category (U.S. Bureau of the Census, *Statistical Abstracts*, 1975, Table 47). In both sexes, the nonwhite life expectancy is much lower than that of the white population (U.S. Bureau of the Census, *Marital Status*, 1972).

Widows and widowers experience many similar problems in modern American urban society that place great emphasis on the conjugal relation and houses each nuclear family independently of other similar units. Marriage is seen as equal to, or only secondary to, the parental relation in the case of the mother of small children and secondary to the job for the man (Lopata, 1971a). Marriage here is based on mutual choice by the mates and it is expected to involve deep personal feelings of love or at least attachment. In the case of the traditional woman particularly, entrance into marriage is expected to create a reconstruction of reality, including particularly the self (Berger & Kellner, 1970). Although not needing to change his name and identity away from home, according to the cultural norm, the man also becomes dependent upon the wife for emotional supports (Berardo, 1970; Bernard, 1973; Harvey & Bahr, 1974). The first problem to confront the survivor of either sex is usually grief, but financial, childrearing—if there are young children—and daily life problems, accentuated by the withdrawal of a partner in the division of labor follow in close succession. In the long run, the financial, *loneliness*, and daily life problems that have not been, and sometimes cannot be resolved remain. Widows and widowers also can have similar positive experiences, or new life styles as a result of the death of the spouse or in repercussive consequences. They can be released from an unhappy or at least unsatisfying marriage, or from one existing only in technical form, as in cases of extreme disability of the spouse or his or her absence from the support systems for other reasons. Leaving behind one role complex or style of social engagement, a widow or widower can be free to develop new ones, changing and even expanding personal resources and life space. They can change former relationships and develop new ones, they can learn new competencies and independencies. In the case of widowers more often than widows, they can enter new marriages. All widows and all widowers do not face the same problems or develop the same new life styles, but all face more or less of a crisis with the death of the spouse, due to the disorganization produced by his or her removal from the support systems, the circumstances of the death and modification of other roles (Lipman-Blumen, 1975). Wives who are economically dependent upon their husband's earnings experience a loss of this income and need to seek new sources (Lopata, 1973a, 1975c, 1979). Husbands dependent upon their wives to manage the household, care for the children, and integrate them into a family and friendship network, experience the loss of these services and a need to replace them through their own efforts or those of others (Berardo, 1968, 1970). The degree to which the spouses are involved in each other's roles and relations influences the degree of disorganization experienced by the survivor in these roles and relations and in the identities emerging from the role complex. On the other hand, the societal, community and personal resources of the survivor influences the long-range consequences of the disorganization.

There is strong evidence that widowers in this society suffer more problems, or are able to cope with them less adequately than do widows (*U.S. News and World Report*, 1974; Berardo, 1970). In fact, Jessie Bernard (1973) has accumulated strong documentation of the benefit men derive from marriage in that the widowed, divorced, and never married males have higher rates of personal disorganization than do the marrieds, whereas the reverse is true of women. In any case, widows are better off than widowers when it comes to mental illness, suicide, or even death rates. *U.S. News and World Report* (April 15, 1974) in a story on widowers quotes figures from Dr. Daniel Gianturco as follows:

THE HEAVY TOLL
AMONG WIDOWERS
People aged 45 to 64

	Deaths per year per 1000 population
Widowers	32.5
Widows	13.2
Married males	13.1
Married females	6.7

People aged 65 and over

Widowers	113.5
Widows	66.9
Married males	57.4
Married females	32.9

[p. 60].

The widower death rates and their causes vary by age group. "The 20–44 age group has the highest suicide rate . . . automobile accidents kill widowers 20–24 years old at an extraordinary rate. . . . Widowers, as well as older divorced and single men, tend to smoke and drink too much. They eat too much highly salted meat, and they rarely get enough exercise [p. 59]." Berardo (1970) found the combined loss of a spouse and a job, through retirement or unemployment, to produce very strong negative effects, experienced in health problems, depression, and social isolation. He quotes several studies showing widowers to be more prone than other groups to various indices of mental illness [p. 20–22]. Bell (1963), on the other hand, concludes that it is the widow who suffers more than the widower because marriage is more important for women than for men, it is hard for her to learn to function alone in society; her financial difficulties are stronger, and it is less possible for her than for the male to remarry (quoted by Berardo, 1970, p. 14). Two studies, one of suicide among the elderly (Bock & Webber, 1972) and the other a comparative analysis of widowhood and morale (Harvey & Bahr, 1974) conclude that it is not so much widowhood as affiliation or isolation that affect the life style of the survivor. To the extent that the death of the spouse increases the isolation of the widow or widower, it will have strong negative effects expressed in low morale and even suicide. In the United States and to some extent in the United Kingdom, the marital unit tends to be relatively isolated from the kinship group and other forms of ascribed or at least stable social engagement, and the death of a spouse can decrease other sources of social contact and support if that spouse served as a connecting link to other people. Widowers are often more isolated than widows because they had depended upon their wives to maintain social contact in these social systems (Berardo, 1970; Bock & Webber, 1972; Harvey & Bahr, 1974). The Harvey and Bahr (1974) analyses of surveys of people in Germany, Italy, and Mexico indicated greater affiliation of the widowed in these countries than in the United States.

The researchers mentioned as well as others trying to separate the influences of other life circumstances from the influence of the death of a spouse on the survivor stress the importance of socioeconomic status. "The present analysis, drawn from a variety of national settings and from samples larger than is typical in studies of the effects of widowhood derives not from widowhood status but rather from socioeconomic status. The widowed have appeared to have more negative attitudes than the married and they have appeared less affiliated for the same reason [Harvey & Bahr, 1974, pp. 195–196]." That is, the widowed have lower socioeconomic status. One reason for this is that people in lower social classes are more apt than their better-off counterpart to become widowed. The other reason is that widowed people are less able to maintain status. Bock and Webber (1972) also found the degree of social integration aside from marriage to be an important variable affecting suicide rates among elderly married and widowed people. Such integration is highly related to social class in American society. Berardo (1970, p. 14) found the "older, relatively uneducated and living in a rural environment" widowers to be the most isolated. My previous research documents the importance of education and middle class lifestyle on the social integration of Chicago area widows (Lopata, 1973a, 1973c, 1979).[3]

The Influence of Education and Social Class on Widowhood

Thus, the Harvey and Bahr (1974), Berardo (1970) and my own research (Lopata, 1973a, 1975a, 1979) indicate the importance of socioeconomic status upon life style in widowhood, and both studies of the Chicago area widows select the one variable of formal schooling as the main foundation for this status. Formal schooling has two main consequences upon a person (a) the development of abilities necessary for voluntary engagement in society; and (b) the availability of other personal opportunities facilitating the utilization of societal resources. Formal schooling, particularily at the high school and over levels, teaches people to analyze a situation in the abstract, to perceive alternate paths and their consequences in reaching goals, to plan action, and to modify it flexibly if the consequences are not as anticipated. People who are successful in the school system also build self-confidence in their actions and learning abilities, and trust in their own judgement. These abilities are necessary for planned engagement in social relations and social roles and in planned rather than reactive life styles. In addition, formal schooling increases the person's ability to integrate other resources into an upward or at least stable middle-class life style, in terms of occupation, income, and association with others. In the case of a woman in American industrial and urban society until very recently this also meant that increased formal schooling improved her opportunity to marry a man whose earnings guaranteed resources by which they could build together a better life style.

Most, if not all, research focusing on American class differences concludes that middle class, higher educated couples communicate with each

[3] The study involved lengthy interviews with a modified area probability sample of 301 metropolitan widows aged 50 or over. The research was funded by an Administration on Aging grant (Grant No. AA–4–67–030–01–A1) with the cooperation of Roosevelt University in Chicago. Interviews were conducted in 1970.

other and share their lives, particularly in leisure time, much more than
do lower class couples (Blood 1972; Blood & Wolfe, 1960; Gans, 1962;
Komarovsky, 1967; Lopata, 1973a, 1973c). Working class couples tend to
live in a sex-segregated world, his part shared with men at work, those seen
in taverns, or park benches among the retired, hers limited to contact with
relatives if they are easily available, and to neighbors if she is living in a
stable community. If the wife is not working in paid employment, her contacts are often quite limited, the church usually being the only voluntary
association in which she is involved. The man's work guarantees contact,
some men also belong to unions or lodges, but these sources of social
engagement dissolve with retirement, often leaving the husband dependent
upon his wife for social contact even with the kinship group (Berardo,
1970; Bock and Webber, 1972). Middle class couples usually belong to a
couple-companionate friendship clique and are more apt to be members
together in a church and voluntary associations than are their less educated
and more restricted counterparts. The wife is usually the social secretary,
but she tends to draw from a variety of sources for their friends, dipping
even into the husband's work group (Babchuk & Bates, 1963; Lopata,
1971a, 1975a, 1979).

The type of social engagement in which a couple is embedded affects the
social life space of the survivor, not so much because the foundation remains but because reengagement requires the same set of skills and interests. However, there appears to be a difference between widows and
widowers in this respect. The widower appears to be less able to reengage
socially than is the widow of equal social class life style because of the
tendency in American society for the woman rather than for the man to be,
as stated above, the social secretary of the unit. That is, women, particularly middle class ones, are taught the skills of arranging for social contact
with relatives and friends. This situation is particularly true of women who
do not work outside the house, but the pattern seems to carry over even to
women who are in paid employment, though with lesser frequency of contact (Lopata, 1971a).

The study of the older Chicago area widows revealed that the wife with
higher education and with a more middle-class life style developed with her
husband when he was still living was subject to a more disorganized life
upon his death (Lopata, 1973a). This fact is a consequence of the greater
mutual dependency such a couple develops. The degree of disorganization
also depends on other circumstances of life and of his death, such as age,
the presence and ages of children, sources of income, content of the support
systems in which the couple is engaged, and the widow's ability and willingness to continue these in modified form. Of course, the same variables
affect what happens to the widower. Generally speaking, widowhood in

middle years of life appears to be most difficult, partly because it is "off time" and there are few associates who are in the same marital status who can assist in the process, and partly because of the feelings of "unfairness" frequently experienced by the widow (Blau, 1961; Neugarten, 1968). If she is not employed for pay outside the home, she may be under heavy financial strain, even if she is receiving social security benefits, and especially if she has several children. Widowers may be able to continue working, but their costs can rise sharply if they have to purchase child and home care. The presence of children can be a deterrent to loneliness and a help, or a problem if they themselves react negatively to the death of the parent. The circumstances of death are important because of costs and often the need for prolonged care (Glick, Weiss, & Parkes, 1974).

The disorganization of life resulting from the death, which depends on the depth of involvement of the deceased in the lives of the survivors, may be compounded by other events accompanying or following that event. Health problems may arise, as can the need to change other roles such as labor force participation, friendships, involvement in the in-law kinship group, or other life circumstances, such as residence. It is also often, if not usually, accompanied by grief lasting varying amounts of time and of varying depth and accompanying symptoms.

Early Problems of Widowhood

As mentioned before, there has been considerable recent attention given to grief. Much of the literature comes from two research centers, a team of psychiatrists and sociologists at the Harvard Medical School, and a team of psychiatrists at the Washington University School of Medicine in St. Louis. The basic formulation of the concept of grief work was developed by Erich Lindemann (1944) following Freud's (1917) "Mourning and Melancholia." As phrased by Maddison and Walker (1967), who were part of the Harvard Medical School team, "A widow is faced with two concurrent tasks: she is required through the processes of mourning, to detach herself sufficiently from the lost object to permit the continuation of other relationships and the development of new ones; at the same time she has to establish for herself a new role conception as an adult woman without a partner [p. 1059]." Of course, the same process applies to the widower. Glick, Weiss, and Parkes (1974) summarized this research in *The First Year of Bereavement.* Much of their work was with relatively young widows, although they also dealt with widowers, and one of their chapters centered on "widowers as a contrasting group." In it they state that "insofar as men reacted simply to the loss of a loved other, their responses were similar to those of widows, but insofar as men reacted to the traumatic disruption of their lives, the responses were different [p. 262]. The shock, numbness, feelings of pain, "yearning for the dead spouse," need to cry, anger, disorganization, and physiological reactions such as trouble with sleeping, restlessness, or loss of weight were the first reactions of both widows and widowers. However, men were more unwilling to cry or to show their emotions, a finding which fits the American maleness norms for men, although they felt it would be helpful to them if they could express these emotions. The men tried to prevent what the psychiatrists called obsessional review of the past and of the death of the spouse.

The Harvard team found the men to be much less apt to withdraw from social contacts during the period of grief and much more willing to remarry than were the women. Of course, they had a better statistical probability of finding a new partner, but there seemed to be a greater eagerness on their part. We shall return to the subject of remarriage later.

Clayton and her associates at Washington University (see particularly Clayton, Halikes, & Maurice, 1971; also see Clayton, 1973a, 1973b, 1974) also examined at length the symptoms of grief of both widows and widowers, reporting less concern, however, with "losing one's mind" and a more nonpathological set of symptoms than did the Harvard group. Their work also stresses the "anniversary reaction" (Bornstein & Clayton, 1972) experienced 1 year after the death. Most researchers define the first year as the most difficult, although movement from acute grief to other forms and stages seemed to occur after only a few weeks (Glick, Weiss, & Parkes, 1974, p. viii). It is during the first year that, according to Silverman (1972, 1974), the widowed most need help from other people who have gone through the same experience. Silverman's (1972) work evolved out of the research at Harvard Medical School and took the form of a widow-to-widow program. The program is based on the assumption that a new widow has problems in relating to her friends and relatives who "do not understand" what she is going through and whose offers of help are not of much assistance, even serving to drive her away from social contact. A new widow is contacted by a member of the widow-to-widow group who provides both practical supports in the form of information needed for solving immediate problems and emotional supports. The latter supports are designed to allow the widow to mourn, assisting her in the process of grief work. The widow-to-widow program is now being organized in other cities throughout America, and the new interest in the problems of the widowed is leading to the formation of similar groups. Widowers with children are particularly drawn to Parents Without Partners. Most of the groups, however, have a mainly female membership.

Even after the heavy period of acute grief is over, the widowed often face loneliness, particularly in a society with independent conjugal households in which the death leaves the survivor as the only living member, because the children, even if there had been some in the past, are already dispersed. This loneliness is of two forms, as Weiss (1973) pointed out, emotional and social. The survivor is lonely for the intimacy of the relation as well as for the whole life style of sociability of the past. In fact, there are many forms of loneliness experienced by the widowed, and there seems to be some class variation in the weaving of these forms, depending on the nature of the past marital relation (Lopata, 1969). The widowed can miss having and being a love object to a significant other. Often the death robs them of the only person to whom they were a really important human being, even when the importance was one of being an antagonist. The widowed can miss having a partner, a companion in activities, often but not necessarily shared with other couples. Even watching television can be a lonely experience if the person is accustomed to exchanging comments on what is being viewed. The absence of a partner is particularly important to the traditional woman who is unaccustomed to going to public places alone and who was brought up to value the company of a male escort more than that of a female partner. The loneliness can be limited only to having a partner in the division of labor, the widowed being irritated and conscious of the loneliness when having to perform a task which had fallen in the province of the other in the past. This is particularly true of the parental role. The survivors complain of an inability to be "a mother and a father" at the same time and numerous studies of the single-parent family point up this form of loneliness. For people not having children at home, there is the loneliness of being alone, usually for the first time in life. Widows complain of not having someone around for whom they can organize their time and work, much as men miss schedules after they retire from a job. The social aspects of the loneliness, besides the companionship of activity also include missing the whole life style of the past. Women are no longer invited to social events of the late husband's employer or organization. In-laws are often dropped, by choice or because of withdrawal from contact by these relatives. Widowers become socially isolated if they depended on the wife to make the social arrangements and they are unable or unwilling to take over this activity. Friendships often become strained, many widows believing that their still married female friends are dropping them because of jealousy of the husband's attentions. Widows believe that widowers have a much better time because the married women want an extra man around (Lopata, 1973a; 1975a). Whatever the reason, there seems to develop strain with married friends, particularly at younger ages of widowhood. Hunt (1966) reports the same situation for the divorced in his *The World of the Formerly Married.*

The Reconstruction of Social Life Space
in Widowhood

Whatever the problems facing the newly bereaved, whether they are grief and loneliness, childrearing, or financial or relational strain with prior associates, sooner or later, most of the social relations and social roles must be modified to create a new social life space without that particular person who has died. Of course, no change need be introduced in those roles in which the deceased was not involved at all, unless his or her absence necessitates modification of life style. The latter situation occurs, for example, in relations the wife had with neighbors if her current marital status forces her to move, or the performance of the occupational role by the husband if the absence of the mother in the home necessitates his refusal to work late or to travel on the job. One way of preventing major role changes is replacement of the deceased with a new spouse.

Remarriage and Other Relations
with the Opposite Sex

Even remarriage requires some changes in the former widow's or widower's relations with others. Unless the offspring are tiny and not conscious of the replacement, relations with a stepfather or stepmother are different than with one's own parents, resulting in changes in the relations with the surviving parent (Bernard, 1956; Ney & Berardo, 1973). Part of the problem in stepparent–stepchild relations following the death of the original parent is the tendency of the children to idealize the deceased to an extent that makes it impossible for the living to match. Not only the role of parent, but other roles must be modified with remarriage. The relatives of the late husband are likely to be even less often seen than during widowhood. A new set of in-laws is often introduced by the new spouse. Friends who were attached to the deceased may not be able to transfer allegiance, and the new spouse may bring into the relation new friends (Babchuk & Bates, 1963).[4] Remarriage often means geographical mobility, and each family unit develops its own rhythm of life (see Bernard, 1956).

Not many of those who are widowed remarry, because of a lack of opportunity or desire (Bernard, 1956). The Williams and Kuhn (1973) analyses of remarriages in the United States, based on Bureau of the Census

[4] The support systems study contains interviews with 1169 widows drawn from lists of previous or current beneficiaries of social security who, when weighted by the ratio in which they were drawn to insure sufficient cases among the young, represent 82,085 widows in the metropolitan Chicago area. Interviewing was conducted in 1974.

data, points that the "remarriage rates for men are more than three times those for women [p. 1]." Due mainly to the age difference, widowed women are less apt to remarry than divorced women (10 per 1000 compared to 135 per 1000, respectively). Widowers remarry at the rate of 39.3 per 1000. "Although the rates for the widowed were also (as for divorced) higher at younger ages, they were much lower than the rates for the divorced [p. 5]." The rates for the divorced are much higher at all age groups. As of 1969, the median age of the widows entering remarriage was 51 years and that of the widowers was 59 years. Finally, although most people who remarry do so fairly soon after the dissolution of the late marriage through divorce or death, "widowed men remarried much sooner than widowed women [p. 13]." There is a general tendency, however, for the widowed to marry each other.

Most commentators on the infrequency of remarriage among widows point to the statistical distribution of widows and widowers and to the tendency in American society for men to be able and wish to marry younger women than themselves, even by many years. The society simultaneously frowns on women marrying younger men, although such a pattern would be a reasonable solution to the prevalence of widowhood at a relatively young age of the wife created by the combination of the man being older and dying younger (see Nye & Berardo, 1973). However, several studies indicate the possibility that some women are not remarrying by choice (Bernard, 1956, 1973; Lopata, 1973a, 1979; Steinhart, 1975b). When asked if they would like to remarry, over 75% of the older metropolitan area widows responded "No" (Lopata, 1973a). When asked to explain this decision, some stated that they do not want to give up their independence or to enter the role of wife again. Many simply do not consider the possibility of being able to remarry. Others do not wish to care for another sick man. In fact, there is a strong belief among some widows that second marriages bring nothing but trouble. Bernard (1956) lists many reasons for not wishing to remarry, including unhappiness in the prior marriage, the possibility that income will stop at remarriage or the "fear of fortune hunters [p. 117]." Widows can also worry about the relation between a new husband and the children still remaining in the home or even those living independently out of it. Finally, many widows idealize the late husband to the point of sanctification and are thus unable to look objectively at living men (Lopata, 1973a, 1975b, 1976, 1979). Sanctification can interfere with the social relations of a survivor if it leads her or him to compare living associates with the idealized former spouse in a manner obvious to companions. Hunt (1966) states that divorced men do not like to date widowed women because they can not live up to the image of the deceased. Also, persons in these two marital status situations have little in common as far as past biography is concerned, especially if it is modified by memory and often have different attitudes toward marriage and their future biography.

The study of the support systems of metropolitan widows of all ages finds remarried women to be younger, with several young children and higher incomes prior to their husbands' fatal illness or accidents than are those who have not remarried (Lopata, 1979). They are apt to have had complex social life spaces, including engagement in jobs outside the home, and they define their networks as supportive during the period when they were trying to build new lives. They are now financially better off than are the widows who do not have the earnings or social security of new husbands, particularly if they are working for pay themselves. The remarrieds report the late husbands as the main contributors to their emotional support systems prior to their illnesses, and they also report their new husbands as active in many supports. The most bitter and unhappy are women who were widowed, then remarried and had that marriage end in divorce. There is a distinct difference along many attitudinal dimensions between them and most of the women who are either remarried or still widowed.

BOYFRIENDS AND SEXUAL RELATIONS

The absence of a new spouse in the lives of people who have been widowed does not mean an absence of boyfriends or of sexual involvement (Lopata, 1979). Unfortunately, we know very little about the sexual behavior of the widowed, mainly because of the societal attitudes toward them which somehow desexes them both as objects and as experiencers of sexual desire. The societal and sociological neglect of the sexual desires of the widowed, particularly of the widows, reflects the traditional view of such women, as well as the bias against any but the young members of this society. It does not necessarily mean, however, that the associates of the widowed refrain from sexual advances. One-fifth of the older widows studied in the Chicago area agree with the statement: "Widows are constantly sexually propositioned, even by the husbands of their friends [Lopata, 1973a, 1975a]." The U.S. News and World Report (1974, p. 60) article on widowers defined one of their problems to be the "hungry woman hazard." The widowers seem frightened by the abundance of attention they get from several women whereas there is frequent anger in the widow's reactions to such propositioning, even when they feel sexually deprived. Such advances confuse the relationship with the friends. In addition, they do not lead to desired relations. The widows who are interested in sexual interaction often want a multidimensional relation, not a short encounter.

In one of the few studies of "Postmarital Coitus among Widows and Divorcees," Gebhard (1970) found the divorcees to be much more sexually active than are the widows. For example, 73% of the divorcees but only 42% of the widows aged 21 to 25 were sexually active. The proportion increases for widows to 55% in the years between 26 and 30, while the divorcee rate for some reason drops to 70%. The highest rate of 78% is found among divorces aged 31 to 40; among the widows it never again reaches the high twenties. The rates for widows indicate greater sexual activity than remarriage.

LIVING ARRANGEMENTS

There has been a dramatic change in the living arrangements of the widowed, particularly of widowed women, in recent decades made possible by their increasing economic and personal independence (Chevan & Korson, 1972, 1975; Lopata, 1971b 1973a). "Proportionally, more than two and one-half times as many widowed lived alone in 1970 as in 1940, and the percentage increase of widows in this category was slightly higher than that for widowers [Chevan & Korson, 1972, p. 45]." Those who live with others are mostly mothers with dependent children, and they are heads of their own households (Lopata, 1971). The independence of even older widows is documented by the fact that a total of 78% of the women aged 65 and over are heads of their own households and 80% of these women are the primary individual in it, 77% of the total heads living alone and only 3% have unrelated individuals living with them. Most of the 22% of older widows who live with others are in households headed by family members (Lopata, 1979).

There are several reasons why widows live alone or at least do not live with married children. When asked what the problems of such an arrangement are, the older Chicago area widows organized their answers along two general lines: desire for independence and management of their own home and work as well as the disadvantages of living in homes managed by another woman. Unlike some of the traditional ancestral homestead situations in which the widow could remain in her own home until she turned over its management to a younger woman, modern familial patterns involve the children all moving away from the parental home and being unilling to return to it when the parents age or become widowed. This means that the widow or widower must break up her or his own household and move into the homes of a daughter or daughter-in-law. Although many modern women disparage the role of housewife as a source of status and identification, many of the older widows do not want to give it up. They want to control the space and management of their dwelling and do not want to fit into the system run by another woman. They are afraid of strain over spacial rights if they move. Additionally, their contact with adult children and grandchildren warns them of potential conflict. They expect to disapprove of many of the actions of their children and children-in-law vis-a-vis the grandchildren, money, time and work organization and so forth. Finally, they feel that they have earned the right to rest and relaxation, having reared one family, sometimes even more than one, and managed a complex home in the past. Now they want life to be easy, rejecting extensive demands for baby sitting and housework services (Lopata, 1971b, 1973a). All in all, they wish independence and, as Rosenmayr and Kockeis (1963) called it, "intimacy at a distance." There are, however, some "age, race, sex, educational achievement, income, labor force status, ethnicity, place of residence, fertility and marriage" influences on who lives alone (Chevan & Korson, 1972, p. 51). The least apt to be living alone are the poor, white, less educated, very old, and ethnic widows.

Support Systems Involving Widows

As mentioned before, widowers seem dependent upon their work roles and remarriage for their support systems. Defining a support system as a set of exchanges of objects or services which the giver, the receiver, or both define as necessary or helpful in maintaining a style of life (Lopata, 1979), we can list as many as 65 separate economic, service, social, and emotional supports in which urbanites can be involved. The contributions to these have been studied in the case of metropolitan widows who were given the chance to list three contributors for each support. Most of these women were not involved in extensive economic supports (Lopata, 1975c, 1978, 1979). They obtained most of their income either from their own earnings or from their late husband's social security. A few have investments, take in boarders, or depend on welfare, but the majority maintain themselves from their own or their late husband's work backgrounds. This does not necessarily mean they are affluent. Over a third are living on incomes falling below the poverty line by Social Security Administration or the Department of Labor standards (Kim, 1975). As of 1970, the mean income of women now widowed was $2952, that of women known to have been widowed at any time was $2963 and that of all women aged 14 and over was $3158 (U.S. Bureau of the Census Marital Status, 1972, Table 7). The widowers were better off, the mean for men who are now widowed was $4262 for those known to have been widowed it was $5343 and for all men it was $7434. The figures indicate less of a gap in total family income for women by marital status than for men, but a large gap between all women and all men.

Very few widows get financial contributions in the form of gifts of money, payment, or help in payment of rent, food, clothing or bills from family or other personal associates. Few are recipients of service in the form of transportation (45% are not), household repairs (57%), housekeeping help (77%), help with shopping (61%), yard care (68%), child care (96%), car care (87%), care during sickness (44%), help with making decisions (59%) or legal aid (81%). If they are engaged in such exchanges, it is almost inevitably with their children in and outside of the home. The extended family enters the service supports very rarely (see Lopata, 1978, 1979).

Many of the Chicago area former or current beneficiaries of social security do not engage in leisure time activities, which pretests showed to be the most frequent activities shared by urbanites with other people: 51% never go to public places such as movie theaters, 21% do not visit and 40% do not entertain anyone, 37% do not go out to lunch or share lunch with anyone, 24% do not go to church with anyone, 58% do not engage in sports, card, or other games, 40% do not travel out of town, but only 8% do not celebrate holidays in the company of others. The companions in these activities of those women who do engage in them are predominantly children and friends. Grandchildren enter in the celebration of holidays, the widows go to church or travel out of town, when they do, alone, and coworkers appear as sharers of lunch. Many widows who do not engage in these activities explain that they cannot afford the expense, or that they do not care to do such things. There are strong social class differences in the answers. Working class women are less apt than are their middle class counterparts to engage in many of these activities, and if they do, they are restricted mainly to the company of their children. When education and income are held constant, the younger women are more active socially than are the older, unless they have many children still in the home, and then their circle of contributors is narrowed to them. Remarried widows carry out more activities and are accompanied very often by the new husband.

Children, the new husband, and boyfriends and less often friends, appear in the emotional support systems of these Chicago area widows. These are the people she feels closest to, who she most enjoys being with, who comfort her when she is depressed, to whom she tells her problems or turns to in crisis, who make her angry or make her feel important. They also most often make her feel respected, useful, independent, accepted, self-sufficient and secure. Another major contributor to emotional supports is the widow herself, which is not surprising in feelings of self-sufficiency and independence. In fact, she appears most often after the children. There are many widows, however, who state simply that no one contributes to their emotional supports. There was an unexpected absence of listings of siblings, grandchildren and other extended kin folk. Most of the widows do not have living parents, but there is a greater absence of mothers and an even greater one of fathers from the supports. Young widows are much more apt to list parents than are older widows, even when parents are living, undoubtedly because the parents themselves are younger and able to be more active. There is a relative absence of men from the support systems of widows and an underutilization of friends in the emotional supports, in spite of expectations to the contrary as a result of the literature on the confidant (Blau, 1961, 1973; Lopata, 1979; Lowenthal & Haven, 1968).

Role Changes of People Who Are Widowed

Proportionately more widowers than widows are able to hold down jobs, because of the family pattern which was discussed at the beginning of the chapter, in which marriage or at least motherhood removes the woman from the labor force, often for many years or never to return again. Proportionally more widows of employable age work than do married women, especially when they do not have small children at home and social security coming in regularly. However, a smaller proportion of widows age 65 or over are in the labor force than are in the female population (U.S. Bureau of the Census, *Marital Status*, Table 6). The most apt to work are women with no children or mothers of one child or of several children, because of convenience of making baby sitting arrangements in the first case, and of financial need in the second. Steinhart, (1975a, 1975b) documented an economic push to work in his analysis of the Chicago area widows. In addition, education and occupational prestige are motivating factors for the employment of widows as it is of women in other marital situations (see Department of Labor, *Handbook on Women Workers*, 1975, and Bureau of the Census, *Marital Status*, 1972). Generally speaking, however, the women most apt to be widowed and not to be working are the poorest and least educated women.

Although the role of wife or husband vanishes in its main features with the death of the spouse, there are some vestiges of it in widowhood. The widow usually continues to carry the name of the deceased, unless she remarries. Care of possessions and of the offspring is part of the obligation to the late spouse. One of the main sets of duties, however, is grief, and the guarantee of continued social existence of the deceased through talking and thinking about him or her even though the acute grief is over. It is here that the duty to remember the late spouse, privately and publicly, often acquires idealization dimensions even to the point of sanctification (Bernard, 1956; Lopata, 1973a, 1975b, 1976, 1979; Nye & Berardo, 1973). The wake and the funeral start this process of purifying the deceased. Listening to widows describe the late husband in the exploratory phase of research made evident this process to such an extent that I finally created a sanctification scale in the study of the support systems of metropolitan widows. The scale, which consists of 13 items, including a call of agreement with the statement "my husband had no irritating habits" finds the majority of the widows at the extreme level of idealization to the point of sanctification. The process by which the husband becomes saintly in the eyes of his surviving wife—and it is quite possible that wives, parents, and offspring who die are also sanctified by their survivors—performs several functions. One is to enhance the status of the survivor; after all, this perfect person chose the spouse in marriage or was otherwise associated with her or him. Even more importantly, the sanctification process cleanses the spirit of the deceased from mortal feelings such as jealousy or the insistance on constant grieving. Placement of the other in the position of saint insures noninterference in the daily life of the survivor. It also contributes to the completion of some of the unfinished business that death always leaves (Blauner, 1966). Of course, sanctifying the late spouse may be easier for some survivors than it is for others because of differences in the quality of the relation prior to death or throughout its existence.

The consequences of the death of the parent of the children can have a variety of different effects on the surviving parent, as stated before, depending on factors such as the age of the children, the circumstances of the death, the closeness of the relationship, the restructuring of the family unit after death and the position of the child in the new alliances, and changes in financial or other supports. Many of the metropolitan widows reported little influence of the death of the father on a vast majority of offspring, because the latter were either too young or already adult, and some children were relieved by the death, living their own lives (Lopata, 1975c, 1979). The most frequently reported effect was sadness, but there were mothers who reported severe emotional effects or problems that made life difficult for them. Some of the mothers attempted to get professional or familial help or emotional supports for their children, particularly for the sons, others simply talked the whole problem over with the offspring.

There have been some very interesting changes in the relations of the widowed to their friends. Both widows and widowers often report some social isolations from their former friends who are still married. Their lives become different, and the other factors mentioned earlier operate to produce strain. On the other hand, traditional women considered their relatives to be their friends, and the feministic movement can be expected to increase the significance of friendship in future lives of women in all marital situations. As we saw, only the more educated women have developed strong friendships that result in the active contribution of such associates to the support systems of the widows. This relation attracts greater emphasis as the "sisterhood is powerful" movement increases.

One of the changes reported by the older Chicago women as a result of widowhood was experienced in the self (Lopata, 1973a, 1973b). Although the more traditional, older, and particularly the less educated and more isolated women report no change in themselves as a result of becoming widows, the more educated and more socially integrated report feelings of greater independence and competence. This does not mean that they look back at their marriages negatively; these are usually the same women who are positive but not extreme in their evaluation of their late husbands and of marital life with them, only that they experienced a positive change in themselves after the acute grief period was over. These women would therefore be defined by Lindemann (1944) as having successfully completed the second task of grief work, that of reconstructing the self into a partnerless person.

Summary and Conclusion

The analysis of the available data on the support systems and life styles of widows and widowers in American society indicates many common problems of grief and loneliness, financial and relational strains as the immediate effects of the death of the spouse. The evidence points to many widowers being unable to cope with the effect of the loss of a wife with high incidence of personal disorganization as well as the tendency to rapidly remarry. Widows fall into three types (a) those who are able to reengage in new support systems and life space after the main grief work is accomplished; (b) those for whom the death of the husband is another step in disengagement from a life previously already peripheral to the social system; and (c) those who remain embedded in a set of supports and a social network in spite of the death. Although such a typology has not emerged in the case of the widowers because of the absence of comparable research, it possibly could be applicable. There is evidence that the same factors are operating to isolate both widows and widowers. These include a lack of formal schooling to a level enabling voluntary engagement in social relations and social roles and the lack of other personal resources. Modern American urban society has developed innumerable resources for the engagement of its members, but these require knowledge, initiation of behavior and flexibility in the life course. There are historical generations of Americans who have not developed the knowledge and skills for such engagement.

The detailed studies of American metropolitan widows indicate the emergence of a new kind of woman who is able to reconstruct her own self and her support systems to insure a complex and multidimensional social life space as a partnerless person after the death of her husband and after the grief work following it is accomplished. As both sexes become more educated and competent at all stages of life, and as both the women's and the men's liberation movements expand, we can expect an increase in the proportions of independent people after the mutual sharing of life in marriage is no longer possible because of the death of the spouse.

Acknowledgments

Many thanks go to the staff of the Survey Research Laboratory of the University of Illinois; to Drs. Henry P. Brehm, Chief of Research Grants and Contracts Staff, Social Security Administration; Adam Kurzyrowski of the Szkola Glowna Planowania i Statystyki, Warsaw, Poland; and Nada SmolicKrkovic of the Institute of Social Work in Zagreb, Yugoslavia, for all their help in construction of the schedule, to the staff of the Center for the Comparative Study of Social Roles including Frank Steinhart, Carla Christiansen, Sister Gertrude Kim, Terry Baumer, and Monica Velasco for all the help throughout the stages of work.

References

Aries, P. *Centuries of childhood.* New York: Random House, Vintage Books, 1965.

Babchuk, N., & Bates, A. Primary relations of middle-class couples: A study of male dominance. *American Sociological Review,* 1963, *28,* 374–384.

Barrett, C. J., & Schneiweis, K. M. An empirical search for stages of widowhood. Paper presented at the Gerontological Society Annual Meeting, New York, 1976.

Baum, J. An exploration of widowhood: coping patterns adopted by a population of widows. Unpublished dissertation, Department of Social Welfare, University of Wisconsin-Madison, 1979.

Bell, R. R. *Marriage and family interaction.* Homewood, Ill.: The Dorsey Press, 1963.

Berardo, F. Social adaptation to widowhood among a rural–urban aged population, *Washington Agricultural Experiment Station Bulletin 689,* College of Agriculture, Washington State University, 1967.

Berardo, F. Widowhood status in the United States: perspective on a neglected aspect of the family life-cycle. *The Family Coordinator,* 1968, *17,* 191–203.

Berardo, F. Survivorship and social isolation: The case of the aged widower, *The Family Coordinator* 1970, *1,* 11–25.

Berger, P. L., & Kellner, H. Marriage and the construction of reality. In H. Dretizel (Ed.), *Recent sociology* (Vol. 2). London: Collier–Macmillan, 1970. Pp. 50–73.

Bernard, J. *Remarriage, a study of marriage.* New York: The Dryden Press, 1956.

Bernard, J. *The future of marriage.* New York: Bantam Books, 1973.

Blau, Z. Structural constraints of friendship in age. *American Sociological Review,* 1961, *26,* 429–439.

Blau, Z. *Old age in a changing society.* New York: Franklin Watts, 1973.

Blauner, R. Death and social structure, *Psychiatry*, 1966, *XXIX*, 378–394.

Blood, R. O. *The family*. New York: The Free Press, 1972.

Blood, R. O., & Wolfe, D. M. *Husbands and wives*. New York: The Free Press, 1960.

Bock, E. W., & Webber, I. L. Suicide among the elderly: isolating widowhood and mitigating alternatives. *Journal of Marriage and the Family*, 1972, *34*(1).

Bohannan, P. J. *Social anthropology*. New York: Holt, Rinehart and Winston, 1963.

Bornstein, P. E., & Clayton, P. J. The anniversary reaction. *Diseases of the Nervous System*, 1972, *33*, 470–471.

Chevan, A., & Korson, H. The widowed who live alone: an examination of social and demographic factors. *Social Forces*. 1972, *51*, 45–53.

Chevan, A., & Korson, H. Living arrangements of widows in the United States and Israel, 1960 and 1961. *Demography*, 1975, *12*(3), 505–518.

Clayton, P. J. Anticipatory grief and widowhood. *British Journal of Psychiatry*, 1973, *122*, 566. (a)

Clayton, P. J. The clinical morbidity of the first year of bereavement: a review. *Comprehensive Psychiatry*, 1973, *14*(2) 151–157. (b)

Clayton, P. J. Mortality and morbidity in the first year of widowhood. *Archives of General Psychiatry*, 1974, *30*, 747–750.

Clayton, P. J., Halikes, J. A., & Maurice, W. L. The bereavement of the widowed. *Diseases of the Nervous System*, 1971, *32*, 597–604.

Cohn, A. R. Influences of selected characteristics on widows' attitudes towards self and others. Masters thesis, Department of Psychology, Illinois Institute of Technology, 1973.

Cumming, E., & Henry, W. E. *Growing old: the process of disengagement*. New York: Basic Books, 1961.

Freud, S. Mourning and melancholia. In J. Strachey (Trans and Ed.), *Standard edition of the complete psychological works of Sigmond Freud, XIV*. London: The Hogarth Press and the Institute of Psychoanalysis, 1853.

Fulton, R. L. (Ed.). *Death and identity*. New York: John Wiley and Sons, 1965.

Gans, H. *The urban villagers*. New York: The Free Press, 1962.

Gebhard, P. Postmarital coitus among widows and divorcees. In P. Bohannan (Ed.), *Divorce and after*. Garden City, N.Y.: Doubleday, 1970. Pp. 81–96.

Glick, I., Weiss, R., & Parkes, C. M. *The first year of bereavement*. New York: John Wiley and Sons, 1974.

Gorer, G. *Death, grief and mourning*. New York: Doubleday, 1965.

Harvey, C. D., & Bahr, H. M. Widowhood, morale and affiliation. *Journal of Marriage and the Family*, 1974, *36*(1), 97–106.

Hunt, M. *The world of the formerly married*. New York: McGraw-Hill, 1966.

Kim, Sister G. Income of widows, size and sources. In H. Z. Lopata (Ed.), *Support systems involving widows in American urban areas*, Social Security Administration, 1975.

Komarovsky, M. *Blue-collar marriage*. New York: Random House, 1967.

Kubler-Ross, E. *On death and dying*. New York: Macmillan, 1969.

Kuber-Ross, E., (Ed.). *Death, the final stage of growth*. Englewood Cliffs, N.J.: Prentice-Hall, 1975.

Laslett, P. *The world we have lost* (2nd ed.). New York: Charles Scribner's Sons, 1973.

Lindemann, E. Symptomatology and management of acute grief, *American Journal of Psychiatry*, 1944, *101*, 141–148.

Lipman–Blumen, J. A crisis framework allied to macrosociological family changes: marriage, divorce and occupational trends associated with World War II, *Journal of Marriage and the Family*, 1975, *37*(4), 889–902.

Lopata, H. Z. Loneliness: forms and components. *Social Problems*, 1969, *17*(2), 248–262.

Lopata, H. Z. *Occupation: Housewife*. New York: Oxford University Press, 1971. (a)

Lopata, H. Z. Living arrangements of urban widows and their married children. *Sociological Focus*, 1971, *5*(1), 41-61. (b)

Lopata, H. Z. Role changes in widowhood: a world perspective. In D. Cowgill & L. Homes (Eds.), *Aging and modernization*. New York: Appleton-Century Crofts, 1972.

Lopata, H. Z. *Widowhood in an American City*. Cambridge, Mass.: Schenkman Publishing Company, General Learning Press, 1973. (a)

Lopata, H. Z. Self-identity in marriage and widowhood. *Sociological Quarterly*, 1973, *14*(3), 407-418. (b)

Lopata, H. Z. The effect of schooling on social contacts of urban women. *American Journal of Sociology*, 1973, *79*(3), 604-619. (c)

Lopata, H. Z. Couple-companionate relations: wives and widows. In N. G. Malbin (Ed.), *Old families—new families*. New York: Van Nostrand, 1975. (a)

Lopata, H. Z. Grief, the sanctification process and support systems involving widows. Proceedings of Council on Aging and Human Development, Duke University, 1975. (b)

Lopata, H. Z. Support systems involving widows. A report to the Social Security Administration, 1975. (c)

Lopata, H. Z. Grief work and identity reconstruction. *Journal of Geriatric Psychiatry*, 1975, *8* (1), 41-55. (d)

Lopata, H. Z. Widowhood and husband sanctification. A paper presented at the American Sociological Association Meetings, New York, 1976 (submitted for publication).

Lopata, H. Z. Contributions of extended families to the support systems of metropolitan area widows: limitations of the modified kin network. *Journal of Marriage and the Family*, 1978, 355-364.

Lopata, H. Z. *Women as widows: Support systems*. New York: Elsevier-North Holland, 1979.

Lowenthal, M., & Haven, C. Interaction and adaptation: intimacy as a critical variable. *American Sociological Review*, 1968, *33*, 20-30.

Maddison, D. The relevance of conjugal bereavement for preventive psychiatry. *British Journal of Psychiatry*, 1968, *41*, 223-233.

Maddison, D., & Agnes, V. The health of widows in the year following bereavement. *Journal of Psychosomatic Research*, 1968, *12*, 297-306.

Maddison, D., & Walker, W. L. Factors affecting the outcome of conjugal bereavement. *British Journal of Psychiatry*, 1967, *113*, 1057-1067.

Marris, P. *Widows and their families*. London: Routledge and Kegan Paul, 1958.

Neugarten, B. Adaptation and the life cycle. Paper presented at the FFRP Conference, Puerto Rico, June, 1968.

Ney, F. I., & Berardo, F. M. *The family*. New York: Macmillan, 1973.

Rosenmayr, L., & Kockeis, E. Propositions for a sociological theory of aging and the family. *International Social Science Journal*, *XV*, 410-426.

Sarasvati, P. R. *The high-caste Hindu woman*. Philadelphia: James B. Rodgers, 1888.

Shorter, E. *The making of the modern family*. New York: Basic Books, 1975.

Silverman, P. Widowhood and preventive intervention. *The Family Coordinator*, 1972, *21*, 95-102.

Silverman, P. R., MacKenzie, D., Pettipas, M., & Wilson, M. *Helping each other in widowhood*. New York: Health Sciences Publishing Corporation, 1974.

Steinhart, F. The social correlates of working widows. Paper presented at the Annual Midwest Sociological Society Meetings, Chicago, 1975. (a)

Steinhart, F. Labor force participation as a resource for support systems. In H. Z. Lopata, *Support systems involving widows in American urban areas*. Social Security Administration, 1975. (b)

Strauss, A., & Glaser, B. *Awareness of dying*. Chicago: Aldine, 1965.

Strauss, A., & Glazer, B. *Time for dying*. Chicago: Aldine, 1968.

The plight of America's two million widowers. In *U.S. News and World Report*, 1974, *15*, 59–60.

United States Bureau of the Census. *Marital status*. Washington, D.C.: Government Printing Office, 1972.

United States Bureau of the Census. *Statistical abstract of the United States*. Washington, D.C.: U.S. Government Printing Office, 1975.

United States Department of Labor, Wage and Labor Standards Administration, Women's Bureau. *Handbook on women workers*. Washington, D.C.: U.S. Government Printing Office, 1975.

Vernon, G. M. *Sociology of death*. New York: The Ronald Press, 1970.

Weiss, R. S. *Loneliness: the experience of emotional and social isolation*. Cambridge, Mass.: MIT Press, 1973.

Williams, K. M., & Kuhn, R. P. Remarriages, United States. *Vital and Health Statistics*, 1973, Series 21 N. 25 DHEW Publication No. (HRA) *74–1903*, National Center for Health Statistics; Rockville, Md.

Znaniecki, F. *Social relations and social roles*. San Francisco, Calif.: Chandler Publishing Company, 1965.

Chapter 7

The Clinical Psychology
of Later Life:
Developmental Paradigms

DAVID GUTMANN
JEROME GRUNES
BRIAN GRIFFIN

This chapter will report some early, tentative attempts to relate the developmental paradigms of middle and later life, of the sort generated by life-cycle researchers, to the psychopathologies of older adulthood. This work is being carried out by faculty and students of the Older Adult Program of Northwestern University Medical School; and our goal is to generate the bases for a new, functional rather than descriptive, typology of clinical disorders in the latter half of life. The current clinical nosologies in geropsychiatry are mainly based on the manifest features of presenting symptoms, and on the distinctions, originally established for *younger* patients, among the affective disorders, the thought disorders, and the organic brain syndromes. Furthermore, our conceptions of the older patient tend to be consistent with such a descriptive category system in that they lack either a dynamic or a developmental focus. With a degree of unanimity that is rare in the social sciences, most schools of psychiatry view the older patient as a creature compounded of multiple *losses* and depletions in the somatic, psychic, social, and existential spheres. When clinicians turn their attention to earlier life periods, they are prone to consider the developmental contributions to phase specific pathology: It may reflect maturational lesions, or derailments. Not so in regard to the aging patient: Despite the wealth of cross-cultural and research evidence sug-

TRANSITIONS OF AGING

gesting that the aged develop executive capacities that are relatively unavailable to the young, established psychiatry and clinical psychology continue to view the older patient in the most catastrophic and benighted terms. In part, the trouble is due to sampling error: Older patients have not been socialized into the culture of therapy, and psychiatry is stigmatized for them. Consequently, they tend to bring their psychological troubles, coded as physical symptoms, to internal medicine; and the internists hang on to older patients, and do not make psychiatric referrals, until they become unmanageable. Accordingly, the psychiatrist mainly sees older patients who are drastically and irreversibly damaged; in effect, he sees *terminating* rather than aging patients. But technical and theoretical problems arise when the psychiatrist confounds the later with the earlier stage, makes termination retroactive across the distinctively different period of *aging*, and defines the aging patient as a metaphor of irremediable loss. In effect, the psychiatry of aging is transformed, more or less unwittingly, into the psychiatry of termination. As a result, even the middle-aged are regarded from the "loss" perspective as creatures of irreversible loss. Thus, like the terminating patient who suffers from the loss of neurones, trained capacities, and the social world, the middle-aged patient is also seen from the deprivational perspective, as suffering the loss of career opportunities in the case of men, and the "empty nest"—including the loss of procreative capacities—in the case of women. And again, therapy with the aging—of whatever age—is designed to reconcile them to inevitable loss and to blunt, *via* the various somatic therapies, the pain and depression occasioned by loss.

The result is a therapeutic philosophy that essentially disparages the aged and which enacts the basic themes of the bias which has come to be called ageism—the tendency to view all older individuals as hapless victims of external circumstance, and to consider them as suffering from the same troubles and as amenable to the same general remedy. However, in recent years the development of a new body of life-cycle developmental research, particularly in Chicago, has made the point that the later, postparental years are not a prelude to death, but a complex set of life periods, each with its own specific developmental *potentials* as well as its specific risks and losses. We begin to find that in the later years powerful energies no longer bound to the service of parenthood and production and no longer repressed in their service assert themselves within the personality. As these new potentials surface, the outcome of the transitions that they provoke is still in doubt: Depending on the history, temperament, and psychosocial circumstances of the individual, these new endowments of motive, appetite, and energy can provide the basis for new executive capacities of the personality or for phase-specific versions of psychopathology.

In our work at Northwestern, while we have been guided by the growing body of research into the developmental potentials of later life, we make few assumptions as to what we might find; we only assume that the various life-cycle paradigms will function as a kind of mediating lens between ourselves and the clinical data, a lens that will sensitize us to regularities, across individual cases, that we would otherwise have missed. Consistent with the canons of naturalistic science, we do not test a priori theories; instead, we generate data out of the unpredicted regularities that are manifested to us in the course of close, collectively examined clinical observations. Presently, we concentrate our diagnostic and treatment efforts on those patients, without significant brain syndromes, who have sought inpatient or outpatient psychiatric treatment *for the first time* in their middle or later years. Whatever the nature of their complaint, these are by and large individuals who have lived reasonable adult lives, founded in some degree of love and work, and without a prior history of diagnosed psychiatric illness. This focus on the "late-blooming" patient allows us to test the utility of a dynamic psychology of later life. If there are phase-specific developmental pathogens of later life, then the effects of these will be most clearly observed in late-onset patients—in those patients for whom the effects of the new pathogens are not obscured by the effects of long established, chronic weaknesses of the psychological organism. The more recent the onset, the greater the likelihood that the disease is responsive to novel inner or outer forces, of the sort that we wish to identify, classify, and treat.

At this point, we are most sensitive to the pathogenic possibilities inherent in midlife changes and developments that have already been identified in "normal" older adult populations in this and other societies. Thus, Gutmann (1969, 1975) noted (and these observations have been supported by investigators in a variety of cultures) that the transition to the postparental phase of adult life has important consequences for the psychological organization of senior men and women. Men relinquish some part of their active, competitive, and production-centered stance in favor of a more socioemotional, communalistic emphasis; women, in their turn, take on some of the managerial and "political" stances that their husbands appear to be abandoning. In effect, there takes place, in both sexes, a universal "return of the repressed," in which the psychological structures maintained by men and women during the period of active parenthood are dismantled in the postparental period. Men are freed to live out "feminine" aspects of the self that they previously had to submerge in the service of their particular parental task; while women regain a "masculine" potential that was previously submerged, or lived out vicariously, through identification with the prestige and exploits of the husband. Thus, each sex reestablishes, internally, a sexual bimodality that was previously partialled out externally, between the self and the mate. With these developments, there is a movement toward the normal androgyny of later life.

Research suggests that most older individuals, perhaps after some period of mild dislocation, accommodate to their sexual bimodality, and begin to live out and even enjoy the hitherto submerged aspects of the self. Accordingly, men can become more openly sensual, more openly dependent, and more openly emotional; whereas women can become happily assertive, less needful of love, more ready to risk the loss of love in trials of strength. In most individuals, the postparental psychological shifts lead eventually to new capacities for enjoyment, to new sensitivities, and to the maturation of new executive capacities, for each sex.

However, one man's meat can be another man's poison; and by the same token, psychic potentials that can provoke growth in one individual can be toxic to another. We know that some adolescents become, at least temporarily, the casualties of their own developmental potentials: They are devastated by the onset of sexual and aggressive feelings that do not grossly trouble their peers, and that they themselves might later come to enjoy. We make a similar assumption in regard to older patients, estimating that they too may be, if only temporarily, unhinged by the emergence of new appetites, new feelings, and even new growth potentials. Again, we are not trying to "prove" these assumptions; rather, they provide a unique context for our clinical interviews, and sensitize us to themes within cases and regularities across cases that, lacking these paradigms, we otherwise would have overlooked.

Thus far, the application of developmental conceptions to the clinical data of older patients has led us to identify two major precipitants of late-blooming psychopathology. On one hand, we have identified a number of cases where the onset of symptoms—usually of the depressive variety—reflects the intersection of midlife developmental potentials with long-standing but hitherto latent lesions of the personality structure. These tend to be younger patients, in their late forties through the fifties. A second group of patients are victims of what might be called existential stress: They have been shocked, often to the point of psychosis, by the threat of death, by the awareness of the life cycle itself ("life-cycle shock"), or by the loss of some significant person. As might be expected, it is mainly the older patients—those in their late sixties and seventies—who group under the heading of *existential stress*. Thus, our studies do not lead us to rule out deprivation as a major theme in later life pathology; but they do lead us to view the "loss" pathogen in a more circumscribed fashion, as affecting certain kinds of individuals, with particular vulnerabilities, mainly located within a delimited and older age range.

We will begin by describing the types found under the general heading of *developmental casualties.*

Men: The Masculine Protesters

Patients in this category range in age from the middle forties to the late fifties. Hospitalized or seeking outpatient treatment for the first time, they are generally in a state of agitated depression: anxious, insomniac, without appetite for food or sex, and unable to concentrate on their work despite a prior history of steady employment or even high achievement. Their presenting complaints have to do with difficulties regarding love and work: There is trouble on the job, and almost invariably they are in contention with a newly assertive, newly achievant, sometimes unsupportive wife. They view the wife's developmental move toward independence and self-direction as a kind of dismissal: "It's like she fired me from my job." Besides sharing clear similarities in symptoms and presenting complaints, these men have parallel histories. Typically, they were the youngest children of aging parents, separated by at least 7 years from the next oldest sibling. The father is almost invariably seen as absent or weak—though he may get some recognition for his gentle and nutritive qualities. By contrast, the mother is omnicompetent, filling the domestic space with her presence. The mother's strength is both admirable and fear provoking: These patients sometimes indicate that they hold her responsible for the father's "castration." Lacking an alternate, "transitional object" in the father, these sons seemingly remained to an important degree bonded with the only source of ultimate security that they knew—the omnicompetent mother. Their failure to separate from the mother has a variety of consequences, each of which is amplified in different character structures, and in different forms of later-life pathology. These consequences in most cases entail heightened dependency on maternal figures, coupled with a tendency to view them as dangerous and castrating toward men; a reliance on outer structures for direction and control; and strong though unconscious feminine identifications. While these predilections toward a dependent and feminine stance are generally managed with some success during the parental and productive years of early adulthood, they are brought to crisis by the developments and the depletions which characterize the middle and postparental years.

Thus, the men who have retained the maternal bond in its outward form, through their dependent liaison with a nutritive and managerial wife, are generally stabilized through their adult, parental years. In their postparental years, satisfied that they have done their duty as providers, they move into the family niche that their grown children have abandoned: In effect, they propose to replace the now departed children as the object of the wife's affection and concern. Thus, these men are not troubled by their *own* postparental shift, toward dependency and passivity; rather, their crisis is brought on by the postparental shift in the wife toward autonomy, assertion, and self-definition along more masculine lines. These dependent men are ready to revive the role of indulged child; their problem is externally rather than internally based, and has to do with the fact that the wife is now interested in self-fulfillment, and is no longer interested in being the indulgent mother to her husband. The husband's resulting breakdown toward depression is stimulated not by his own inner rejection of his own aggravated dependency, but by his wife's rejection of these qualities; and by her developmental move away from altruistic maternalism.

In at least seven case that we have studied, men who have these dependent vulnerabilities have also managed to stave off a breakdown by shifting their maternal transference away from the defecting wife and toward a grown-up daughter. In these cases, the illness announces itself at the time when the daughter leaves home, usually to get married. Incidentally, the men who are able to shift their dependencies in this flexible fashion, from the wife to the daughter, are also more apt to develop somatic, rather than depressive symptoms.

The second group of casualties comes from men who have preserved the maternal bond inwardly, through identification, rather than externally, through the adoption of passive roles. Moreover, the feminine identification is denied, and these men adopt a counterdependent and sometimes hyper-*macho* stance toward the world. The masculine world of work provided opportunities for the enactment of this defensive stance, and it also provided the outer structures that compensated for poorly developed structures of the self. Thus, their work—as directed by bosses, patrons, and mentors—provided direction, tokens of prestige, and admirable "fathers." In a real sense, their work organization served, in the absence of a reliable superego, as a predictable source of control and self-esteem. Thus, in their work these men seem to have reconstituted the absent father; and in their marriage to nutritive but nonassertive women, they have—though in a less threatening form—recreated the unrelinquished bond to the mother. Accordingly, during their early adulthood and parental years, these men are stabilized, the missing parts of self compensated for by the outer structures that are provided by work and marriage.

However, midlife changes involving both depletion and development threaten these precarious logistics of the self. We understand these dislocations as follows: On the depletion side, work becomes less challenging and less compelling; it no longer promises opportunity and an open future. Work can no longer support grandiose fantasies, or stringent controls; and it no longer provides a buffer against the more domestic aspects of the other world, or the more "feminine" *persona* of the inner world.

Besides relying on work, these men had also relied on their wives to defend against their closeted femininity. In her more docile days, the wife represented a projective ecology through which the husband could live out, or externalize, the more passive, "feminine" aspects of the self. That is, the younger wife represented both the external and the internal tie to the mother—the bonding through outer relationship, as well as the bonding through inner identification; and as she individuates, she compromises both. Besides taking away the "good mother," she also takes away the projective ecology through which the husband lived out the maternal identification—the more "womanly" aspect of self. As a consequence, the husband is faced with the frightening, albeit unconscious, recognition of his own sexual bimodality: The mother is not out there, in the wife; she is inside, as part of himself. Thus, as the wife "comes out of the closet" and refuses to be a metaphor of the husband's denied femininity, the husband is confronted with his own closeted maternal self, and senses uneasily that his masculine *persona* is reduced. The consequent sense of emasculation is heightened by the seeming threat from the wife: As she becomes bolder, especially toward him, she is confounded with the domineering mother; in the husband's eyes, the wife is castrating him as the mother once castrated the weakened father.

The husband's consequent loss of self-esteem is heightened and underlined by the developmental shift toward a more emotional and "maternalistic" stance within himself: These intrinsic changes add to the wounds that are imposed extrinsically, by the phasing out of work, and by the midlife development of the wife. Given normal development in early life, these toxic factors would not have been sufficient, by themselves, to bring about a crisis of clinical proportions; what we see are the clinical effects of *overdetermination:* the mutual facilitation, between the developments and the depletions of later adult life, and the *specific* vulnerabilities left over from earlier failures to achieve adequate separation from maternal figures. In any event, the pathologic outcomes, as we have seen, are much the same across cases—an agitated depression, mingled with panic. Indeed, given the fears of emasculation which underlie that panic— and which are sometimes expressed as a fear of homosexuality, this midlife syndrome can be seen as a version of homosexual panic.[1]

The various acting-out behaviors that we see clinically in men of this background and symptom picture represent desperate attempts to deny

---

[1] When such fears are at the forefront, the danger of suicide must be taken very seriously. The mingling of rage and shame toward the hidden aspects of self can, under conditions of temporary psychosis, take the form of a murderous attack against the inner enemy. This danger was illustrated most graphically in the Rorschach responses of a 50-year-old man who

sexual bimodality, to seek new but disguised sources of oral supply, or to reexternalize the "feminine" and needful aspect of the self. They represent often unsuccessful attempts to stave off depression. For example, alcoholism—a syndrome that typically intensifies in the middle life of men—serves these multiple functions very well. It is an ideal vehicle for externalizing the ambivalence around active and passive modalities. On the one hand, strong drink is instant *machismo:* Because it releases inhibitions on aggression, it is confounded—as "fire water," or "Dutch courage"—with the energies that it sponsors, and as such becomes a liquid metaphor of male power. On the other hand, drinking is an oral activity, a recapitulation of infantile sucking in which the individual takes in a liquid that has analgesic, soothing (as well as stimulating) qualities. Thus, within the course of the same drinking bout, the alcoholic is both a god and a helpless baby. He starts the evening by claiming that he can "lick anybody in the house," but ends it impotent, like an infant: unable to walk, and smeared with his own mess. Under the cover story, "It's the liquor talking," the alcoholic has been permitted to externalize—and enjoy—both aspects of his troubling duality without having to take personal responsibility for either of them.

Psychosomatic symptoms, even including the heart attacks that proliferate in later life, may also support these midlife reexternalizations. In effect, the ailing man brings his troubling passive needs to the one major institution in our society that recognizes and even insists on a dependent stance—the hospital. By becoming a patient, the middle-aged man says, "It is not I, but my diseased organs that ask for help. My spirit is still willing; but my heart, liver, or stomach is weak." In effect then, psychosomatic illness also serves, at great price, to restore the *status quo ante:* The damaged organ takes on the role of the weak, dependent "feminine" entity that was once played by the wife. The damaged aspect of self is reexternalized onto the damaged, "castrated" organ, rather than onto the "damaged" wife.

Threats to the Older Woman

Our own experience with first admission midlife women also confirms the clinical usefulness of the developmental approach that is outlined here. We find that the typical diagnostic label attached to women in their late

---

had made a very dedicated suicidal assault against himself. The Rorschach imagery consisted almost exclusively of soft, squashy forms that had been crushed, and stamped upon. Through these images, the patient was telling us of his destructive intentions toward the feminine "softness" that he felt to be growing within himself.

forties and fifties is "depression," and the symptoms associated with that label usually lead, almost automatically, to diagnostic assumptions based on the "loss perspective": The depressed patient is seen to be suffering the menopause and the loss of her procreative capacities, she is suffering the "empty nest," she is suffering from her husband's disinterest, or she is suffering the pain of widowhood. But intensive interviewing as well as analysis of projective fantasy reveals another story: Just as in the case of men, the *real* losses are more apt to be internal than external, based on a loss of self-esteem rather than a loss of some external object. Thus, in case after case, we are surprised by the energetic quality of the fantasy—particularly by the vigor and dominance assigned to the female stimulus figures. It is as though the unacknowledged aspects of the self, expressed through the TAT, are more dynamic and assertive than the acknowledged version of the self, which is focused on depletion and victimization.

For example, consider the case of a woman, hospitalized for depression, who is diagnosed as suffering from a kind of preemptive mourning for a terminally ill husband. The patient had been going to school, and was soon to begin a postgraduate career. However, these plans were aborted by the patient's decision to stay home and nurse her dying husband. The couple had been close, and the diagnostic formulation presented the patient as suffering and depressed in anticipation of the husband's oncoming death. However, the projective test data were full of images of imprisonment, claustrophobia, and rage. Clearly, the patient was bitter over her imprisonment in a nursing role, at a time when she was looking forward to an expanded and self-expressive life. Again, the patient was not chiefly suffering the pain of loss, but the pain of guilt and self-reproach: She could not forgive herself for desiring the quick death—the death that would free her to an expanded life—of a beloved husband. Clearly, in such cases, the therapist should not concentrate on the irreversible loss (which is no news to the patient), but on the guilt which is both unconscious and reversible.

We cannot integrate these findings without moving away from the simple-minded and externalized "victim" hypothesis toward a formulation which is at the same time more dynamic and more complex. Clinical experience shows us that the major defensive mode in hysteria is the assumption of a plausible passivity: The ego of the hysteric adopts a passive position toward events that it has unconsciously conspired to bring about; or toward wishes and drives that it has unconsciously conspired to satisfy. This idea matches our tentative formulation concerning these patients. Their depression is, in many cases, an assertion of passivity in the face of phase-specific but inadmissable strengths and capacities of the sort that normal development brings to the fore in the later years. For reasons that probably have to do with early socialization and idiosyncratic vulnerabilities, they insist, *via* depression, that they are not the bold creatures of their own covert fantasy. Our present hunch is that these women are afraid of the energy, and the capacity for autonomy, that is revealed in their fantasy.

In earlier years, they tend to live out their assertiveness vicariously, by identifying with the exploits of the husband, and by relying on him to control their own aggressive impulses. When the postparental husband becomes more mild, they can no longer call their fury by his name; and they cannot rely on him to control and punish them for their rage. Again, as in the case of men, these women are faced with the submerged aspects of their own *bimodality*. They fear that if they permit themselves to live out their tougher qualities, they may end by leaving the husband, or by threatening him to the point where he abandons them. They seem to find a new rationale for abjuring autonomy and for continuing in a dependent but protected state by becoming physically and/or emotionally ill.

Alternatively, instead of protecting themselves through becoming ill, these women may be protecting their vulnerable midlife husbands. *Via* their symptoms, our female patients may be telling their husbands—in the face of their own developmental unrest and his own emergent passivity—that they (and not he) are still weak and damaged creatures. By becoming ill, they may perhaps magically preserve the status quo of the early years of marriage, the years when the husband was the strong provider and protector of a seemingly weak and inadequate woman. In effect, by becoming ill, they protect the husband against *his* bimodality: They provide him with a new opportunity to re-externalize the "feminine" fantasies and strivings that his own developmental progression is bringing to awareness.

There appears to be a "deep structure" in the human psyche, a universal which dictates that candidates for aggressive power must endure the assault of that power *against themselves*, before they can own it and deploy it outwardly. By the same token, women in many cases appear to be enduring their own anger, in the form of depression, before they can own it, enjoy it, and turn it to alloplastic uses. Thus, at least in some cases, the hospitalized midlife woman can be seen as suffering a kind of token death in depression, as a prelude to her "rebirth" in a more active stance.

Thus far, we have been describing men and women who appear to be victimized by their own growth potentials, when these are *experienced* as threats, as *deprivations* rather than as increments.

Now we turn to those usually older patients who do indeed suffer from *real* depletions. These are not imposed by development, but by the exigencies of fate and circumstance. In the main, whatever their early backgrounds, these patients have reacted catastrophically to personal losses in the cosmetic, social, or existential domains. They respond to loss of youthful beauty as though it were a personal insult; they respond to average expectable social losses—of kinsmen, mates, or friends—as though they had lost a part of themselves; and they are terrified and/or enraged (as though fate had singled them out) by evidences of finitude, and by the looming threat of mortality.

Narcissistic characters, those whose self-esteem depends on profoundly unrealistic convictions about themselves and others, are ubiquitous in our time. However, in our first-admission older population, we seem to be studying a particular group, whose difficulties may be traceable to developmental failures of *adulthood*, and not exclusively to the developmental lesions of early life (though these too may well be present).

Classical psychoanalytic theory holds that all significant events influencing psychological maturation take place in the early years, certainly no later than adolescence. But our clinical investigations of women hospitalized for the first time in their late sixties indicates that *parenthood*, an aspect of adulthood, represents a pivotal developmental period of the human life cycle. Thus, it often transpires that older first-time patients—most of whom are women—have never been parents. They may have been successful in many nutritive roles, as teachers, missionaries, or nurses. But, though they may have *tried* to have children, they have *not*, in the large majority of cases, been fully *parental.*

In general, these women are admitted, in their late sixties or late seventies, for the *first time*, with transient psychoses, usually featuring diffuse paranoid ideas (about landlords or neighbors). While these later life casualities share *childlessness* in common, they are divided into two major camps, depending on their early identifications.

First, those we call *aging tomboys:* These women are likely to be the oldest daughters of idealized fathers. In their early life they tended to have a particularly close relationship with the father of the sort that excluded a disparaged mother. Seemingly, they solved the problem of Oedipal rivalry by defining themselves as the father's favorite son—the son who would live out his dreams, and take up his causes better than the real sons could. They solved the erotic problem with the father by joining him through the fleshless intellect, rather than through the senses. Whereas the mother was loved, she was not respected; and the daughter sensed that the father did not take the mother seriously, being more interested in the significant world of men. These patients have joined with the father in derogating the mother, and women in general, as weak and silly. They are likely to marry idealized older men with whom they have a collaborative and "spiritual" relationship, based on shared intellectual and/or aesthetic interests. In most cases, they did not have children: "Our life together was too exciting;

and it never occurred to me to have them." In their later life, as widows, they often devote themselves to continuing the work that they shared with their husbands, and in embellishing their legends. Aging—usually in the form of some potentially disabling disease—terrifies them; they have spent their lives denying that they are women, denying that they are the weak and damaged creatures that the father would have despised. Aging, with its attendant crippling, is seen as the process which deprives them of their prized independence, which finally castrates them, *which finally turns them into women.* This assault on their narcissism is then managed through primitive means: Either the inner sense of blemish or the responsibility for that blemish is projected away from the self.

Second, we find the *perpetual daughters.* As with the "tomboys," many of these women are too narcissistic to have children. But in their case, it is the demand for exclusive possession of the mother, rather than the father, that has been conserved. These women may have failed to beget children because they had never really given up the "little girl" posture. They could not allow themselves to become mothers because this would imply that they had renounced their claim on *being mothered.* Thus, for the majority of these women, parenthood has been deliberately avoided for reasons having to do with narcissistic injury in early life; but in the case of some others, parenthood had been attempted, in the face of repeated miscarriages. But whatever their motives for or against parenthood, the nonparental women appear to be particularly susceptible to late onset depressions and transient psychoses, particularly following the death of an aging mother, or the appearance of a potentially lethal disease. These specific vulnerabilities reflect developmental failures: These women never accomplished the vital maturations that result from maternity—the decisive separation from the mother; and the entry into, as well as the acceptance of, the finite life cycle. Thus, research by psychoanalytic investigators, notably Ballou (1975), has shown that *primaparas,* as they reestablish the mother–infant bond with their own child, can finally relinquish the archaic tie to their own mothers. As a consequence, they can tolerate the death of the mother; while nonmaternal women of the sort that we see, respond more catastrophically, as though the mother's demise was an arbitrary and tragic separation.

Her maternity also introduces the new mother to her own mortality, and to the life cycle: she is no longer shocked by the idea of her own death, but rather by the possibility that the child might predecease the mother. For the first time, the new mother can accept her own death as a *real* event, and one that is, under certain circumstances, even desirable. By the same token, childless women have never experienced that great transformation of narcissism that renders the child's life more precious than their own; accordingly, they remain disastrously vulnerable to the later life intimations of mortality. When they become ill, when they are faced with the irreversible, they experience "life-cycle shock," and in their attempts to deny their condition, they do so to psychotic lengths.

These findings have theoretical as well as clinical implications: They suggest that, at least in the case of women, significant psychological development around separation and individuation continues long after childhood and adolescence, and that the later versions of maturation, which take place in adulthood, have vital and *independent* consequences for the psychological functioning, and the mental health of the older women. Feminists like to point up the psychic costs, for women, of marriage and motherhood; but, whereas childless women can never have a postpartum psychosis, being maternal may protect women—perhaps, even narcissistic women—against the psychoses of *later* life.

While these findings are still tentative, they do suggest promising lines for future investigation; moreover, they indicate the value of a developmental approach to the clinical problems of the second half of life. Such an approach helps us to identify genetic and dynamic patterns that previously would have gone unrecognized; it points up later life resources that are usually overlooked, or coded as weakness; and it suggests treatment approaches that will precisely address the identified problems, and that will draw on and amplify the strengths that may be unique to the older patient. Finally, the application of the comparative and developmental perspective to later life phenomena suggests the outlines of a more sophisticated psychodynamic approach to the older adult; and to the human life cycle as a whole.

Acknowledgments

We wish to acknowledge the particular contributions of our colleagues in the Older Adult Program of Northwestern University Medical School. These include staff and graduate students who have participated in the process of clinical investigation that has given rise to a number of the conceptions reported in this chapter.

References

Ballou, J. W. The influence of object-relational paradigms on the experience of pregnancy and early motherhood. Unpublished doctoral dissertation, University of Michigan, Ann Arbor, 1975.

Gutmann, D. The country of old men: Cross-cultural studies in the psychology of later life. *Occasional Papers in Gerontology*, 1969, 5, Institute of Gerontology: University of Michigan—Wayne State University, April 1969.

Gutmann, D. Parenthood: A key to the comparative psychology of the life cycle. In N. Datan & L. Ginsberg (Eds.), *Life-span developmental psychology: Normative life crisis*. New York: Academic Press, 1975.

Chapter 8

Economic Status of Late Middle-Aged Widows

GAYLE B. THOMPSON

Women widowed in middle age are in a vulnerable economic position. Loss of the husbands' earnings may necessitate late life-style changes, even among widows who have had substantial labor force experience and continue to work at well-paying jobs after widowhood. Most middle-aged widows have either worked intermittently, entering and leaving the labor force as the needs of their families required, or they have been full-time homemakers. These widows are confronted with the additional burden of entering or reentering the labor force, even though many lack the necessary marketable skills and the confidence and experience required to seek and obtain decent jobs. Some are unable to find work, whereas others remain unemployed for long periods of time. Those who do find work often hold part time or poorly paying, jobs which provide little opportunity for advancement.[1]

[1] For a discussion of the work-related problems faced by middle-aged women, see the following articles in U.S. House of Representatives, Select Committee on Aging and the Subcommittee on Retirement Income and Employment, *Women in Midlife—Security and Fulfillment* (Part I), 95th Congress, 2nd Session, December 1978: Andrew J. DuBrin, "Psychological Factors: Reentry and Midcareer Crises"; Janet Z. Giele and Hilda Kahne, "Meeting Work and Family Responsibilities: Proposals for Flexibility", Tish Sommers and Laurie Shields, "Problems of the Displaced Homemaker"; and Elizabeth Ann Kutza, "Passed Over by Progress: Women at the Bottom."

TRANSITIONS OF AGING

Widows under age 60 are eligible to receive benefits under the old-age survivors, and disability insurance (OASDI) program, more commonly known as the social security program, on two conditions (a) if they are disabled; or (b) if they are caring for dependent children. Disability benefits are payable at any age to widows who are insured on their own earnings records and who meet certain medical and recency of work criteria. A widow also may receive benefits beginning at age 50 on the basis of her late husband's earnings records if she is disabled.

Mother's benefits are payable (on the basis of the deceased worker's covered employment) at any age to widows caring for entitled children under age 18 or disabled. These widowed mothers' benefits provide economic protection and enable a mother to remain at home with her young children. They may also act as a work disincentive, however, and thus make it more difficult for widows to reenter the labor force when they are no longer eligible for mothers' benefits, but are not yet eligible for aged widows benefits at age 60. This gap in the social security protection of widows is referred to as the "blackout period." Failure to return to work as early as possible also has potentially negative effects on retirement income security by impeding the accumulation of savings and the earning of an employee pension.

The purpose of this chapter is to examine the economic status of late middle-aged widows immediately prior to their eligibility for social security aged widows benefits at age 60. The analysis is divided into three parts. The first part describes the income, labor force, and demographic characteristics of these widows. The second part analyzes the impact of employment on their economic status. The final part analyzes the labor force determinants of economic status among employed widows. Because the West Virginia University Gerontology Center is interested in the rural aged, urban-rural differences are discussed.

Methodology

THE SAMPLE

The data are drawn from the Retirement History Study (RHS), a 10-year national sample panel study of the retirement process (Irelan, Motley, Schwab, Sherman, & Murray, 1976). Initial inverviews were conducted in 1969 with 11,153 married and unmarried men and unmarried women aged 58–63. ("unmarried" persons were defined as the widowed, divorced, separated, never married, and married with spouse absent). The sample members and their surviving spouses have been reinterviewed at

2-year intervals since 1969. The final interview year is 1979. The present analysis focuses only on the 446 widowed women sample members who were aged 58–59 in 1969 and who were still in the sample through the fourth biennial interview in 1975. These particular widows were selected because in 1969 they were not yet eligible for aged widows benefits and few were receiving mothers' benefits; that is, most fell within the social security blackout period. By 1975, these widows were aged 64–69 and most had begun to collect social security benefits either as aged widows or as retired workers.[2]

VARIABLES

Six major categories of variables are included in the analysis: economic status, health, demographic characteristics, labor force characteristics, length of work history, and other economic characteristics. *Economic status* is measured by total money income and earnings in 1968. *Health* is measured by a widow's 1969 estimate of whether or not she was limited in the amount or kind of work or household work she could perform. The *demographic characteristics* are: education, length of widowhood (in years), living arrangements (alone or with someone), presence of own children in household, and urban–rural residence in 1969. Urban–rural residence is determined by the Bureau of the Census' assignment of an area for the 1960 Census.[3] *Labor force characteristics* include employment status in 1969 and, if employed, characteristics of the job: annual salary, occupation, extent of employment (full time versus part time), job tenure (years), and employee pension coverage. *Length of work history* is measured by the number of years (up to the 1975 interview) that a widow had been without work since age 21. It is also measured by an indicator of the amount of employment in jobs covered by social security: quarters of coverage from 1951 through 1974. Prior to 1978, a worker earned one quarter of coverage for each calendar quarter in which he or she earned $50 or more on jobs covered under social security. The rules were somewhat different for agricultural workers, self-employed persons, and workers who earned the taxable maximum. Quarters of coverage is not a good measure of length of work history for persons employed on jobs not covered under social security for much of their work history (long-time federal civil servants, for example). The vast majority of jobs are covered under the program,

---

[2] Widows who qualify for their own worker benefits are eligible for retired worker benefits at age 62. Retired worker and aged widow benefits are both actuarially reduced for each month they are received prior to age 65.

[3] For a detailed description of an urban area, see U.S. Census of the Population, 1960, *Geographic Identification Code Scheme*, PHS (2) –1.

however, and, therefore, the quarters of coverage variable is a reasonable measure of length of work history for most persons.[4] *Other economic variables* include: receipt of income from selected sources such as assets, earnings, employee pensions, and public assistance in 1968 and the size of asset income in 1968.

Results

ECONOMIC AND DEMOGRAPHIC CHARACTERISTICS, 1968–1969

Before analyzing the determinants of economic status among late middle-aged widows, it is important to understand how they are distributed across the demographic and economic characteristics that bear some relationship to that status (Table 8.1). Widows aged 58–59 in 1969 had been widowed for an average of 11 years. About 75% of them lived in urban areas. Thirty-three percent were living with children, but only 6% with children under 18 years of age. Only 38% of the widows had a high school diploma and 32% experienced some limitation in the amount of paid work or housework they could perform.

These demographic and health characteristics varied substantially by urban–rural residence. Although widowed for about the same number of years, rural widows were more likely to have been living with children under 18 years of age. They also were less well educated and much more likely to have had work limitations.

The economic status of widows in the 1–2 years prior to the availability of aged widows benefits under the social security program was less than enviable (Table 8.2). Their median total income in 1968 was $2913, and slightly over one-third of the group was poor.[5] Rural widows were much worse off financially than urban widows. Their median income was only 37% of the income of urban widows, and they were almost two and one-half times more likely to have been poor.

---

[4] For a detailed description of quarters of coverage, see U.S. Department of Health, Education, and Welfare, Social Security Administration, *Social Security Handbook*, July 1978.

[5] Poverty rates are based on the weighted average poverty threshold for one-member, female headed families living in nonfarm areas. The poverty threshold for nonfarm families in 1968 was somewhat higher than that for farm families ($1700 compared to $1441). Substantial urban–rural differences undoubtedly still would exist if this $259 difference in thresholds had been built into the calculation of the rates. The 1968 weighted average thresholds at the poverty level for families of various sizes and types are reported in Bureau of the Census, *Current Population Reports: Poverty in the United States 1959 to 1968*, Series P–60, No. 63, December 1969, Table 1.

Table 8.1

Demographic and Health Characteristics by Urban-Rural Residence: Widows Aged 58-59 in 1969[a]

Characteristics	All widows	Urban widows	Rural widows
Years widowed as of 1969 (mean)*	11	11	9
Urban-rural residence (Percentage urban)	74	—	—
Living arrangements (Percentage alone)	53	54	47
Presence of children in household*			
Percentage with any children	33	31	40
Percentage with children under 18	6	3	15
Education (Percentage with high school diploma)**	38	42	26
Work limitation (Percentage limited)***	32	27	45

[a] Starred characteristics are significantly related to urban-rural residence:

  * $p = .05$

  ** $p = .01$

  *** $p = .001$

Table 8.2

Total Money and Poverty Status in 1968 by Urban-Rural Residence: Widows Aged 58-59 in 1969

	All widows	Urban widows	Rural widows
Total money income			
Total number	446	332	114
Number reporting	385	283	102
Total percentage	100	100	100
Under $1000	22	16	39
1000–1999	18	16	24
2000–2999	11	12	8
3000–3999	12	14	9
4000–4999	12	15	6
5000–6999	12	13	6
7000 or more	13	14	8
Median	$2913	$3500	$1310
Mean	$3538	$3955	$2378
Standard error	314	206	303
Poverty status			
Percentage poor	35	25	62
Percentage poor and near poor	42	35	64

The income position of late middle-aged widows compared unfavorably with that of most other members of their age cohort (Table 8.3). Although their median income was not significantly different from that of divorced women, it was only 60% of that of never married women and 40% of that of married men. Furthermore, only 3% of the widows compared with 10% of the never married women and 25% of the married men had incomes of $10,000 or more.

Substantial proportions of late middle-aged widows received income from earnings and assets in 1968: 72% from earnings and 44% from assets (Table 8.4). Although many widows received asset income, the median annual income received from that source was very small ($295) and thus did not make a major contribution to total income.

Earnings were by far the most important income source both in terms of the number of widows receiving them and the amount of income obtained from them. Among earners, median 1968 earnings were $3545. Although the vast majority of widows received earnings, it is noteworthy that 28% did not receive income from this source. Again, rural widows compared unfavorably with urban widows. They were not only less likely to receive earnings, they also earned substantially less.

Few widows received income in 1968 from sources other than earnings and assets. Although 35% of the widows were poor and 28% received no earnings, only 6% received public assistance, less than 1% received private welfare, and only 4% received contributions from relatives or friends outside the household. Income from an employee pension was received by 8% of the widows, and about the same proportion received social security benefits (disability and mothers' benefits). Rural widows were about as likely as urban widows to have received income from each of these sources

Table 8.3

Total Money Income in 1968 for Persons and Couples Aged 58–59 in 1969

	Median income	Percentage with incomes of	
		$2000 or less	$10,000 or more
Women			
Widowed	$2913	40	3
Divorced	3125	33	3
Never married	4818	24	10
Men			
Unmarried	4208	29	12
Married	7035	9	25
Married couples	8208	5	40

Table 8.4

Income Sources in 1968 by Urban–Rural Residence: Widows Aged 58–59 in 1969[a]

Income and income sources	All widows	Urban widows	Rural widows
Percentage with income from			
Earnings*	72	74	64
Assets	44	44	43
OASDI**	9	7	16
Railroad retirement	1	1	1
Employee pension:			
Any type	8	9	8
Private	3	3	4
Government employee, military	6	6	4
Public assistance	6	6	5
Private welfare	b	b	0
Outside contributions	4	4	4
Unemployment, workmens' compensation	3	3	2
Insurance or annuities	3	4	2
Size of income by recipients from			
Assets			
Median	295	268	344
Mean	679	696	627
Earnings***			
Median	3545	3970	1875
Mean	3815	4177	2651

[a] Starred characteristics are significantly related to urban–rural residence:
* $p = .05$
** $p = .01$
*** $p = .001$
[b] Less than 1%.

except social security. They were more likely to receive social security benefits, which is not surprising in view of the fact that they were more likely to have had work limitations and to have been living with children under age 18.

At the time of the 1969 interview, 66% of the widows were employed (Table 8.5). Among the employed, the vast majority worked full time. Close to 50% of the employed widows were white-collar workers and 37% had jobs on which they were covered by an employee pension. The median number of years they had been employed on their current job was 9, and their median annualized salary was $3855.

Looking at these labor force characteristics in reverse, a large proportion of widows were not employed in 1969. Even when they did hold jobs, it was sometimes on a part-time basis, usually in blue-collar positions, and

Table 8.5

Job Characteristics and Length of Work History by Urban-Rural Residence: Widows Aged 58–59 in 1969[a]

Labor force characteristics and work history	All widows	Urban widows	Rural widows
1969 Labor force characteristics			
Employment status (Percentage employed)***	66	71	56
Job characteristics, 1969			
Extent employment (Percentage full-time)***	80	85	60
Occupation (Percentage white-collar)**	47	50	32
Tenure*			
Median years	9	9	5
Percentage with 16 or more years	30	33	22
Annual salary***			
Median	3855	4146	3077
Mean	4143	4437	2980
Pension coverage (Percentage covered)**	37	41	22
Length of work history			
Years without work since age 21 (mean)***	17	15	22
Quarters of coverage, 1951–1974 (mean)***	45	50	28

[a] Starred characteristics are significantly related to residential location:
* $p = .05$
** $p = .01$
*** $p = .001$

usually on jobs which did not provide them with retirement income protection through a private or government employee pension.

Rural widows were less likely to have been employed. If employed, they were more likely to have worked part-time and in blue-collar positions. They also had somewhat shorter tenure, were less likely to have been covered by an employee pension, and had lower salaries.

Many of the widows aged 58–59 in 1969 had long and continuous work histories but many more had worked intermittently or for short periods of time. The proportion of the widows who had never experienced a period of one or more years without work from 1930–1932 to 1975 was 15% and 27% had only 5 or fewer years without work during the same time period. Furthermore, these widows had an average of 45 quarters of coverage from 1951–1974, which is comparable to an average of 11 years of covered employment during the 24-year period.

Nevertheless, nearly one-third of the widows had been without work for 26 or more years or had never worked at all. The work histories of rural widows were substantially shorter than those of urban widows. They had more years without work and substantially fewer quarters in covered employment.

The findings pertaining to the work histories of RHS widows are supported by Mallan's (1974) analysis of the work experience of all women becoming entitled to retired workers benefits in 1970. Most of the women in the Mallan study were born between 1905 and 1908 and came from approximately the same cohort as the RHS widows. Mallan found that 12% of the women retired workers had worked in covered employment continuously for 27 or more years during the 33-year period from 1937–1970. An additional 18% had worked 27 or more years but had one or more breaks in employment lasting for at least a year. At the other end of the spectrum, 35% of the women had worked in covered employment for 14 or fewer years.

EFFECTS OF EMPLOYMENT ON ECONOMIC STATUS

As expected, the economic status of late middle-aged widows is highly related to their employment status (Table 8.6). Among widows without jobs in 1969, median 1968 income was only $1130. Almost two-thirds of these nonemployed widows had incomes below the poverty line and over three-fourths had incomes at or below the near poverty line (the near poverty line is 125% of the poverty line). Although having a job provided economic protection to many (median income equalled $4095), it was no

Table 8.6

Total Money Income and Poverty Status in 1968 by Employment Status in 1969: Widows Aged 50–58 in 1969.

	Employed	Not employed
Total money income		
Total number	296	150
Number reporting	253	132
Total percentage	100	100
Under $1000	10	45
1000–1999	12	30
2000–2999	11	11
3000–3999	16	5
4000–4999	17	5
5000–6999	17	1
7000 or more	18	3
Median	$4095	$1130
Mean	4429	1830
Standard error	187	314
Poverty status		
Percentage poor	19	65
Percentage poor and near poor	24	78

guarantee against poverty. Approximately 2 out of every 10 widows with jobs were poor and about one-fourth were either poor or near poor.

Employed and nonemployed widows differed on some demographic and work characteristics that were related to their income as well (Table 8.7). The nonemployed were more likely than the employed to reside in rural areas where jobs may be scarce and transportation inadequate, they were less well educated, they were much more likely to have experienced work limitations, and they had substantially shorter work histories.

It was hypothesized that employment status intervenes between these demographic and work characteristics, on the one hand, and economic status, on the other. The partial correlations presented in Table 8.8 support this hypothesis. They suggest that length of the work history—as measured by quarters of coverage—education, and work limitations influence employment status, which in turn influences economic status. Urban–rural residence, however, does not have much impact on the employment–economic status relationship. Introducing it as a control had little effect on the magnitude of the correlation between employment status and total money income.

Late middle-aged widows who have had little or no labor market experience over the years, who have not graduated from high school, and who are limited in the amount of work or housework they can perform are at a disadvantage compared with others in their peer group. They are less likely to find, or perhaps seek, a job in their later years even though their failure to hold a job hurts them financially.

Of the variables analyzed, length of the work history appears to play a particularly important role in this process. The bivariate correlation coefficient between employment status and total money income is $r = .356$. The correlation between these two variables controlling for quarters of

Table 8.7

Demographic Characteristics and Length of Work History by Employment Status: Widows Aged 58–59 in 1969[a]

Characteristics	Employed	Not employed
Urban–rural residence (Percentage urban)***	80	64
Education (Percentage with high school diploma)***	46	23
Work limitations (Percentage limited)***	18	59
Quarters of coverage, 1951–1974 (mean)***	60	16

[a] Starred characteristics are significantly related to employment status:
  * $p = .05$
  ** $p = .01$
  *** $p = .001$

Table 8.8
Bivariate and Partial Correlations between Employment Status in 1969 and Total Income in 1968: Widows Aged 58–59 in 1969[a]

Bivariate correlation	.356***
Partial correlation controlling for	
Urban–rural residence	.334***
Education	.294***
Work limitations	.269***
Quarters of coverage	.163***
Quarters of coverage and work limitations	.121**
Quarters of coverage and education	.122**
Quarters of coverage and education and work limitations	.092*

[a] $N = 377$.
* $p = .05$
** $p = .01$
*** $p = .001$

coverage, however, is $r = .163$. In other words, the basic correlation is substantially smaller after quarters of coverage has explained all of the variance it can in both variables. Widows with short or nonexistent work histories may be less positively disposed to work in the marketplace and undoubtedly are less likely to possess the skills and experience necessary to get and keep a job in their later years than widows with long work histories.

LABOR FORCE DETERMINANTS OF ECONOMIC STATUS AMONG EMPLOYED WIDOWS

The third and final part of the analysis examines labor force characteristics that account for the variation in the 1968 economic status of late middle-aged widows who were employed in 1969 (see Table 8.6, page 141, for distribution of total income). Not surprisingly, earnings level was highly related to total income ($r = .944$ among earners). Therefore, in order to see how other characteristics impact on economic status, the analysis examines factors related to earnings level and is restricted to widows who were employed in 1969 and who also received earnings in 1968.

The predictor variables examined are those hypothesized to have an effect, either direct or indirect, on earnings. They are grouped into two major categories. The first category consists of historical variables: education, length of widowhood, and length of work history, as measured by quarters of social security coverage. The second category consists of two job characteristics: occupation and extent of employment.

The basic analytical model hypothesized is that a widow's job characteristics have a direct bearing on her earnings. Historical factors, on the other hand, indirectly affect earnings through their impact on job characteristics. To illustrate, it is hypothesized that long-term widows and high school graduates have longer work histories than more recent widows and nongraduates. Their long work histories presumably result in the development of more marketable skills and a stronger attachment to work, which are reflected in higher occupational status, a greater propensity toward full-time work and, ultimately, higher earnings.

The bivariate relationships among the variables under consideration are shown in Table 8.9. As hypothesized, earnings level was positively related to each job characteristic, quarters of coverage, and education. In other words, earnings increased with increases in quarters of coverage. They also were higher among full-time workers, white-collar workers, and high school graduates than among those with the opposite characteristics. Length of widowhood, however, was not significantly associated with earnings. Although length of widowhood was positively related to quarters of coverage, the relationship was not very large ($r = .139$). Moreover, the effect of length of widowhood on earnings through quarters of coverage may have been offset by the fact that long-term widows were more likely than recent widows to have been employed in blue-collar positions and no more likely to have worked full time.

Quarters of coverage and education were related to both earnings and job characteristics in the direction and manner hypothesized. Widows with many years of covered employment had higher earnings than those with few years, and they were more likely to work full time and in white-collar positions. High school graduates had higher earnings than nongraduates and also were more likely to work full time in white-collar positions.

A path analysis was performed to examine more fully the basic analytical model previously described. Figure 8.1 outlines the causal relationships assumed to exist among earnings, occupation, extent of employment, quarters of coverage, and education. Length of widowhood was dropped from the analysis because it was not significantly related to earnings. The path model contains four major assumptions. First, it assumes that education has a direct effect on quarters of coverage and both direct and indirect effects on the other variables in the model. High school graduates presumably have higher earnings than nongraduates because they are more likely to work full time and in white-collar postions and to have worked longer in covered employment. Their more positive job characteristics result partly from the fact that they have had longer work histories.

Second, it assumes that quarters of coverage has some direct effect on earnings, but that most of its impact is mediated by its effects on occupa-

Table 8.9

Correlations among Selected Demographic and Economic Characteristics: Widows Aged 58-59 in 1969 Who Were Employed in 1969 and Received Earnings in 1968 [a]

Characteristics	Earnings	Extent employment	Occupation	Quarters coverage	Education	Years widowed
Earnings in 1968	1.000					
Extent employment, 1969 job (1 = full-time)	.496***	1.000				
Occupation, 1969 job (1 = white-collar)	.545***	.297***	1.000			
Quarters of coverage (1951–1974)	.310***	.275***	.218***	1.000		
Education (1 = high school diploma)	.468***	.301***	.504***	.132*	1.000	
Years widowed	.065	.067	-.116*	.139*	-.050	1.000

[a] Listwise deletion, N = 231.

* p = .05
** p = .01
*** p = .001

145

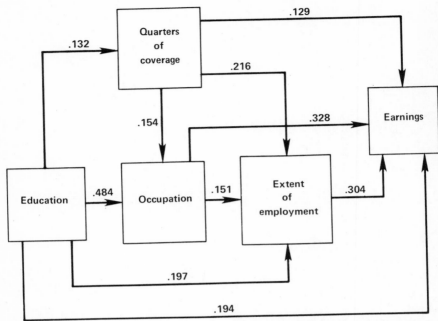

Figure 8.1. Path analysis model of earnings in 1968 with occupation, extent of employment, quarters of coverage, and education: Widows aged 58–59 in 1969 who were employed
in 1969 and received earnings in 1968.

tion and extent of employment. In other words, widows with long work
histories are assumed to have higher earnings than those with short work
histories primarily because they have had a greater opportunity to develop
marketable skills and possibly move up the occupational ladder, and
because they are more likely to seek full-time positions.

Third, it assumes that white-collar workers are more attached to the
labor force and therefore are more likely to seek full-time employment.
Consequently, the effect of occupation on earnings is viewed as both direct
and indirect through extent of employment. Finally, it assumes that the effects of extent of employment on earnings is entirely direct.

The four predictors together explained 46% of the variance in earnings.
The results of the path analysis indicate that, as expected, a major portion
of the effects of both education and quarters of coverage on earnings are indirect through occupation and extent of employment (Table 8.10 and
Figure 8.1). Examination of the components of the total indirect effects indicates that, given the model specified here, education has little impact on
earnings through quarters of coverage. Most of its impact is felt through
extent of employment (.060) and occupation (.159), especially through oc-

Table 8.10

Path Analysis Statistics for Model of 1968 Earnings with Occupation, Extent of Employment, Quarters of Coverage, and Education: Widows Aged 58–59 in 1969 Who Were Employed in 1969 and Received Earnings in 1968[a]

Bivariate relationship	Total bivariate correlation (r)	Causal effects			Noncausal effects
		Direct (Beta)	Indirect	Total	
Education, quarters of coverage	.132	.132	0	.132	0
Education, occupation	.504	.484	.020	.504	0
Education, extent of employment	.301	.197	.104	.301	0
Education, earnings	.468	.194	.274	.468	0
Quarters of coverage, occupation	.218	.154	0	.154	.064
Quarters of coverage, extent of employment	.275	.216	.023	.239	.036
Quarters of coverage, earnings	.310	.129	.123	.252	.058
Occupation, extent of employment	.297	.151	0	.151	.146
Occupation, earnings	.545	.328	.046	.374	.171
Extent of employment, earnings	.496	.304	0	.304	.192

[a] $N = 231$.

cupation. In other words, widows with high school diplomas have higher earnings than widows without diplomas partly because they are more likely to be white-collar workers and are more likely to work full time. Their higher earnings, however, do not appear to be connected with their longer work histories to any large extent.

The indirect effects of quarters of coverage on earnings are about equally divided between their effects through occupation (.050) and through extent of employment (.066). Widows with many years of covered employment earn more than widows with few years for the same reasons that high school graduates earn more than nongraduates: They are more likely to be white-collar workers and to work full time.

To summarize, the earnings of late middle-aged widows who hold jobs are largely dependent upon their occupational level and the amount of time they work per week. Each of these characteristics is in turn the product of education acquired at a much earlier age and the amount of time spent in the labor force over the life course. In short, economic status in late middle age among employed widows results partly from actions taken at a younger age.

Summary and Conclusions

Economic deprivation was not an uncommon phenomenon among late middle-aged widows in the 1 to 2 years prior to the availability of social security aged widows benefits. As expected, their economic level depended to some degree on whether or not they were working. An important question, then, is why so many widows were without jobs. Although the data provide no definitive conclusions, they suggest that education, length of the work history, and work limitations have some influence on a widow's decision to work or on her ability to get a job.

Having a job provided income protection to many, but it was no guarantee against financial hardship. Not surprisingly, the earnings of employed women varied substantially by occupation and extent of employment. Widows who worked part time or in blue-collar positions earned less than widows who worked full time or in white-collar positions. It is interesting, though not unexpected, that education and length of the work history appear to have an indirect effect on earnings through occupation and extent of employment. They also have a direct effect on earnings, that is, an effect independent of their relationship to job characteristics.

In short, the data suggest that education and work decisions made early in life have an impact on economic status among late middle-aged widows.

They affect the probability of employment, and among the employed, job characteristics and ultimately the level of earnings.

The data presented here are part of a broader longitudinal analysis of the economic status of late middle-aged widows.[6] Subsequent reports will address two major questions. The first concerns the characteristics of widows who begin to receive social security aged widows benefits as soon as they reach age 60 compared with those who postpone benefits to age 62, 65, or later. The second relates to the impact that social security benefits have on the economic status of these late middle-aged widows and whether they bring financial relief to the most disadvantaged.

References

Irelan, L. M., Motley, D. K., Schwab, K., Sherman, S. R., & Murray, J. *Almost 65: Baseline Data from the Retirement History Study* (Research Report No. 49), Social Security Administration, 1976.

Mallan, L. B. Women born in the early 1900's: Employment, earnings, and benefit levels. *Social Security Bulletin*, March 1974 (second reprint).

[6] The analysis will appear in the *Social Security Bulletin* in early 1980.

PART

ENVIRONMENTAL TRANSITIONS IN AGING

Chapter 9

Growing Old "Inside": Aging and Attachment to Place in an Appalachian Community[1]

GRAHAM D. ROWLES

Graham: "I'm interested in trying to understand what this place means to you, what Colton means to you?"

Audrey (81 years old): "Oh, it means a lot to me and I believe it means causing me to live longer."

The term *transition*, "passing from one condition . . . to another [Webster, 1975]," provides a fitting motif for considering the evolving transaction between person and environment which characterizes growing old in contemporary American society. Several dimensions of transition are involved. First, well-documented physical and psychological changes in the capability of the aging individual trace a path of *declining personal competence* (Birren & Schaie, 1976; Finch & Hayflick, 1977). This transition necessitates progressive modification of the old person's relationship with his or her environmental context—an adjustment of life style. Unraveling the main features of this adjustment is a daunting task, given the considerable variation in personality and competence among old people.

[1] The research reported in this paper is supported by a grant from the National Institute on Aging—AG00862.

The issue becomes even more problematic when we acknowledge that the old person's environment is also liable to change. *Environmental change* may result from relocation—to a new neighborhood, to a special housing project, or to an institutional setting. Environmental change also occurs *in situ* as a tangible expression of the history of a place. New buildings are constructed and others are razed. Resident populations wax and wane in numbers and ethnic composition. Services and social resources proliferate or disappear. Indeed, over the span of an individual's life, a familiar setting may undergo total transformation.

Societal change represents a third dimension of transition pertinent to understanding the relationship between old people and their environmental context. As American society has changed—from the essentially rural and small town society of the time when most of today's elderly were in their youth, to the pervasive urban technological culture of the 1970s[2]—successive cohorts have accommodated to new mores of aging and have evolved distinctive life styles. In the following pages, I will illustrate how sensitivity to complex interrelationships among all three dimensions of transition is necessary to grasp the richness of the old person's evolving relationship with environment. First, however, it is useful to assess the current status of research in this area.

In recent years, several conceptual frameworks have been proposed to represent the main features of the old person–environment transaction as it evolves in later life (Lawton & Nahemow, 1973; Rowles, 1978a; Windley, Byerts, & Ernst, 1975; Wiseman, 1979). In addition, empirical studies of old people's lifestyles and adjustments within specific urban, public housing, and institutional environments have been completed (Berghorn, Schafer, Steere, & Wiseman, 1978; Carp, 1966; Clark & Anderson, 1967; Gubrium, 1975; Lawton & Kleban, 1971; Lawton, Kleban, & Singer, 1971; Myerhoff, 1978; Townsend, 1970). However, there are two areas in which the burgeoning field of research into aging–environment relationships is poorly represented. First, there is an epistemological deficiency. A paucity of phenomenologically based research limits our understanding of important subjective dimensions of environmental experience in old age. Existing demographic inventories, assessments of changing accessibility potential and transportation needs, studies of housing and living conditions, accounts of increasing social isolation, even surveys of environmental satisfaction, can furnish only a limited array of insights. They do not reveal many subtle dimensions of the old person's *lifeworld*—"the taken-for-

---

[2] In the early twentieth century, the United States was still predominantly a rural nation. It was not until the U.S. Census of 1920 that more than 50% of Americans were classified as urban residents.

granted pattern and context of everyday life by which the person routinely conducts his or her day-to-day existence without having to make it constantly an object of conscious attention [Seamon, 1979b, p. 2]." Inquiry on this level is essential for developing sophisticated understanding of the aging person's changing relationship with environment. It is necessary to explore the older person's lifeworld—to reveal the values, meanings, and intentionalities permeating everyday experience.

A second area of omission is substantive. In 1970, 7,822,629 people over 60 years of age were classified by the U.S. Census as residing in rural environments. In addition, many of the urban elderly had spent their formative years in rural settings. Yet, with the exception of work by Youmans (1967) and by Britton and Britton (1972), few studies existed on rural aging. There has been a recent stirring of interest in the rural aged (Atchley & Byerts, 1975; Harbert & Wilkinson, 1979; Wilkinson, 1978). However, there is still an almost total absence of work concerned with old person–environment relationships in rural settings. This chapter is offered as a contribution to filling both the epistemological and substantive void. Employing an experiential perspective on aging in a rural setting, I will focus on one often recognized but little studied theme within the evolving transaction between the old person and his or her environmental context—*an apparent intensification of attachment to place.*

Intensification of attachment to place has long been an implicit theme within the public image of the old person's changing relationship with environment. The image is reinforced in literary portrayals of old age and in the writings of gerontologists. Gelwicks (1970), for example, notes that:

> As more time is spent in the same setting, more and more psychological support is derived from objects near at hand. The proximal environment assumes an importance in the aged not often perceived by the mobile young adult [p. 157].

Unfortunately, most observations on this issue are anecdotal. Little attempt has been made to probe the old person's presumed increased affinity for place, even though there is some evidence that severance from familiar place can have pathological consequences.[3] The lack of gerontological research on attachment to place is hardly surprising given the difficulty of pinning down such an amorphous phenomenon.

---

[3] Much work on relocation of the elderly reveals increased mortality rates and higher incidence of morbidity. However, it should be noted that there is growing ambivalence regarding this issue as a result of recent studies, which have failed to support the relationship. For useful reviews of this domain see Lawton and Nahemow (1973), Schooler (1976), and Tobin and Leiberman (1976). In the context of this ongoing debate, it would appear that research into the old person's relationship with place is extremely pertinent.

Recent work by humanistic geographers raises the prospect of a break-through in developing an understanding of the role of place in facilitating well-being in later life (Buttimer, 1976; Buttimer & Seamon, in press; Ley & Samuels, 1978; Tuan, 1977). A persistent theme within this research is an insideness–outsideness dualism explored by Relph (1976). "To be inside a place," he notes, "is to belong to it and to identify with it, and the more profoundly inside you are the stronger is this identity with the place [p. 49]." He distinguishes four levels of insideness; vicarious, behavioral, empathetic, and existential, representing successively deeper levels of involvement with place. Relph's analysis, building on the insight of phenomenologists, writers, and artists, has spawned writings on what it means to be "inside," "at home," or "centered" in a place (Buttimer, 1978; Seamon, 1979a).

In this chapter I consider the rural old person's attachment to place from a similar perspective. I will develop the hypothesis that being physically, socially, and—most important—autobiographically "inside" a place is a significant ingredient of successful accommodation to both personal and environmental transitions which attend the process of growing old.

The Appalachian Aging Project

The empirical grounding for my argument is an ongoing experiential exploration involving elderly residents of Colton, an Appalachian mountain community.[4] Nestled in an isolated valley, the community was a prospering coal mining settlement of some eight hundred persons by 1880. Shortly after this, a major mining disaster presaged the decline of mining and eventual abandonment of the Colton "shaft." However, the community experienced economic revival shortly after the turn of the century, emerging as a railroad center where steam engines could refill their boilers and be coupled to "helper" engines which would provide additional power for the long climb over the mountains to the east. By 1911 the town was once again thriving. A post office, company store, and an array of additional commercial establishments made Colton a service center for the surrounding hollows. There was even talk of the community becoming the county seat.

The demise of the rail yard in the 1920s, quickly followed by the

---

[4] In order to honor the confidential nature of some material in the research upon which this chapter is based, the names of all individuals and locations have been changed. Quotations are directly transcribed from tapes of conversations. In a few places, phrases from more than one exchange pertaining to a single theme have been fused. Such splicing of quotations is indicated by . . . .

Depression, transformed the community. By 1931 when the bank closed, Colton was beginning a process of decline that continues even today and has left the community as yet another of Appalachia's dying towns. The 1970 U.S. Census enumerated more than 450 residents in Colton. More recent estimates suggest the population has fallen to approximately 350 souls.

Many of the remaining people are elderly. A 1977 list of members of the Colton Senior Center included 197 names. Some of these persons were from outside the community. However, the numbers indicate the degree to which Colton is a community of the aged. These are people who have experienced the environmental transitions that colored the last century of the community's history. They experienced this space in childhood and adolescence as a vibrant bustling community. This was a place pervaded by the unsettling aura of depression as they worked and raised their families. Now, as personal capabilities decline, it is the setting in which they are adjusting to the realities of later life amidst decaying physical surroundings.

During the past year, employing an experiential methodology (Rowles, 1978b), I have been working with a panel of 12 old Colton residents ranging in age from 62 to 91 years. During periods of residence in Colton, and through biweekly visits at other times, I have sought to develop sensitive interpersonal relationships to foster an appropriate context for the participants to reveal the nature of their involvement with place.

The people I have come to know are part of a complex subtly differentiated "society of the old" that exists in Colton. Some individuals are central figures in this society. Others fulfill a more marginal role. However, the majority, including both central and marginal members, are bonded to the space of Colton in a manner that is clearly a function of the degree to which they sense themselves to be "insiders" within this place.

RELUCTANCE TO LEAVE

The sense of being "inside" is reflected by an implacable reluctance to leave despite the deteriorating contemporary physical setting. In part, this expresses attachment to a familiar house. Eighty-four year old Beatrice tells a story that poignantly illustrates this sentiment:

> This spring, my son talked. He says, "Now Mom, you just can't stay in this house forever. You got to get a smaller place and live someplace where you can be on the level." And he took us, just by force almost, to look at mobile homes and trailers. . . . And we almost bought one. They were so beautiful. And I said, "Well, are we going to sign?" And Pop said, "Well, let's think

about it till morning." So we come home, and he just sit down and started to cry. "I can't do it. I can't do it," he said. He lived in this house 57 or 8 years. And he said, "I just can't do it. We'll stay here."

A similar, although perhaps less intense, bonding with the environment outside the house reinforces reluctance to relocate. This is more than a manifestation of inertia. It expresses a need for rootedness in place, which Audrey considers "human nature." Such a sense of belonging, she explains, underlay her husband's desire to return, after an absence of three decades, to spend his final years in Colton. She talks of the bewilderment of her surviving family in Pittsburgh at her decision to stay in Colton after his death.

They don't understand why I want to live here in this little town when I could be in Pittsburgh where I lived 30 years. I lived in Pittsburgh for 30 years and had a good, oh a good life. . . . But my roots were here you know.

What is the attraction of Colton that fosters the desire to return and makes the elderly so reluctant to follow the path of most of their children who have long since departed? What exactly does having "roots" and being "inside" this place entail?

ON BEING INSIDE

Being "inside" Colton encompasses several levels of involvement in both a *contemporary* and a *historical* place. First, consider contemporary involvement. Clearly, being inside Colton has a physical dimension. *Physical insideness* represents functional existence within the setting manifest in the immediacy of everyday activity—the network of paths traced in the rhythm and routine of utilizing services and making social trips. Considerable variation exists among elderly residents in the degree to which they participate physically in Colton space. Reclusive Mary rarely leaves her house. Ellen, who has a heart problem and is subject to "spells," limits herself to a 200-yard walk to the trailer which functions as a post office once every 2 or 3 months. Audrey makes weekly visits to church. By contrast, Albert is an extensive user of Colton space. His daily walks trace consistent paths encompassing the post office, Eddy's store, and the area around the railroad tracks.

Over the duration of their residence in Colton, the participants have, however, developed a more subtle form of physical involvement with the space they use. There is a physical intimacy, transcending cognition, that provides an implicit physiological insideness within the setting—a body awareness of the physical space. Tuan (1975) has eloquently described this phenomenon. He writes:

> In carrying out . . . daily routines we go regularly from one point to another, following established paths, so that in time a web of nodes and their links is imprinted in our perceptual systems and affects our bodily expectations. A "habit field," not necessarily one we can picture, is thus established: in it we move comfortably with the minimal challenge of choice [p. 242].

The concept of body awareness of place has been explored in some depth by Seamon (1979b, 1979c). Borrowing from the French phenomenologist Merleau–Ponty, he uses the phrase "body subject" to define:

> the inherent capacity of the body to direct behaviors of the person intelligently, and thus function as a special kind of subject which expresses itself in a preconscious way usually described by such words as "mechanical," "automatic," "habitual," and "involuntary" [Seamon, 1979b, p. 10].

Body awareness derives from and is enhanced through familiarity with a setting, through the very process of living within a place. It comes to be taken-for-granted. Beatrice who has lived her entire life within half a mile of her birthplace, comes close to directly articulating the role of such awareness as a component of physical insideness:

> As long as you're on your own stomping ground . . . you can get a lot done, but if you're out in strange territory . . . if I get in a strange store, I don't know, it sort of bewilders me.

From my interaction with the elderly residents of Colton, it is apparent that body awareness facilitates continuing negotiation of space, which declining physiological and cognitive capabilities might otherwise render inaccessible. Indeed, for Beatrice and her peers, physical insideness on this level provides a crucial support in old age.

Being inside contemporary Colton also involves *social insideness*, clearly manifest in the sense of belonging permeating the "society of the old." All the participants share Audrey's view that people and relationships existing among them are essential components of the place. "Friends," she explains, "I can't be away from my friends. Here's where I want to die, right here, if I can." Social insideness involves integration within Colton's elderly society and adherence to a shared value set. It requires awareness of, and willingness to conform to, local norms of appropriate behavior as an old person. There are degrees of insideness within the social order of the community which emanate from status attributed on the basis of age itself, social capital accumulated through contribution to the community during one's past life, and being a "good" person as indicated by the sacrifices made for one's family and by continuing contributions to the community (Lozier & Althouse, 1974, 1975). Asel, at 91 the oldest resident of Colton, enjoys a social status within the community on the basis of his age, although he has long since ceased to participate as an active member of the elderly society. Jason, 84, is socially inside, even though his deteriorating mental capability and frequent disorientation are often a source of embarrassment. He made many contributions as a younger man when he was Superintendant of Schools for the county and a leading figure in the community. He has paid his dues. Sixty-six year old Bill is very much a social insider in a more contemporary sense, because of his willingness to provide his age peers with rides to the doctor or to obtain services. Lucinda, 62, is also an insider on this level because of frequent contributions of time and energy to the fund-raising activities of the Volunteer Fire Department, the Senior Center, and other local community groups.

The complex set of social commitments and relationships that characterize Colton's "society of the old" finds distinctive geographical expression as an intricately balanced hierarchy of social spaces. As Buttimer (1972, p. 287) notes, "places and spaces . . . assume spatial dimensions that reflect the social significance they have for those who use them." The aura of a shared social space is apparent on the level of the entire community. However, clusters of old people living within one or two houses of each other sustain more intense social spaces on a very local scale. Spatial proximity fosters intimately linked support networks with high levels of functional and social reciprocity among neighbors. This phenomenon is similar to the "face block" or immediate vicinity social networks which have been identified in metropolitan neighborhoods (Jacobs, 1961: Suttles, 1972). In several instances I have found that a local cluster of old people is not only mutually self-supportive, but is also sustained by one or two younger families in the immediate vicinity who provide services and social support in times of crisis for individual members of the cluster.

Social insideness on both the community and local level is maintained and reinforced by contact mechanisms, including attendance at church and the Senior Center, and intensive participation in an active telephone network. Most elderly residents make at least half a dozen calls every day—many of them of considerable duration. Often these calls are to persons no more than a few houses away or even next door. Pairs of old people, especially those who spend most of their time at home, have an arrangement whereby they call each other and talk at a prescribed time every day.[5] There is a telephone network that activates to spread snippets of

[5] These relationships are fairly widely acknowledged within the community. On several occasions when I have encountered a busy signal when calling from one old person's home to another, my host has noted that, "She must be talking to. . . ."

"news" or information providing the social currency of the elderly society. Such information ranges from the latest events in the soap operas, through news of the death of someone linked (often in the most oblique way) to Colton, to elaborate planning and preparation for forthcoming community events. Perhaps the most reinforcing and strongly appreciated indication of being an insider is provided by the calls received upon returning from a sojourn away from the community. Audrey comments on her return from a vacation in Pittsburgh.

> I came home on Monday, and on Tuesday I never was away from that telephone. And I said to Jean (a middle-aged neighbor), "How in the world did people know I was back in town, even Monday night?" . . . And she said, "My lands, at least 6 weeks, every day somebody was wanting to know when you are coming home." And they called and called. . . . I have so many friends. . . . Oh, it was wonderful, felt wonderful, if people would like me. They must have liked me or they wouldn't phone: And that made me feel good.

There is, however, a much deeper level of being inside which moves beyond physical and social dimensions of contemporary affinity. Bonding to Colton involves not only the place of the present but also an *autobiographical insideness* within a place, or more accurately a series of remembered places, of which the drab contemporary physical setting is but a remnant. Participation in the evolving history of Colton has fostered a commitment which is the essence of rootedness in place. For each old person in Colton, the place is not the physical setting I can view, nor the contemporary social milieu I have described. It is a mosaic of incident–places which together constitute a "lived in" place conveying a sense of ongoing affinity and forming a repository of personal identity. It is difficult to comprehend fully the temporal texture of this commitment. One can merely describe some of its more overt manifestations.

One day I took a ride with 87-year-old Bertha to visit some of the places in and around Colton where she lived in her youth. We drove down a muddy, partially graveled country lane enclosed by woodland occasionally giving way to a clearing containing a run-down shack or more modern mobile home. This pleasant but essentially unremarkable pathway was transformed into a living landscape as Bertha, responding to the cues of place, graciously revealed the dimensions of her being inside this environment.

We passed "old Graveney's cabin" which Bertha explained, was known as the place "where the slaves used to stay." Nearby was the "swimming pond" where her "kids" used to go swimming. The cabin was gone, and the pond had become clogged with mud and weeds and "all overgrown." We passed the remnants of a tree which, 80 years previously, provided a lofty vantage point from which she was able to sight the dentist as he rode into the valley and, having done so, to make herself scarce before his arrival in Colton. Farther on, she showed me a crevice in a large boulder. "We used to get dirt back in underneath there . . . for our house lawn, and for the porch box where flowers growed so good." We came to the "Green Tree," an imposing oak which served as a childhood rendezvous. "The kids on that end of the country road and us kids would come over here and meet and play." We passed the place where she was born and raised in a family of 21 children. The farmhouse had disappeared. In its place stood a mobile home. But for Bertha the old "home place" still existed. There was the now abandoned farmstead where a daughter died of pneumonia, the family gravesite, indeed, a host of places richly imbued with meaning in terms of events that transpired within them.

These illustrations provide one example of a pervasive phenomenon among the long time elderly residents of Colton. Each of them has heavy historical investment in this place. Each has created an environment richly differentiated as an array of places laden with personal meaning in relation to a life history. Over the years, each one of them has become more and more a part of the place to the point where it has become an autobiography —literally an extension of self. In the same way that each person is generally unaware of the movement of his limbs—the clasping of his fingers, the extending of his arm, the process of walking across a familiar room—so too does being a part of Colton on this level of intimacy come to be taken-for-granted by the existential insider.

VENTURING OUTSIDE

Understanding the nature of the participants' "being inside" Colton is enhanced by considering their relationship with space outside the community. It would be easy to reinforce a contemporary Appalachian myth by extending an image of the independent, reclusive, fearful mountaineer, sheltering in the protective isolation of the mountains. To do so would be a misrepresentation. The old people of Colton, with few exceptions, have geographically extensive and intensive contact with the world outside. Such contact is not limited to service trips to larger communities in the surrounding area. Many old residents have taken vacation trips organized by the county Senior Citizen group to Florida, Canada, and New England. Visits to relatives who left Appalachia during the lean times of the 1950s and 1960s and settled in distant metropolitan areas are also made once or twice a year. Indeed, many old residents of Colton undertake a regular seasonal migration to winter with their families and avoid the harsh weather of the mountains.

In addition to physical participation, there is also considerable social and psychological involvement in the world outside Colton. Continuing social and emotional links with children and family beyond the mountains are sustained through the mail and via the telephone. Such social linkages often span considerable distances and provide opportunity for vicarious participation in places far beyond Colton.[6] Finally, there is frequent contact with the world outside through the media. Television provides an extension of space embracing not only the environments of the soap operas but also the world of current events (Graney & Graney, 1974).

In sum, the old people of Colton are neither physically or psychologically restricted to this place. Nonetheless, in a significant sense, the milieu beyond the circle of hills surrounding the community is viewed as "outside." Developing a more refined understanding of how this outsideness is qualitatively differentiated from being inside Colton is facilitated by considering the process of coming inside in terms of the levels of insideness I have identified.

COMING INSIDE

Return from a trip evokes strong feelings of coming home; but the process of coming inside varies according to the duration of time spent outside. Return from a shopping trip, although it may have recurrent cognitive and emotional correlates, primarily requires reentry on a physical level as the Colton resident once more traverses intimately known space. A winter vacation may necessitate not only reacquaintance with the physical setting but also reintegration within the social fabric of Colton space—a reestablishment of social insideness (Schutz, 1971). Finally, after a lengthy sojourn outside, there may be the more subtle reaffirmation of autobiographical insideness provided by revisiting the locations of incident–places from the past. Parenthetically, it should be noted here that these event–places, due to their constitution in consciousness, may in fact never have been abandoned. The reacquaintance is with the cues provided by place, which reaffirm the event and serve to revive it in reminiscence.

Each reentry involves partial reenactment of the more fundamental process through which the person originally became an insider. Lucinda, one of the younger members of Colton's elderly society, provides an illustration of this process. She has resided within the community for 11 years. Formerly she lived "up a hollow" several miles from Colton where she raised 11 children on a farm that did not have running water or electricity. For many years she walked into town to order groceries, so she was

---

[6] For elaboration on this theme, see Hochschild (1973, pp. 96–111) and Osterreich (1965).

"known" to the community. Since moving into her house in the center of town she has, of course, become physically inside through the very fact of her presence in this space. She has developed a body awareness of her environmental context as a result of increasing familiarity with the detail of its physical configuration. In Lucinda's case, becoming a physical insider was closely intertwined with the attainment of social insideness.

At first a sense of being a social outsider pervaded her image of the social space of Colton:

> I felt like somebody was looking at me, or over my back. . . . I didn't feel like I was a part of it. . . . I felt they were so much bigger than I was . . . [I] didn't know what to talk about. . . . I don't know what people thought of me. . . . I didn't get out, it must have been two years. It took me two years to be going to the post office [less than 200 yards from her house] . . . that's when my kids were home. I'd send them to the store if I needed anything. I didn't have to get out. Once they all left me, then I had to get out. . . . After a while, [I got] used to it, and it [went] away.

As she became more fully an insider in a physical sense, Lucinda gradually gained acceptance within the contemporary social space of the elderly society. Today she is a central figure, serving on committees, participating in the social life of the elderly community, and fully integrated within the telephone network.

However, Lucinda has yet to attain the deepest level of insideness. She has not developed the intensity of insideness pervading Bertha's affinity for Colton: For Lucinda is not inside the history of this place. For her, the Colton environment does not have the temporal depth which, for Bertha, transforms it into a rich mosaic of incident–places. Because of this she is more conscious of the contemporary physical setting.

> I don't really care that much for Colton. . . . I like the people, but as far as the town, I don't like the town. It's too dirty. . . . I don't really like it here.

Indeed, it is hard to find evidence of Lucinda being inside this place on an autobiographical level. The only indication of such affiliation I have thus far discovered is provided by her desire to be buried in a location outside Colton somewhat closer to her former "home place."

> I don't think it makes any difference where I die. I want to be buried in a certain place. . . . I want to be buried beside my husband. The grave is already there and the marker and everything. But as far as where I die . . . don't make any difference to me.

Such autobiographical alienation from place contrasts strongly with the sentiments of Audrey, Beatrice, Bertha, and many of the other older elderly Colton residents. However, Lucinda is not alone. A significant number of old people in Colton, particularly the young-old who have not experienced their childhood or lived all their lives in this place, reveal a similar lack of autobiographical insideness. It is important to note here that many of these individuals may possess an affinity for a place, but this place is not Colton. As Bill, a 15-year resident and very much a physical and social insider in contemporary Colton comments:

> Actually, I haven't spent too much time in Colton in my life. I spent the biggest part of my younger days over around Saltsman and Bowers; so Colton really don't have as much for me as it does for those other old people because I never spent that much time here. . . . Saltsman would be my home place because I spent most of my younger days there.

In sum, a generational difference appears to exist in the nature of attachment to place between the young–old and the more senior members of Colton's elderly population. What is the significance of this difference for understanding the evolving person–environment transaction of the aging person in a rural environment? To answer this question we need to consider the way in which being autobiographically inside a place influences accommodation to aging.

AUTOBIOGRAPHICAL INSIDENESS AS A FACTOR IN ACCOMMODATION TO AGING

Acknowledging different levels of insideness is a key to understanding how place can affect well-being in old age. As people grow older, and physiological and psychological capabilities become progressively impaired, physical participation in environment becomes increasingly supplemented, and gradually supplanted, by emotional and vicarious participation in place.[7] As this occurs, and as reminiscence and processes of life review become more significant (Butler, 1963; Lewis, 1971; McMahon & Rhudick, 1967), place past and hence *autobiographical insideness assumes increasing importance.* Place becomes a scrapbook, a repository for the drama of one's life as selectively construed with the vision of hindsight—it conveys ongoing *identity.*[8] As Lowenthal (1975, p. 9) notes: "Buffeted by

[7] This argument is elaborated in detail in Rowles (1978a).

[8] The selective creativity of memory with regard to incident–place is clearly illustrated by White (1973, pp. 3–4): "When I tell the story of my life, it is largely made up of the images I create of the places in my life. Remembering the places and the emotions as I once experienced them is a tricky business. I don't exactly discover the past of my life by remembering events. In

change, we retain traces of our past to be sure of our enduring identity."
For Audrey, Beatrice, and the other *older* participants in my research, the
past is retained through the place. Colton provides identity even though its
buildings are deteriorated or have disappeared, and even though the place
is no longer peopled by those who molded its social character throughout
its history.

Both physical and social insideness within a place can be recreated and
sustained following relocation. It is also possible to transport images of
place which provide a remembered sense of autobiographical insideness—to be residing in an institution for example, and yet "living" within a
home place one has physically abandoned. However, unlike physical and
social insideness, *autobiographical insideness can rarely be created within a
new setting.* A long-term care facility cannot accumulate the necessary temporal depth of meaning.

To migrate as an old person is to give up the support to autobiographical insideness provided by living within the place where significant incidents occurred. Such support emanates from both physical cues and the
presence of a particular group of peers. Audrey provides a mellow illustration of the way the environment harbors *physical cues* enhancing a sense of
autobiographical insideness. I asked her if she could visit places in Colton
without thinking of the people who frequented them.

> Oh no. No. No. Well, when I walk into that church and sit down. You see
> where I sit all the time? We came back to Colton. First time [we] went to
> church. . . . We went in that church and sat down right there. We always sat
> there. I never changed places after that. I always sit there.

Memories of her husband were powerfully evoked. How did she feel when
she sat in this pew?

> I don't know, sudden mixed emotions. I feel sad sometimes. Sometimes I feel
> happy. If I seem too sad, I go up and kneel down at the altar for a few minutes
> and talk to the Lord and that helps.

To be surrounded by *age peers who have shared in the evolving history*
of a place is also a source of support to autobiographical insideness. The
small surviving cadre of the very old, through their telephone interaction,
sustain a selectively retained social mythology of Colton's past. Occa-

---

fact I invent my past as a grand fiction, the myriad details of which fit into a coherent pattern
that is called a self-concept. There is much twisting and bending of the original event so that it
can fit into the model of what I say I am, and what I say the world is."

sionally they talk about events of the distant past, such as the time at the turn of the century when the schoolhouse burned down. However, it is more their symbolic presence as representatives of a departed era, rather than the stories they tell, which reinforces an ongoing sense of autobiographical insideness.

SOCIETAL CHANGE AS A THREAT TO
AUTOBIOGRAPHICAL INSIDENESS IN OLD AGE

If my hypothesis, that being physically, socially, and in particular, autobiographically inside a place is a source of support in old age, is accepted, there follow some rather unsettling implications with regard to well-being and perhaps even survival in old age. These implications result from acknowledging societal transitions that are transforming the experience of aging for present and future generations of old people. As the essentially rural and small town society existing in the America of my study participants' formative years becomes increasingly pervaded by the homogenizing influences of urban technological culture, and as people become increasingly mobile, there is occurring an alienation from place. As individuals spend less and less time in one place, it becomes more difficult for them to identify with a "home place" imbued with the depth of autobiographical insideness I have suggested is adaptive for the older old people of Colton. Such alienation is already revealed by Lucinda, Bill, and other members of Colton's younger elderly population.

To summarize in the context of my observations at the beginning of this chapter, I suggest that the experience of aging in the existing rural environment of Colton embraces a constellation of transitions influencing attachment to place. With advancing years, physiological and psychological decrements in the study participants' capabilities have been accommodated through adaptations made possible by familiarity with the setting. The process has been one of carving a personal niche in this place—of becoming a physical, social, and autobiographical insider. Familiarity with the setting, known not only as a physical context for contemporary existence, but as the arena of one's whole life, has facilitated this process. It has enabled the older old residents to cope with environmental transitions because the place is imbued with a temporal depth of meaning transcending its remaining physical structures and present day social identity. But such insideness is only fully attainable in situations of limited mobility such as are characteristic of traditional rural communities. As a strategy of accommodation to aging and environmental change, it is threatened by the increased mobility and alienation from place that marks contemporary cultural change and that is transforming rural society.

There is a potentially tragic irony here. Through sensitive environmental design, we can enrich the places where old people reside by making them barrier free and fostering a sense of physical insideness. Through developing congregate housing, retirement communities, and other group living arrangements, and supporting these with an array of social programs, we can encourage a sense of social insideness. Such innovations reflect a technological society's growing reliance on services and programs for the elderly as a replacement for community support. As we become more proficient at providing supportive environments for old people on these levels, we may come to delude ourselves into the belief that we are creating optimum places in which to grow old. Perhaps in a purely functional sense we are: But by ignoring autobiographical insideness, we are neglecting the very thing which gives place a depth of meaning for old people. In so doing we arrogantly dismiss the possibility that there is indeed some substance to Audrey's assertion that dwelling in Colton "means causing me to live longer."

Acknowledgments

Thanks are due to Linda Levi for her assistance in transcribing tapes and the preparation of this manuscript.

References

Atchley, R. C., & Byerts, T. O. (Eds.). *Rural environments and aging*. Washington D.C.: Gerontological Society, 1975.

Berghorn, F. J., Schafer, D. E., Steere, G. H., & Wiseman, R. F. *The urban elderly: A study of life satisfaction*. New York: Universe Books, 1978.

Birren, J. E., & Schaie, K. W. (Eds.). *Handbook of the psychology of aging*. New York: Van Nostrand Reinhold, 1976.

Britton, J. H., & Britton, J. O. *Personality changes in aging*. New York: Springer, 1972.

Butler, R. N. The life review: An interpretation of reminiscence in the aged. *Psychiatry*, 1963, 26, 65–76.

Buttimer, A. Social space and the planning of residential areas. *Environment and Behavior*, 1972, 4, 279–318.

Buttimer, A. Grasping the dynamism of lifeworld. *Annals of the Association of American Geographers*, 1976, 66(2), 277–292.

Buttimer, A. Home, reach, and the sense of place. In *Regional identitet ouch forandring i den regionala samverkans samhalle*. Uppsala: Acta Universitatis Upsaliensis Symposia, 1978. Pp. 13–39.

Buttimer, A., & Seamon, D. (Eds.). *Place and journey: Excursions in human geography*. London: Croom Helm, in press.

Carp, F. *A future for the aged*. Austin: University of Texas Press, 1966.

Clark, M., & Anderson, B. *Culture and aging: An anthropological study of older Americans.* Springfield, Ill.: Charles C. Thomas, 1967.

Finch, C. E., & Hayflick, L. (Eds.). *Handbook of the biology of aging.* New York: Van Nostrand Reinhold, 1977.

Gelwicks, L. E. Home range, and the use of space by an aging population. In L. A. Pastalan & D. H. Carson (Eds.), *Spatial behavior of older people.* Ann Arbor: University of Michigan–Wayne State University, Institute of Gerontology, 1970.

Graney, M. J., & Graney, E. E. Communications activity substitutions in aging. *Journal of Communication,* 1974, *24,* 88–96.

Gubrium, J. F. *Living and dying at Murray Manor.* New York: St. Martin's Press, 1975.

Harbert, A. S., & Wilkinson, C. W. Growing old in rural America. *Aging,* 1979, *291–292,* 36–40.

Hochschild, A. R. *The unexpected community.* Englewood Cliffs, N.J.: Prentice Hall, 1973.

Jacobs, J. *The death and life of great American cities.* New York: Vintage Books, 1961.

Lawton, M. P., & Kleban, M. H. The aged resident of the inner city. *The Gerontologist,* 1971, *11,* 277–283.

Lawton, M. P., Kleban, M. H., & Singer, M. The aged Jewish person and the slum environment. *Journal of Gerontology,* 1971, *26,* 231–239.

Lawton, M. P., & Nahemow, L. Ecology and the aging process. In C. Eisdorfer & M. P. Lawton (Eds.), *The psychology of adult development and aging.* Washington D.C.: American Psychological Association, 1973. Pp. 619–674.

Lewis, C. N. Reminiscing and self-concept in old age. *Journal of Gerontology,* 1971, *26*(2), 240–243.

Ley, D., & Samuels, M. (Eds.). *Humanistic geography: Prospects and problems.* Chicago: Maaroufa Press, 1978.

Lowenthal, D. Past time, Present place: Landscape and memory. *The Geographical Review.* 1975, *65*(1), 1–36.

Lozier, J., & Althouse, R. Social enforcement of behavior toward elders in an Appalachian mountain settlement. *The Gerontologist,* 1974, *14*(1), 69–80.

Lozier, J., & Althouse, R. Retirement to the porch in rural Appalachia. *International Journal of Aging and Human Development,* 1975, *6*(1), 69–80.

McMahon, A. W., & Rhudick, P. J. Reminiscing in the aged: An adaptational response. In S. Levin & R. J. Kahana (Eds.), *Psychodynamic studies on aging: Creativity reminiscence and dying.* New York: International Universities Press, 1967. Pp. 64–78.

Myerhoff, B. *Number our days.* New York: Dutton, 1978.

Osterreich, H. Geographical mobility and kinship: A Canadian example. In R. Piddington (Ed.), *Kinship and geographical mobility.* Leiden: E. J. Brill, 1965. Pp. 131–144.

Relph, E. *Place and placelessness.* London: Pion, 1976.

Rowles, G. D. *Prisoners of space? Exploring the geographical experience of older people.* Boulder, Colorado: Westview Press, 1978. (a)

Rowles, G. D. Reflections on experiential fieldwork. In D. Ley & M. Samuels (Eds.), *Humanistic geography: Prospects and problems.* Chicago: Maaroufa Press, 1978. Pp. 173–193. (b).

Schooler, K. K. Environmental change and the elderly. In I. Altman & J. F. Wohlwill (Eds.), *Human behavior and environment: Advances in theory and research* (Vol. 1). New York: Plenum Press, 1976. Pp. 265–298.

Schutz, A. The homecomer. In *Collected papers: Studies in social theory* (Vol. 2). The Hague: Martinus Nijhoff, 1971. Pp. 106–119.

Seamon, D. Newcomers, existential outsiders and insiders: Their portrayal in two books by Doris Lessing. Paper presented at Annual Meeting of the Institute of British Geographers, Manchester, England, January 4, 1979. (a)

Seamon, D. Body subject, time–space routines, and place ballets. Paper presented at Special Session, Experiential Perspectives on Place, Association of American Geographers, Annual Meeting, Philadelphia, April 24, 1979. (b)

Seamon, D. *A geography of the lifeworld: Movement, rest, and encounter.* New York: St. Martin's Press, 1979. (c)

Suttles, G. D. *The social construction of communities.* Chicago: University of Chicago Press, 1972.

Tobin, S. S., & Leiberman, M. A. *Last home for the aged.* San Francisco: Jossey–Bass, 1976.

Townsend, P. *The family life of old people.* London: Penguin Books, 1970.

Tuan, Y. F. Space and place: Humanistic perspective. In C. Board, R. J. Chorley, P. Haggett, & D. R. Stoddart (Eds.), *Progress in geography: International reviews of current research* (Vol. 6). London: Edward Arnold, 1975.

Tuan, Y. F. *Space and place: The perspective of experience.* Minneapolis: University of Minnesota Press, 1977.

Webster's new twentieth century dictionary (2nd ed.). New York: William Collins and World, 1975.

White, E. A. Environment as human experience: An essay. Unpublished Masters' Thesis, Clark University, 1973.

Wilkinson, C. W. *Comprehensive annotated bibliography on the rural aged (1975–1978).* West Virginia University Gerontology Center, *Occasional Papers on the Rural Aged, 1,* 1978.

Windley, P. G., Byerts, T. O., & Ernst, F. G. (Eds.). *Theory development in environment and aging.* Washington D.C.: Gerontological Society, 1975.

Wiseman, R. *Spatial aspects of aging.* Washington D.C.: Association of American Geographers, Resource Paper, 78–4, 1979.

Youmans, E. G. (Ed.). *Older rural Americans: A sociological perspective.* Lexington: University of Kentucky Press, 1967.

Chapter 10

Environmental Change: The Older Person as Initiator and Responder

M. POWELL LAWTON

A first point of departure for examining environmental change is the distinction, for heuristic purposes, among three types of change: change in the individual, environmental change that does not involve a change in residence, and environmental change that entails a physical relocation of the individual. At first glance, changes in these three elements may be clearly independent of one another. The individual learns new skills or declines in competence through internal processes; the housing or neighborhood becomes old, weathered, or outmoded in style; a new residence has a different address, and with it a complete new package of attributes. As Nahemow and I have suggested repeatedly (Lawton & Nahemow, 1973), however, individual and environment interact in an intricate fashion. In more extreme terms, they are said to "transact" in such a way as to make the separation of person and environment impossible (Ittelson, 1976).

Thus, whereas individuals do change in biology, cognition, personality, and so on, when they behave, they are doing so somewhere; their behavior is being shaped, facilitated, or constricted by their environment; their behavior, in turn, is altering or using their environments. We must first begin with the idea that not only are person and environment inextricably

TRANSITIONS OF AGING

related, but that change in each is constantly interacting with change in the other.

A second point of emphasis is the distinction between the external ("objective") environment, expressable in terms of grams, centimeters, seconds, numbers of people, and so on, and the "subjective" environment. One's internal representations of a changing environment may operate so as to accentuate or deny the changes occurring in the external environment. More generally, the process of apprehending the objective environment involves the transformation of all that is "out there" into manageable chunks, complete with simplification, shorthand, filtering, accentuation, and distortion. Comprehension of the environment is conditioned by the quality of the sensory apparatus, cognitive skills, personal needs, personality styles, and past experience.

The third point of departure concerns the directionality of action between person and environment. Many of us who have written about persons and environments have, for one reason or another, apparently implied a one-way causal link from environment to person, such that the individual appeared to be the passive respondent to environmental press. In some ways this environmental–deterministic position feeds the optimistic view that all would be well for humanity if only the design sector could construct the right kinds of environments. Clearly, no such suggestion is intended.

This naive deterministic position is related to another traditional assumption of much dynamic psychology, namely, that tension reduction is the major goal of behavior. Suffice it to say that important streams of research have reinstated into the behavioral system the neglected other side, the motivation to *create* tension. Diverse psychological processes such as the preference for complexity (Berlyne & Madsen, 1973), sensation-seeking (Zuckerman & Link, 1968), and sharpening (Gardner, Holzman, Klein, Linton, & Spence, 1959) represent some of what underlies the more general human needs to know, to create, to look for problems to solve. To link these two somewhat neglected directions of action: It is *people* who create, alter, or choose among environments, and they may do this so as either to reduce or to create tension.

Wohlwill (1966) called attention to the "optimization principle" as a basis for understanding environmental behavior. Invoking Helson's (1964) concept of adaptation level, Wohlwill suggests that the hedonic experience is neutral at the point where the individual has adapted to incoming stimulation, but that pleasure is experienced as stimulation either *increases beyond* or *decreases below* adaptation level (see Figure 10.1). Lawton and Nahemow (1973) incorporated this principle into their ecological model of aging (Figure 10.2). We saw the outcome of interaction between the indi-

DISCREPANCY FROM ADAPTATION LEVEL

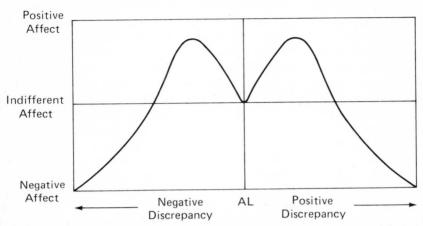

Figure 10.1. Changes in affective response to stimuli as a function of extent of deviation from adaptation level. (After Helson, 1964. From J. F. Wohlwill, The physical environment: A problem for a psychology of stimulation, *Journal of Social Issues,* 1966, *22,* 29–38. Reprinted by permission.)

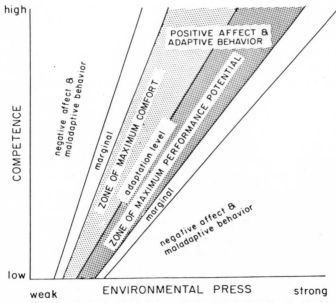

Figure 10.2. Ecological model. (From M. P. Lawton & L. Nahemow, Ecology and the aging process. In C. Eisdorfer & M. P. Lawton (Eds.), *Psychology of adult development and aging.* Copyright 1973 by the American Psychological Association. Reprinted by permission.)

173

vidual and the environment as being represented by behavior (capable of being ranged on a continuum from adaptive to maladaptive) and affect (on a continuum from positive to negative). We conceive of the person in terms of competence at several levels and environment in terms of press strength, or demand character. Most of the time we are at adaptation level, that is, we have tuned out the environment so that we can pay attention to the important task of the moment. The details of this model are explicated at greater length elsewhere (Lawton, in press a) and need not be elaborated here. Two details of the model are relevant for the present purpose.

First, we proposed that the affective outcome of mild increases or decreases in press level was as Wohlwill (1966) had proposed. However, we suggested that the behavioral outcome of an increase in press leads to extra effort, learning, and higher-quality adaptive behavior; sustained or repeated performance at above adaptation-level press strengths may lead to a lasting increase in competence. Therefore, we named the surface area where press slightly exceeds adaptation level as the "area of maximum performance potential." By contrast, the area containing outcome points where press is below adaptation level leads to relaxation, mild dependence, and passable quality task performance—the "area of maximum comfort." Sustained exposure to press below adaptation level conceivably could lower competence. Both of these directional responses are "normal." Presumably the dynamics of everyday life lead each of us through both zones, flirting occasionally with the limits of stress on one side, or stimulus deprivation on the other, but lingering most of the time near the adaptation level line. But the point is that within limits change is enjoyable, some change leading to the positive affective experience of diversion and new learning, and other change leading to the pleasures of letting things slide for a while.

The second point to be emphasized is that the model itself says nothing about *how* press level changes. It is perhaps a deficiency in our presentation that we have not emphasized more clearly that press level may change *either* through forces outside the individual (e.g., encroachment of an expressway on a neighborhood) *or* by the instrumentality of the individual (e.g., looking for an unfamiliar route home as a diversion). This latter observation brings us back to this chapter's first general point, that is, that the individual may change press level by shaping or reshaping his or her immediate context or by choosing and going to a new context. Figure 10.3 demonstrates our original conception of behavior change, where in addition to the instrumentality dimension already mentioned (the self as the initiator of change versus the respondent to change) another dimension describes the application point of the force toward change—this point may be the individual or the environment.

Much of the environmental psychology of later life is based on the

ECOLOGICAL CHANGE MODEL

The Individual's role

Point of application	Respondent	Initiator
The environment	A Social and environmental engineering	B The individual redesigns his environment
The individual	C Rehabilitation, therapy	D Self - therapy growth

Figure 10.3. Ecological change model. (From M. P. Lawton & L. Nahemow, 1973, Ecology and the aging process. In C. Eisdorfer & M. P. Lawton (Eds.), *Psychology of adult development and aging.* Copyright 1973 by the American Psychological Association. Reprinted by permission.)

thought that significant change may be accomplished through designing an external environment with press acting in the direction of eliciting desirable behavior or affect. This "behavioral engineering" accounts for only one of the change cells, however. Equally important is the improvement that occurs to the individual as he chooses and shapes the external environment to his liking.

The greater emphasis placed on the older individual in the reactive, rather than the shaping, role must be understood in light of the fact that some of aging is decremental, competence-reducing. It is precisely for those whose competence is reduced that environmental interventions may be selectively effective. This conclusion is an alternative statement of my "environmental docility hypothesis," which suggested that environmental factors account for an increasing proportion of the variance in behavior as competence decreases (Lawton, 1970). But the thrust of this presentation will be to give equal time to the older individual as change initiator.

Following in logical fashion from the individual-as-environmental-change-agent perspective, the last point of departure reminds all of us that the effects of change range on a continuum of quality from negative through neutral to positive. Such a great proportion of both gerontological folklore and gerontological research has focused on the negative aspects of change, that it is possible to fall into the trap of considering only such questions as "How can we avoid change?" or "How can we counteract the effects of change?" rather than equally valid questions such as, "How can options be maximized?" or "How can we introduce positive change into the lives of people?" or "How can we determine which changes would be beneficial for which person?"

Again, the Lawton–Nahemow model of adaptation and aging and the

Wohlwill optimization principle illustrate that affect may be made more positive by the deliberate search for an increased level of environmental press. A correlate of the model, however, is that to the extent that competence is impaired, the range of tolerability for press above adaptation level is also reduced. Therefore, while we affirm strongly the idea that change can have a positive outcome for anyone, to the extent that the older person deviates from ideal competence, the probability that change may have a negative impact is increased.

Thus properly reminded that all aspects of the behavioral system may change, that change may be subjective or objective, that the individual varies along the continuum from active to passive agent in change, and that the results of change vary along the continuum from positive to negative, we can begin to examine some of the implications of person–environment transitions for the elderly. Wherever possible each type of change will also be discussed in terms of its objective versus subjective, active versus passive, and positive versus negative quality.

Environment-Relevant Changes in the Individual

Having suggested that all behavior represents an individual–environment transaction, it is perhaps inconsistent to single out some individual-level changes and not others as relevant to environment. To do so simply acknowledges that some changes have a more obvious relationship to environment than others. It should not be surprising that the balance of the quality of individual change is strongly on the negative side. Biological aging does move on a downward trajectory, and at this level we shall be talking about coping with negative sensory, motor, cognitive, and other changes (see Carp, 1976, for a treatment of this topic in depth).

Changes in physical vigor and health may underlie behavior at all other levels. The list of environment-relevant behaviors where reduction in energy level may be evidenced is limitless: Climbing stairs, doing heavy chores, home maintenance, carrying shopping bags, walking to the store, mounting a bus, and so on. One's perception of such changes in the self may compound the feeling of vulnerability. Perceived reduction in potency may explain, for example, the extreme level of fear of crime in some older people, as compared to their statistical risk of victimization (Lawton, in press b).

Sensory changes occur with normal aging and will affect the way one negotiates the environment (Pastalan, in press), whether it be within the dwelling unit, walking in the neighborhood, crossing a street, or driving a car. To an unknown degree, the texture and variety of experience may be leveled. The positive aspects of the adaptation process are evident in this sector, however. Being conservative in deciding when to cross a street may be an unconscious response to recognition that poor sight or hearing could give mistaken cues as to when crossing would be safe. In the affective realm, how many of us past age 30 notice and bemoan the fact that musical sounds have become less rich as overtones in the higher frequencies are no longer heard? I, for one, am glad that I never notice.

While cognitive changes of many kinds are not inevitable concomitants of aging, information-processing efficiency has been shown to decline. The results of this kind of change are very clear in the performance of complex skills like automobile driving, which can be self-paced only within very narrow limits. It may well be that slowing of information processing is responsible for the anxiety that some people feel about going into an unfamiliar neighborhood, taking a new public transportation route, or dealing with a fast-talking salesperson.

Changes in health, sensory functioning, and cognition are basic to behavior at the most complex levels of effectance and social behavior (Lawton, 1972). Some opportunities for new experience may be eschewed if one is anxious about one's ability to understand them, about how one will travel to them, and so on. Social isolation may be the alternative chosen to avoid the threat of exposing oneself to these kinds of environmental challenges.

A major missing element in our knowledge is what intrapersonal factors make the difference between those who expand their capabilities in spite of some of these inevitable decrements and those who retreat. I have suggested elsewhere (Lawton, in press a) that some personality–style factors may perform such functions as regulating the intensity of environmental stimulation, its complexity, the mixture of internal and external stimulation, and the content of stimuli to be processed. Thus styles such as repression—sensitization (Byrne, 1961), preference for complexity (Berlyne & Madsen, 1973), reduction versus augmentation (Mishara, 1972), or field dependence–independence (Witkin, Lewis, Hertzman, Machover, Meissner, & Wapner, 1954) may condition whether the individual chooses a challenging or a soporific environment, whether he shapes or reacts to the environment, or whether he retreats in the face of internal changes of the kind discussed earlier.

The most important point to be made regarding intraindividual change, however, is that the amount and type of such change will determine the results of environmental change for that individual. To the extent that none of the decrements associated with aging happen to a given individual, the impact of environmental change will decrease.

Aging-in-Place

The full import of changes in the individual level do not become evident unless we consider the context and changes in the context in which the individual behaves. This section will consider some typical changes that occur in the local environments of older people (dwelling, neighborhood, community) and examine these changes in terms of their relationships to older people's well-being.

Some changes occur truly independently of the older person: The aging of physical structures, the movement of neighborhood populations and significant individuals, changes in neighborhood amenities and services, and changes in household composition due to death. In some of these instances, there is at least a theoretical opportunity for the older person to behave as an active agent. For example, the "functional aging" of the dwelling unit may be counteracted by vigilance to home maintenance needs. Involvement in a strong neighborhood organization might conceivably affect panic selling, zoning restrictions, incentives for services to remain or to move out, and so on. On the whole, however, there are many forces operating to make the older person a respondent rather than initiator.

Take the case of home maintenance. The *Annual Housing Survey* indicates that almost 50% of the units occupied by the elderly were built before 1940, as compared to only 35% of those occupied by younger people (Lawton & Hoover, 1979). The survey also counted indicators of housing quality; of the 19 deficits reported by Lawton (1979) in his analysis of 1976 data, housing occupied by the elderly was of poorer quality in 16. If preventive or ameliorative maintenance is to be done, resources are necessary for the purpose. Yet overall, 29% of older Americans are paying 30% or more of their incomes for housing; the average income of the elderly home owner in 1975 was $6800. If one is to lower costs by performing some of the work oneself, one needs to be in reasonably good physical health, have an adequate sensory–motor apparatus, and have enough expertise from an earlier period of life to be able to do the work. Yet, the decrements in health and the socially determined inexpertise of many older women limit the extent to which the available time for handyperson work may be actually spent in home maintenance. In contrast to the active national program for new construction of senior rental housing, there is no uniformly available housing assistance for the older person living in unplanned "normal" communities (Lawton, 1979).

Thus there is a strong tendency for the older person to be in the passive role while coping with the negative press of a physically declining dwelling unit. The concrete results include exposure to safety hazards, within-unit barriers to mobility, malfunction of utilities, obstacles to the competent performance of instrumental tasks, disincentives to entertaining, and decline in the aesthetic quality of the dwelling.

This discussion has thus far primarily involved the "objective" aspect of the dwelling unit. However, let us consider the more subjective aspects. First, according to the Lawton–Nahemow model, repeated exposure to a moderate press should result in adaptation to that aspect of the environment. Thus, unless press level is too strong, the older person can adapt in diverse situations such as learning to avoid a shock-producing switch, to plan the day so as not to have to go upstairs until bedtime, to bundle in a blanket when there is not enough heat, or to not notice cracks in the wall. A validation of this psychological folk logic was seen in a HUD study (Struyk, 1978) where older people were asked to report deficits to an interviewer. Their homes were then inspected by trained housing inspectors; the inhabitants identified only half of the deficiencies found by the inspectors.

We must look upon this denial of change as an adaptive mechanism. On the positive side, such behavioral and perceptual adjustments enable us to live in our imperfect worlds. If one does not have $40 for an electrician, it is better to learn to avoid the shock than not to avoid it. Looking around an ugly crack in the wall rather than at it is better than being preoccupied with the crack. Thus in some sense, the subjective alterations that we make in our environments are the best that can be done, and in that sense are active and positive.

Another aspect of the subjective dwelling unit is its "meaning," the accumulation of associations, affective responses, and symbolic features associated with the physical entity, about which Rowles (1978) has written so evocatively. Meaning tends to persevere in the face of objective change. The repeatedly documented reluctance of older people to move has been partially ascribed to the associations that the home provokes regarding earlier times of one's life, the presence of children, a friendly neighborhood, or the more symbolic value of the home as an extension of the self, and so on.

There are few research findings that might let us know how important, in fact, such considerations are in an individual's choosing to remain while self and/or environment are changing in a negative direction. Rowles' observations discussed in Chapter 9 are highly relevant to this issue. Another relevant finding was reported by Jirovec (1977), in a study of the connotative dimensions of dwelling unit preferences. His older group's preferences were characterized in terms of dimensions such as friendliness, noise, neatness, aesthetic quality, and texture, as compared to the more formal dimensions that were salient to the younger subjects (i.e., space, shape, and potency). This constitutes at least soft evidence that symbolic meaning may be a stronger determinant of older people's environmental choices than of younger people's.

A "changing neighborhood" is often cited as the reason for residential dissatisfaction or for wishing to move. Physical changes in the neighborhood and changes in the character of the neighborhood's inhabitants are inextricably linked. The phenomenon of "housing succession" denotes the moveout of original occupants as the neighborhood ages, the reoccupancy of the housing stock by less advantaged groups, and the further decline of the housing potentiated by the inability or unwillingness of the new group (or later-cycled similar groups) to engage in proper maintenance. Changes in land use may be concurrent: Single-family to multiple-family or rooming house; residential to commercial; commercial to industrial; and any of these to vacancies, abandonment, and demolition.

Are the elderly selectively exposed to such neighborhood transitions? This question is difficult to answer with hard data. The percentage of central-city residents who are elderly (11.4%, U.S. Bureau of the Census, 1978a) is only slightly greater than the proportional representation of younger people. Within central cities, relatively little is known about the smaller areas where older people live. However, within the Los Angeles area, Kendig (1976) found that census tracts with the highest proportions of elderly were also highest in incidence of fires, of assaults, of commercial resources, and of both rezoning and urban relocation. In terms of the characteristics of people in their neighborhoods, the urban elderly are, in fact, likely to have other elderly as neighbors (i.e., they live in census tracts that tend toward segregation by age [Cowgill, 1978]). However, cities differ markedly in the extent to which this is true. The least segregated, where the aged are distributed approximately as their proportion in the entire population, are small sized cities not undergoing major change in terms of industrialization, land use, or inmigration. The highest degree of segregation occurred in retirement areas and in cities experiencing the fastest recent growth—probably reflecting the pattern of younger people having moved to the suburbs and older people remaining in old city neighborhoods.

We thus have some hints that change on a community or on a neighborhood level is likely to have some very real negative consequences for the elderly: A reduction in physical security, possibly decreases in municipal services, and a new social context in which to orient themselves. On the other hand, such changing areas may be better supplied with local resources and with age peers. Major unknowns, however, are whether the resources are relevant to the needs of the elderly and how *simpatico* nonelderly (usually replacement) residents of the area are to the elderly.

On a more interpersonal level, we know that one result of a changing neighborhood is that any given remaining individual is likely to have fewer intimates, neighbors, familiar shop keepers, or identifiable faces in his or her social space as the change continues. Research evidence is mounting to indicate the crucial function of intimates in weathering stress (Lowenthal & Haven, 1968; Schooler, in press) and the relationship between peer contact and psychological well-being (Lemon, Bengtson, & Peterson, 1972). Disturbance of these supports, as well as the help-giving potential uniquely present in proximate neighbors (Litwak & Szelenyi, 1969) seems highly likely to increase press level above the tolerable range.

Rosenberg (1970) contributed findings on neighborhood social interaction that are helpful in understanding how older people may respond to change in the character of their neighborhood's population. His interest was in social interchange among neighbors. In general, interaction with others on one's block was greater as one's similarities with others on the block (age, socioeconomic status, race) increased. As in Rosow's (1967) study of apartment dwellers, Rosenberg found that interaction depended partly on the number of age peers on one's block, and that poor men were *more* subject to this age-density effect than the "solvent." However, social isolation was more likely for solvent men in "poor" social contexts than it was for poor men in higher socioeconomic contexts. Where older people's neighborhood changes around them, they are very likely to experience the alienating effect of having originated in a somewhat higher socioeconomic position than the inmovers.

The older individual is perhaps least able to behave in an active way where these externally imposed changes in the neighborhood occur. The major possible mode of dealing with such changes, short of "leaving the field" by moving, is largely reactive: Becoming an isolate, using public or private transportation to get out of the neighborhood, having services brought to oneself, or more carefully picking and choosing the nature, time, and frequency of interactions with the neighborhood. Clearly, all of these modes of adaptation may be performed in a positive or negative way. However, because they are primarily reactive rather than active, they do little to enhance the individual's sense of control. Judging by recent evidence demonstrating the favorable outcomes associated with a realistic feeling of autonomy and ability to control one's environment (Langer & Rodin, 1976; Schulz, 1976), it may well be that these uncontrollable changes in one's neighborhood are the most difficult to deal with.

Of course, the same types of subjective transformations of the "objective" environment that occur with the dwelling unit also occur with the neighborhood environment. External changes may be adapted to with the effect of denying the fact of change. The feeling of belonging to a neighborhood, or familiarity with its pathways, hazards, amenities, and landmarks may overshadow the risks associated with continued residence. An interesting takeoff point for the subjective alteration of reality is seen in people's responses to the fear of crime. Elsewhere (Lawton, in press b) I have reviewed a large body of evidence indicating lower than expected correlations between crime risk and fear of crime, victimization and fear of crime, fear of crime and mobility within the local neighborhood, and victimization and local neighborhood mobility. The fact is that some older people are strongly overreacting to the statistical probability of being victims, while others who perhaps "should" be afraid or be limiting their local mobility do not. There are clearly costs either to overreacting or to underreacting. To date, we have no strong indications as to how to predict who will behave which way, or to know whether deliberate attempts to increase one's feeling of or ability to control crime risk would help. We do have an interesting finding by Patterson (1978) showing that older urban residents who marked the exterior of their properties in some territorial manner (either through explicit crime-related markers such as peepholes, "beware of the dog" signs, or more general markers such as a welcome mat or initials on the exterior) were less afraid than those who did not exhibit territorial marking behavior. Do these behaviors represent the achievement of some degree of perceived control?

Jirovec (1977) also studied the connotative meanings of neighborhoods. Age differences were fewer than in the case of the residence, but three old-age-specific dimensions were brightness, age homogeneity, and familiarity. The third term especially underlines the possibility that a feeling of understanding, or a good cognitive map of one's local area, may play a very strong role in determining quality of adaptation.

An insufficiently known research finding of Schooler (in press) is the only one that has succeeded in separating the effects of change-*in*-place from those of change-*of*-place. Schooler studied a large national probability sample of older people, and interviewed subsamples of movers and nonmovers three years later. Among those who did not move, an improvement over time in the subject's perception of dwelling unit quality was associated with an improvement in morale. In the case of another morale factor and a measure of general health, nondirectional change was associated with improvement. Whereas the meaning of this pattern of results is not completely clear, Schooler's results do indicate that both environmental change independent of moving, and nondirectional amount of change are concepts worthy of further investigation.

A special case of neighborhood change is the current phenomenon of "regentrification" of older central-city neighborhoods. This rehabilitation of often interesting or historic homes and their repopulation with affluent middle-class individuals constitutes a classic example of positive neighborhood change, infrequent though positive change seems to be. For the older person in place, the consequences are by no means all positive. First and foremost, the elderly renter may be forced out by inability to pay higher rent or, even more likely, by the purchase of the house by a prospective owner–occupant. Second, neighborhood taxes may increase. Third, sources of inexpensive amenities or those more suited to the needs of the elderly may vanish in favor of those tailored to young, affluent professionals. Finally, the problems of turnover in people, change in familiar pathways, and disappearance of well-known structures occur with positive change as they do with the more familiar negative change. While the specific impact of neighborhood gentrification on the elderly has not been studied, a revealing set of case studies (Myers, 1978) documents the potential magnitude of the problem and provides a rationale for special advocacy for this vulnerable group.

In conclusion, it would seem that aging in place carries with it a very complex and interacting set of gains and losses for the individual. To the extent that individual competence is reduced, reactive means coping with change will be less effective. Active means of effecting environmental change of one's own choice will be even more greatly affected by reductions in competence. More control is possible, and should be further enhanced by both planning effort and service programming, within the sector of the residential unit. Creating one's own proximate environment on the neighborhood or community scale is much more feasible through moving than through shaping the mesoenvironment, however. Substantial transformations of the amount or the quality of change may be produced by the operation of the intrapsychic mechanisms commonly referred to as "environmental cognition." The idiosyncratic way in which the environment is apprehended may well be a more important predictor of environmental behavior than the objective quality of the environment.

Aging in a New Place

Transitions that involve a change of locale bring us to more familiar ground. Much more research has been done on migration, residential mobility, rehousing, institutionalization, and involuntary relocation than has been done on aging-in-place. These moves are objectively countable and perhaps thereby more accessible to evaluative research than is aging-in-place, for which *both* the independent and dependent variables are often difficult to specify and measure.

Long-distance migration and local residential mobility are both less frequent among the aged than among younger groups. The 12-month mobility rate for ages 20–24 was 39%, as compared to 6% for ages 65–74 in 1975–1976 (U.S. Bureau of the Census, 1978b). Many reasons to explain this lower mobility rate have been discussed previously or implied: Declines in competence in a variety of areas, economic barriers, lack of significant-other support, and positive attachment to one's present residence.

Changes of residence by older people in average health and with some financial solvency are of particular interest, because many of these people will presumably be actively *choosing* to move and choosing a *place* to which to move. The motivations to change residence are many and are by no means clear. Let me state first that it is no easy task to determine for a particular individual to what extent the move was voluntary. For example, Kasl (1977) studied a group of older people who faced eviction from their homes in the community because of urban renewal, landlord-initiated eviction, and other very clearly involuntary reasons. Yet, when asked whose choice the move was, 63% *perceived* the choice as their own. But because the probable number of ordinary residential moves that are truly compulsory is relatively small, knowing the characteristics of both movers and their relocation sites will tell us something about what people may be actively seeking when they move.

First we have migration to the traditional retirement areas. Moves to Florida, California, and Arizona constitute more than one-third of all elderly interstate migration. This behavior represents the prototype of active choice or self-determination of one's environment. While we do not have definitive research findings on the outcome of such Sunbelt migration, the sheer volume and continued flow of this type of change attests to its positive attractions.

Second, a milder but distinctly measurable migration trend into rural areas not thought of as traditional retirement country was noted by Beale (1975). Beale characterized those areas as having some scenic and recreational attractions (Ozarks, northern Michigan); we may speculate that they also are characterized by lower living costs and lower crime risk. Another trend beginning in 1975 was noted for migration from central cities to suburban areas (U.S. Bureau of the Census, 1978a), probably directed particularly toward smaller, rather than larger, suburbs (Stahura & Stahl, 1978).

Third, some interstate migrants are going home again. This occurs particularly in the Southern states (Longino & Flynn, 1978; Serow, 1978). The extent to which symbolic–affective attachment, the presence of a relative, lower living costs, greater security, climate, and so on, are involved in the return-migration decision is not known. Some evidence is available suggesting that a significant return-migration flow from Florida to New York also occurs, at an older age than most migration—perhaps this represents the return to family following poor health or loss of a spouse.

I suggest that, other things being equal, these three "place" correlates of mobility favor the idea that such moves represent the active search for a positive outcome, the deliberate choice of a higher press level, with the hope that both behavior and affect may change positively.

Research reviewed at greater length in Lawton (in press d) gives information on individuals who move. Movers are likely to be recently retired (Chevan & Fischer, in press), to have been previous movers (Chevan & Fischer, in press), and renters. Long-distance movers are likely among those with higher incomes (Aizenberg & Myers, 1977) and among husband–wife pairs (Longino & Flynn, 1978), whereas local moving is more frequent among low-income males (Aizenberg & Myers, 1977), people in nonindependent living situations (Aizenberg & Myers, 1977), and the very old (Aizenberg & Myers, 1977; Golant, 1977). One may hazard the hypothesis that since low income, nonindependent living arrangements, and very old age are indicators of reduced competence, that local moves are *more likely* to be involuntary than long-distance moves.

Virtually the only longitudinal study of older people making ordinary residential moves was Schooler's (in press), described earlier. Over the 3 years, 58% of those who did not move reported a decline in dwelling unit quality, as compared to only 21% of those who moved—a strong demonstration of the fact that moves tend to be *toward* an improved-quality residence. Perhaps the most significant finding regarding movers is that those who had expected to move and did in fact move within 3 years were the most adversely affected. And further, among this group the negative effects were ameliorated, though not obliterated, when the quality of the environment improved following the move. Schooler suggests that the perception of threat during the period prior to moving was a stress that resulted in a decrease in health and morale.

A special type of move is one into the household of a younger or more competent family member. This process itself has not been studied. Suggestive information regarding the dynamics of such moves comes from several sources. We know that multigenerational living arrangements may be instituted because of active family wishes (either mutual or unidirectional), moral compulsion, cultural tradition, economic necessity, and needs for physical or psychological support; clearly these reasons will overlap and the list is certainly not exhaustive. The fact that poor older people are more likely to live in households with younger heads than are the more affluent elderly (Soldo, 1979), minorities, and those in poor health (National Center for Health Statistics, 1975) suggests that such an arrangement may often be dictated by necessity. Newman (1976) studied by retrospective reports the responses of older people when faced with a major illness. About half of them made a residential change, and of these, one-third moved to the household of another person, usually a child.

These living arrangement changes with a strong element of compulsion are obviously neither totally self-initiated, nor do they have the prospect of a particularly "happy ending." Yet people do adapt to this way of life. In the Lawton–Nahemow model, press level is reduced by such moves and a positive outcome consistent with the competence of the individual results. More knowledge is needed regarding the outcomes associated with the more actively chosen shared living arrangments.

We also need more study of the way people construe dependent living situations. It is very probable that some redefinition of what constitutes environmental control occurs among those compelled to live dependently. Smaller territories become established as one's home range (DeLong, 1970), their size becoming more consistent with the possible span of control. Thus, it is at least possible that such subjective transformations of reality can expand one's active role and convert what might otherwise be a negative outcome into a positive one.

Moves into planned housing have been one of the most studied transitions. There is no need to review the findings in any detail. Suffice it to say that a variety of positve effects, of modest size, have been documented by most studies (Carp, 1966; Lawton & Cohen, 1974; Sherwood, Greer, & Morris, in press; Wittels & Botwinick, 1974). Whereas there has been no major evidence that moves to planned housing are involuntary (for example, 71% of tenants in three projects studied by Lawton, in press c, indicated that they alone had decided to make the move and only 13% moved under apparent compulsion—urban renewal or strong family pressure), this aspect has not been given the attention it deserves.

Observing the choices made by the most affluent gives some indication of the kinds of environment sought by those free of one major constraint. These choices do include typical luxuries such as a swimming pool, a golf course, a clubhouse, and so on, but they also include more generally sought-after amenities such as informal social interaction, physical security, access to medical assistance, and ordinary activity programming. Thus most of the service package associated with planned housing seems to be of general appeal.

Lawton (1969) suggested that congregate housing (e.g., housing with some package of supportive services including meals served in a common dining room) provided an example of older people's matching their competence to the optimal level of environment press for their needs. This conclusion was based on the finding that initial occupants of congregate housing were significantly older, less socially active, lower in morale, and less healthy than the original occupants of traditional housing without services.

A comparison of older people choosing federally assisted housing with the older population at large indicated that the housing population was much more likely to be female and not presently married, suggesting that these kinds of environments were serving particularly those short on social supports (Lawton & Nahemow, 1975); residents in a high-income retirement community were much less likely to have living or proximate children than the population in general (Peterson, Hamovitch, & Larson, 1973). On the other hand, new tenants in five planned housing environments did not differ initially on most measures of competence (morale, functional health, social activity) from a group of community residents (Lawton, in press c).

From these scattered bits of information, no clear conclusion is possible regarding whether the dominant trend is for people in traditional housing to be seeking a press level slightly above or below their accustomed level. The appeal of such housing for the social underaffiliated argues perhaps for the housing's being used to increase social press level by this segment. The probable key to the better understanding of the function of new planned housing for people will lie in far more finely detailed tracking of the new-housing careers of people with different types of needs or with contrasting degrees of congruence between need and press (Kahana, in press). In fact, the overall positive effect of housing masks other effects—an absence of effect on some, and a negative effect on a smaller group. Attempts to predict these outcomes on the basis of preoccupancy characteristics have not yielded very informative findings, other than the general conclusion that those who began as better off improve relatively more (Carp, 1966; Lawton, in press c).

As it now stands, the best we can say is that both supportive and stimulating functions are served by traditional housing, whereas congregate housing best serves the supportive function. However, again it is important to note that in all kinds of housing, the image of self as maintaining independence, and of the housing as an environment for the healthy elderly is very strongly maintained. No matter how old or frail the person may be, the new tenant's reaction often is, "I didn't know there were going to be all these old people here." As detailed at greater length elsewhere (Greenbaum, Lawton, & Singer, 1970), tenants in highly supportive housing tend to be rather overtly rejecting of visually obvious frailties in others, while covertly tolerating them with the comforting thought that the same thing could happen to themselves.

The final topic to be discussed here is involuntary relocation. Among community residents, urban renewal is the most frequent occasion for compulsory change of residence. Massive relocations of entire neighborhoods no longer occur on the scale that they did in the 1950s. The only studies of mass relocation of the elderly (Niebanck, 1965) demonstrate economic and social losses for the relocation but these studies did not focus on most psychological or behavioral domains. Two other studies of relocation (Brand & Smith, 1974; Kasteler, Gray, & Carruth, 1968) were retrospective, one-occasion studies that did not successfully isolate and test relocation itself. Therefore, Kasl's (1977) study is the only acceptable attempt to evaluate this kind of transition. When compared to a community–resident group, the relocated showed no losses on a variety of social and psychological measures, but some clear decrements in health occurred; the relocated *increased* significantly in their housing satisfaction, as compared to the nonrelocated. Kasl's results are relevant to several of the main issues of this chapter. First, it will be remembered that despite their involuntary dislocation, almost two-thirds perceived the move as voluntary. Perhaps the relative absence of negative effects reflects their subjective apprehension of being in control. But let me now note that the relocation environment was the same for all subjects: a new public housing site for the elderly, the type of environmental change associated with *positive* outcome in almost all published research. Thus on two counts, Kasl's subjects had an easy transition. A good environment and perceived control apparently overcame the potential negatively disposing factor of eviction from familiar home and neighborhood. But a very important final point is that there was a hidden *cost* of change, evidenced in a significant decrease in health among the relocated. A similar decline in health was the only negative effect of rehousing found by Lawton and Cohen (1974) (as compared to positive changes in five other social and psychological measures). Furthermore, the most sensitive indicators of negative change in some of Schooler's (in press) movers were the physical health factors.

The evidence is soft, and not always consistent (e.g., Carp, 1966; Sherwood *et al.*, in press found improvements in health among their rehoused groups) but we may be building up evidence for the mixed blessing involved in the change-of-residence type of transition. Gains may be impressive in the social and psychological domains, but possibly at a cost in the functional health domain (badly needed are data at the physiological and organic health level, to complement those measures in the referenced studies that are primarily self-reports of health, symptoms, or behavioral and performance measures). Neither Kasl (1977), Lawton and Cohen (1974), Lawton and Yaffe (1970), nor Wittels and Botwinick (1974) reported any excess mortality for their relocated groups, while Carp (1975) and Sherwood *et al.* (in press) found reduced mortality among the rehoused.

The situation is totally different with respect to involuntarily relocated nursing home populations, as discussed by Tobin in Chapter 11. Other reviews of these findings may be found in Lawton and Nahemow (1973) and in Schulz and Brenner (1977). Several facets of this work that are especially relevant to the issues raised in this chapter will be briefly mentioned.

First, when institutionalized older people are moved, it is primarily the grossly impaired who exhibit excess mortality. Less impaired populations (Lieberman, Tobin, & Slover, 1971; Markson & Cumming, 1974; Marlowe, 1973) do not, a finding exactly in accordance with the environmental docility hypothesis.

Second, in two large-scale studies (Lieberman *et al.*, 1971; Marlowe, 1973) environmental effects overshadowed effects attributable to the particular individual who was relocated.

Third, and most important, two studies separated a substantial group that *improved* following the forced relocation. Goldfarb, Shahinian, and Burr (1972) found that the most competent relocatees showed a *deficit* in mortality; they speculated that the positive effect might have been attributable to an improvement in environmental quality, though they did not measure this dimension. Marlowe's (1973) results were quite complex. While no overall striking difference emerged between her relocated mental hospital patients and those who were not relocated, where there was decline, it seemed to be more devastating for the relocated. Thus, even though this mental hospital population was less vulnerable than the nursing home populations studied by others, some risk was associated with change; another significant group improved following relocation, however.

A very similar set of results were reported by Lieberman *et al.* (1971), who found no relocation mortality effect among their aged mental hospital discharges. Both of these studies identified relocation environments that were associated with positive outcomes. Favorable psychosocial characteristics of the environment were the degree of autonomy accorded the individual, the supporting quality of the social life, and the amount of individual treatment displayed.

Thus, while research data give considerable support to the idea that enforced relocation should be avoided, they also encourage the search for interpersonal and environmental buffers to increase the chance that the change would be a positive one. The place to look for appropriate intervention points is particularly in the psychosocial area.

For both voluntary and involuntary residential change, the positive associations with taking the active role and with a favorable relative gain in environmental quality are emphasized by findings in several contexts.

Conclusion

The skeleton of conclusions from the foregoing is reasonably clear. Change occurs in both the individual and in the external environment, some cognitive restructuring of both self and environment is made necessary by the change; the change may be initiated by the self or by an agent or process outside the self, and the results of change may be positive or negative. Over all people and all situations, the tendency is for older people to resist change (though the evidence in favor of this proposition has not been reviewed). Empirical findings regarding the outcomes of changes, particularly those chosen or created by the individual, indicate, however, that the potential gains in some kinds of changes may be overlooked if we accept too readily the maxim that old people do not respond well to change. The moral would seem to be that our planning and service delivery should be careful to provide choices for people at all points of the continuum of competence and mobilize all possible means of making people aware of these choices. My congregate-housing research (Lawton, 1969) indicates that people make appropriate choices of environments for themselves when the options are there to choose from. The Lawton–Nahemow model illustrates how there are limits (on both the high-demand and low-demand side) to the kinds of environment where people will find congruence possible. For the less competent, the definition of these limits may require more participation by caretakers or the service sector. However, right down the continuum of competence, we have evidence at every level that there is some range where the individual may select or create an environment for challenge or one for relaxation. Our task is to maximize the opportunity for these environments to be accessible to people in ordinary dwellings, planned housing, or institutions.

References

Aizenberg, R., & Myers, G. C. Residential mobility and living arrangements. Paper presented at the annual meeting of the Gerontological Society, San Francisco, November, 1977.

Beale, C. L. *The revival of population growth in nonmetropolitan America.* Economic Research Service No. ERS–605. Washington, D.C.: U.S. Department of Agriculture, 1975.

Berlyne, D. E., & Madsen, K. B. (Eds.). *Pleasure, reward, preference.* New York: Academic Press, 1973.

Brand, F., & Smith, R. Life adjustment and relocation of the elderly. *Journal of Gerontology,* 1974, *29,* 336–340.

Byrne, D. The repression–sensitization scale: Rationale, reliability and validity. *Journal of Personality,* 1961, *29,* 334–339.

Carp, F. M. *A future for the aged.* Austin: University of Texas Press, 1966.

Carp, F. M. Impact of improved housing on morale and life satisfaction. *Gerontologist*, 1975, *15*, 511–575.

Carp, F. M. Urban life-style and life-cycle factors. In M. P. Lawton, R. J. Newcomer, & T. O. Byerts (Eds.), *Community planning for an aging society*. Stroudsburg, Penn.: Dowden, Hutchinson, and Ross, 1976.

Chevan, A., & Fischer, L. R. Retirement and interstate migration. *Social Forces*, in press.

Cowgill, D. O. Residential segregation by age in American metropolitan areas. *Journal of Gerontology*, 1978, *33*, 446–453.

DeLong, A. J. The microspatial structure of the older person. In L. A. Pastalan & D. H. Carson (Eds.), *The spatial behavior of older people*. Ann Arbor: University of Michigan, Institute of Gerontology, 1970. Pp. 68–87.

Gardner, R. W., Holzman, P. S., Klein, G. S., Linton, H. B., & Spence, D. P. Cognitive control: A study of individual consistencies in cognitive behavior. *Psychological Issues (4)*. New York: International Universities Press, 1959.

Golant, S. M. Spatial context of residential moves by elderly persons. *International Journal of Aging and Human Development*, 1977, *8*, 279–289.

Goldfarb, A. I., Shahinian, S. P., & Burr, H. T. Death rate of relocated nursing home residents. In D. D. Kent, R. Kastenbaum, & S. Sherwood, (Eds.), *Research, planning, and action for the elderly*. New York: Behavioral Publications, 1972.

Greenbaum, M., Lawton, M. P., & Singer, M. Tenant perceptions of health, health services, and status in two apartment buildings for the elderly. *Aging and Human Development*, 1970, *1*, 333–344.

Helson, H. *Adaptation level theory*. New York: Harper and Row, 1964.

Ittelson, W. H. Some issues facing a theory of environment and behavior. In H. M. Proshansky, W. H. Ittelson, & L. G. Rivlin (Eds.), *Environmental psychology* (2nd ed.). New York: Holt, Rinehart and Winston, 1976.

Jirovec, R. L. Optimum residential environments across the lifespan. Paper presented at the annual meeting of the Gerontological Society, San Francisco, November, 1977.

Kahana, E. A congruence model of person–environment interaction. In M. P. Lawton, P. G. Windley, & T. O. Byerts (Eds.). *Theory in environmental context and aging*. New York: Garland, in press.

Kasl, S. V. Effects of "involuntary" relocation on the health and behavior of the elderly. Paper presented at National Institute on Aging Conference on Epidemiology of Aging. Bethesda, MD, March, 1977.

Kasteler, J., Gray, R., & Carruth, M. Involuntary relocation of the elderly. *Gerontologist*, 1968, *8*, 276–279.

Kendig, H. Neighborhood conditions of the aged and local government. *Gerontologist*, 1976, *16*, 148–156.

Langer, E., & Rodin, J. The effects of choice and enhanced personal responsibility for the aged. *Journal of Personality and Social Psychology*, 1976, *34*, 191–198.

Lawton, M. P. Supportive services in the context of the housing environment. *Gerontologist*, 1969, *9*, 15–19.

Lawton, M. P. Ecology and aging. In L. A. Pastalan, & D. H. Carson (Eds.), *The spatial behavior of older people*. Ann Arbor: University of Michigan, Institute of Gerontology, 1970. Pp. 40–76.

Lawton, M. P. Assessing the competence of older people. In D. Kent, R. Kastenbaum, & S. Sherwood (Eds.), *Research, planning and action for the elderly*. New York: Behavioral Publications, 1972. Pp. 122–143.

Lawton, M. P. Housing problems of the community-resident elderly. *Occasional papers in housing and community affairs. 1.* Washington, D.C.: U.S. Government Printing Office, 1979. Pp. 39–74.

Lawton, M. P. Competence, environmental press, and the adaptation of older people. In M. P. Lawton, P. G. Windley, & T. O. Byerts (Eds.), *Theory and the environmental context of aging*. New York: Garland, in press. (a)

Lawton, M. P. Crime, victimization, and the fortitude of the aged. *Aged Care and Services*, in press. (b)

Lawton, M. P. *Environment and aging*. Monterey, Calif.: Brooks–Cole, in press. (c)

Lawton, M. P. Social and medical services in housing for the elderly. National Institute of Mental Health, Washington, D.C.: U.S. Government Printing Office, in press. (d)

Lawton, M. P., & Cohen, J. The generality of housing impact on the well-being of older people. *Journal of Gerontology*, 1974, *29*, 194–204.

Lawton, M. P., & Hoover, S. The housing of 20 million older Americans. Philadelphia: Philadelphia Geriatric Center, 1979.

Lawton, M. P., & Nahemow, L. Ecology and the aging process. In C. Eisdorfer & M. P. Lawton (Eds.), *Psychology of adult development and aging*. Washington, D.C.: American Psychological Association, 1973. Pp. 619–674.

Lawton, M. P., & Nahemow, L. Cost, structure, and social aspects of housing for the aged. Final report to Administration on Aging, DHEW, 1975.

Lawton, M. P., & Yaffe, S. Mortality, morbidity, and voluntary change of residence by older people. *Journal of American Geriatrics Society*, 1970, *18*, 823–831.

Lemon, B. W., Bengston, V. L., & Peterson, J. A. An exploration of the "activity theory" of aging. *Journal of Gerontology*, 1972, *27*, 511–523.

Lieberman, M., Tobin, S. S., & Slover, D. The effects of relocation on long-term geriatric patients (Final Report, Project No. 17–1328). Chicago: Illinois Department of Health and Committee on Human Development, University of Chicago, 1971.

Litwak, E., & Szelenyi, I. Primary group structure and their functions: Kin, neighbors, and friends. *American Sociological Review*, 1969, *34*, 465–481.

Longino, C. F., & Flynn, C. B. Going home: Aged return migration. Paper presented at the annual meeting of the Gerontological Society, Dallas, November, 1978.

Lowenthal, M. F., & Haven, C. Interaction and adaptation: Intimacy as a critical variable. *American Sociological Review*, 1968, *33*, 20–30.

Markson, E. W., & Cumming, J. H. A strategy of necessary mass transfer and its impact on patient mortality. *Journal of Gerontology*, 1974, *29*, 315–321.

Marlowe, R. A. Effects of environment on elderly state hospital relocatees. Paper presented at the 4th meeting of the Pacific Sociological Association, Scottsdale, Arizona, 1973.

Mishara, B. Do people who seek less environmental stimulation avoid thinking about the future and their death? *Proceedings of the 80th Annual Convention of the American Psychological Association*. Washington, D.C.: American Psychological Association, 1972. Pp. 667–668.

Myers, P. *Neighborhood conservation and the elderly*. Washington, D.C.: The Conservation Foundation, 1978.

National Center for Health Statistics. Prevalence of selected impairments. Series 10, No. 99. Rockville, Md.: U.S. Department of Health, Education and Welfare, 1975.

Newman, S. J. Housing adjustments of the disabled elderly. *Gerontologist*, 1976, *16*, 312–317.

Niebanck, P. *The elderly in older urban areas*. Philadelphia: University of Pennsylvania Institute for Environmental Studies, 1965.

Pastalan, L. A. Sensory changes and environmental behavior. In T. O. Byerts, L. A. Pastalan, & S. C. Howell (Eds.), *The environmental context of aging*. New York: Garland, in press.

Patterson, A. H. Territorial behavior and fear of crime in the elderly. *Environmental Psychology and Nonverbal Behavior*, 1978, *2*, 131–144.

Peterson, J. A., Hamovitch, M., & Larson, A. E. *Housing needs and satisfactions of the elderly.* Los Angeles: University of Southern California, Ethel Percy Andrus Gerontology Center, 1973.

Rosenberg, G. S. *The worker grows old.* San Francisco: Jossey–Bass, 1970.

Rosow, I. *Social integration of the aged.* New York: Free Press, 1967.

Rowles, G. D. *Prisoners of space.* Boulder, Colo.: Westview Press, 1978.

Schooler, K. K. Response of the elderly to environment: A stress–theoretic perspective. In M. P. Lawton, P. G. Windley, & T. O. Byerts, (Eds.), *Theory and the environmental context of aging.* New York: Garland, in press.

Schulz, R. Effects of control and predictability on the physical and psychological well-being of the institutionalized aged. *Journal of Personality and Social Psychology,* 1976, *33,* 563–573.

Schulz, R., & Brenner, G. F. Relocation of the aged: A review and theoretical analysis. *Journal of Gerontology,* 1977, *32,* 323–333.

Serow, W. J. Return migration of the elderly in the USA: 1955–1960 and 1965–1970. *Journal of Gerontology,* 1978, *33,* 288–295.

Sherwood, S., Greer, D. S., & Morris, J. N. A study of the Highland Heights apartments for the physically impaired and elderly in Fall River. In T. O. Byerts, L. A. Pastalan, & S. C. Howell (Eds.), *The environmental context of aging.* New York: Garland, in press.

Soldo, B. J. The housing and characteristics of independent elderly: A demographic overview. *Occasional Papers in Housing and Urban Development 1.* Washington, D.C.: U.S. Department of Housing and Urban Development, 1979.

Stahura, J. M., & Stahl, S. M. Intrametropolitan migration of the aged: An explanation of the centralization process. Paper presented at the annual meeting of the Gerontological Society, Dallas, November, 1978.

Struyk, R. J. Research in housing for the elderly: The U.S. Department of Housing and Urban Development. Paper presented at Conference on Community Housing Choices for Older Americans, Philadelphia Geriatric Center, 1978.

U.S. Bureau of the Census. Geographical mobility: March 1975 to March 1978. Current Population Reports Series P–20, No. 331. Washington, D.C.: U.S. Government Printing Office, 1978. (a)

U.S. Bureau of the Census. Social and economic characteristics of the metropolitan and nonmetropolitan population: 1977 and 1970. Current Population Reports, Series 23, No. 75. Washington, D.C.: U.S. Government Printing Office, 1978. (b)

Witkin, H. A., Lewis, H. B., Hertzman, M., Machover, K., Meissner, P. B., & Wapner, S. *Personality through perception.* New York: Harper, 1954.

Wittels, I., & Botwinick, J. Survival in relocation. *Journal of Gerontology,* 1974, *29,* 440–443.

Wohlwill, J. F. The physical environment: A problem for a psychology of stimulation. *Journal of Social Issues,* 1966, *22,* 29–38.

Zuckerman, M., & Link, K. Construct validity for the sensation seeking scale. *Journal of Consulting and Clinical Psychology,* 1968, *32,* 420–426.

Chapter 11

Institutionalization of the Aged

SHELDON S. TOBIN

Institutionalization refers to a specific environmental transition in aging: relocation to a long-term care facility that invariably will be the elderly person's last home. This type of relocation is assumed to have dire consequences, primarily because of the effects on individuals of living in institutional environments. Before considering the effects, as well as the causes for effects, not only of institutional life itself but also during the process preceding entering and living in long-term care facilities, the extent that institutionalization is a frequent transition in aging will be addressed.

Institutionalization as a Ubiquitous Event

Although less than 6% of the elderly reside in long-term care settings, the probability of becoming institutionalized is greater than can be inferred from this statistic. Kastenbaum and Candy (1973) have referred to the statistic as the 4% fallacy, estimating the likely probability of institutionalization as one in four for those who survive beyond 65 years of age. Palmore (1976), using data from the Duke Longitudinal Study of 207 elderly who were followed for 20 years, found that 26% (54) of the sample "had been institutionalized one or more times before death [p. 505]." In turn, this

195

statistic regarding the likelihood of becoming institutionalized beyond 65 does not adequately reflect the role of age in the process. Among all Americans who are 65–74 years of age, for example, only 2% reside in institutions; between the ages of 74 and 84, 7% do; and for those above 85, more than 16% reside in institutions (Office of Nursing Home Affairs, 1975). Currently, the elderly in long-term care facilities average 82 years of age and, in many institutions, 20% or more of the residential population is 90 years of age and over. Thus it is the oldest of the old who are likely to become institutionalized.

The nature of the institutions in which these elderly reside, or will reside if institutional care is sought, helps in understanding institutional effects. The institutions are of three types: mental hospitals in which half the residential populations are likely to be elderly, geriatric and chronic disease hospitals, and nursing and personal care homes. In the third group of facilities live more than 80% of the institutionalized elderly, and 75% of these facilities are proprietary nursing homes (run for profit), 20% are nonprofit homes, and 10% government sponsored (Office of Nursing Home Affairs, 1975). Most institutional elderly, therefore, reside in proprietary nursing homes that have been under repeated investigation for patient abuse (see Mendelson, 1974, for an excellent analysis of the operations of the nursing home industry). Yet studies of the institutionalization process have invariably focused on entering and living in sectarian not-for-profit homes for the aged, the best of contemporary facilities but also not the most common.

The current portrait is unlikely to change. If anything, proprietary nursing homes will become more prominent. Neither new models of service delivery nor medical breakthroughs are likely to occur that will appreciably alter the current scene. Although average life expectancy is increasing, there is no evidence that with longer life, the very old can avoid a period of preterminal deterioration (Tobin, 1975). Indeed it may be argued that if the three major causes of death among the elderly were to be cured (cancer, stroke, and arteriosclerotic heart disease), adding 3 or so years of life, the elderly would be even more physically infirm and mentally impaired preceding death at an advanced old age. The wished for 120 years of life (the biologist yardstick for *Homo sapiens* longevity in an optimal environment), with no loss of physical prowess or mental incapacity preceding death, is still only a vision and not at all a reality for our lifetimes.

If this all too abbreviated sketch is correct—if deterioration is inevitable, if becoming institutionalized is likely to occur to one of four elderly, if the final abode is likely to be a proprietary nursing home—then it is to be expected that thoughts of institutionalization, before there is any visible need for institutional care, should be fearful ones. Indeed, when asked, 3% of community elderly, at the most, select an institutional setting as the preferred living arrangement (1% in Blenkner's, 1965, community sample and 3% in Shanas's, 1962, sample), a selection that invariably refers to a non-profit home for the aged. Thus, in any consideration of the effects of institutionalization, the topic must be extended beyond the actual living in the institution and include the effects during the process preceding entering the institution. It was with this concern in mind that we (Tobin & Lieberman, 1976) designed a study to ascertain the effects throughout the process of becoming institutionalized when old.

A Longitudinal Study

In our study, reported in *Last Home for the Aged: Critical Implications of Institutionalization* (Tobin & Lieberman, 1976), elderly were followed from before admission through entering and then living in long-term care facilities. At each point in time, these respondents, as well as respondents in community and institutional comparison samples, were interviewed for 12–16 hours in 4–6 sessions. In discussing the salient findings from this intensive longitudinal study, I shall expand on a few of the findings that merit further clarification and additional interpretation such as the role of family in the process of becoming institutionalized, both before and after admission; explanations for passivity as a predictor of vulnerability to the stress of institutionalization; and how the experience of those now becoming institutionalized may differ from those we studied (having, for example, launched our study more than a decade ago). Our primary sample consisted of 85 elderly (mean age = 79) who were interviewed, on the average, 4 months before actually entering and living in sectarian homes for the aged when on waiting lists (after applying and being accepted) to enter the homes, interviewed again 2 months after admission, and then interviewed once more 1 year after admission. Two comparison samples, interviewed 1 year apart, were also gathered: an institutional sample of 37 elderly who had resided in the homes for more than 1 year and a community sample of 40. Because of our matching procedures (by demographic and other variables, and also because if institutional care was sought, they would apply to these sectarian homes), the community sample serves as a baseline to study the process of becoming waiting list respondents. Indeed three elderly individuals in the community sample did seek institutional care within 2 years after our first interview and were followed through the first year after entering and living in the homes.

The selection of sectarian homes was purposeful. We chose the best of contemporary long-term care facilities because we were interested in the irreducible effects of institutional life. The choice of a longitudinal design

was also purposeful because in previous studies, cross-sectional comparisons between community and institutional samples (mostly of elderly in
sectarian facilities, as discussed by Tobin & Lieberman, 1976) have resulted
in differences between the two samples being attributed to living in the institution, whereas other factors may be of even greater importance, such as
population differences, effects during the process before admission, and relocation effects.

EFFECTS PRECEDING ADMISSION

To assess the fears of becoming institutionalized, Kuypers (1969) developed an interview guide that permitted the assessment of latent, as well as
manifest, attitudes. Data were gathered from only 14 of the 40 community
respondents because the others had already been interviewed by the time
we went into the field to gather these data. The 14 voiced little concern regarding their personal future, a finding reported for the elderly by others
(see, for example, Heyman & Jeffers, 1965). We were unable, however, to
determine whether the lack of future concern was a function of denial or
stable life situations. Since then, Kulys and Tobin (1980–1981) have determined, on a different sample of 60 persons who averaged 78 years in age,
that lack of future concern is associated with having interpersonal supports
whereas the presence of future concerns, because of the association with
the lack of interpersonal supports, as well as anxiety and dysphoric mood,
reflects preoccupation with events that are uncertain to occur.

The sample of 14, in addition to not being preoccupied with the future,
had a rather positive appraisal of the sectarian institutions to which they
would apply if institutionalization became necessary. For example, they
felt that old-age homes were necessary, that the staff met the needs of the
residents, that a resident could maintain self-respect, and that the home
provided companionship. To them: "People who went into the homes were
different from themselves . . . ." If they themselves were no longer independent "the home would be a necessary alternative." The focused interview that followed the questionnaire, however, revealed more latent attitudes. For 12 of the 14, entering the home would be a calamity. One
respondent said "it would be giving up everything" and that she would go
"only if helpless," another compared it to "a jail," and a third, to "a place
to die." Although it may be giving up everything, a jail, and a death house,
they would enter the sectarian home, as have others before them, to assure
survival.

Given the attitude of elderly toward these homes before admission is contemplated, it is not at all surprising that if admission is later sought, that the process is associated with negative psychological effects. When the waiting list sample was compared to the community sample on the four dimensions assumed to be most affected by the actual living in an institutional environment, respondents in the waiting list sample were found to be less cognitively intact, less emotionally responsive, have worsened affect states, and negative changes in the self system. Moreover the psychological portraits of waiting list respondents were essentially the same as the psychological portraits of elderly who have lived in institutions. This was corroborated in our own data when the community, waiting list, and institutional samples were compared cross-sectionally (Lieberman, Prock, & Tobin, 1968): The waiting list and institutional samples were remarkably alike and the community sample decidedly better on all four psychological discussions. If anything, the status of the institutional sample was better than that of the waiting list.

Differences between the community and the waiting list samples cannot be attributed to population differences; to, for example, physical status, marital status, and personality type. The samples were matched for marital status and other demographic variables and both samples showed a similar diversity of personality types. Regarding physical, as well as mental status, we selected a waiting list sample that was the least impaired among those applying for institutional care because we wished those most able to respond to our lengthy interview. We also assessed adverse changes in the past three years and found that the changes that differentiated the two samples were in the area of interpersonal relationships, reflecting deteriorative changes in relationships that had either led to seeking institutional care or had followed the decision to seek care. In either case, the process of becoming institutionalized is associated with a psychological portrait usually attributed to living in an institutional environment and, in our study, the psychological portrait is primarily a product of adverse interpersonal changes. Corroboration for the role of interpersonal change is found when the latent meaning of the process is explored. Using the reconstruction of the respondent's earliest memory as a projective test (see Tobin, 1972; Tobin & Etigson, 1968), the focal concern when on the waiting list is that of abandonment, separation from significant others without an expectation of reunion, feeling rejected and awaiting an uncertain fate. This experience of being abandoned is attenuated (or, if you wish, defended against) by anticipating physical care, security, and activities (Pincus, 1968). Some investigations (see, for example, Dobroff, 1976), have questioned the universality of feelings of abandonment in focusing on the positive anticipations of residents-to-be.

INSTITUTIONALIZATION AS A FAMILY PROCESS

The findings of feelings of abandonment can best be understood when institutionalization is considered a family process. Indeed families go to extremes to avoid institutionalizing a family member and when a comprehensive picture is obtained of family caring (see Tobin & Kulys, in press, for a recent review of the literature), it becomes quite understandable why there may be three times as many elderly outside of institutions who approximate in status those 5% or so who reside in long-term care facilities. That is, 7–8% of community elderly are homebound, one of four of whom are bedridden, and another 7% or so are quicky becoming homebound (Shanas, Townsend, Wedderburn, Friis, Milhoj, & Stenhouwer, 1968). Residence in long-term care facilities is apparently a result not only of functional status—according to Shanas *et al.* (1968) and it is our impression as well—but is also related to the lack of formal services and to the absence, inability or unwillingness of significant others, really family, to aid the older person in independent living. Thus about 16% of those in long-term care facilities were never married as compared with 6% in the general population of those 65 and over (U.S. Bureau of the Census, 1973). (The corresponding percentages for widowed, 70% in facilities as compared to 40% in the 65 and over population are grossly misleading because for the people whose ages approximate those in long-term care facilities, the percentage of widows in the general population is probably a similar 70%.)

Although a disproportionate percentage of those who reside in long-term care facilities may be without nuclear family members, most do have families. The Survey of Institutionalized Persons (1978) revealed, for example, that 9 of 10 institutionalized persons have a next of kin, and that over one-half have at least one living child. Among those elderly who do have family members involved in the decision-making process to seek institutional care, the situation evokes problems in family relationships that are persistent, but often veiled, and the family manifests, according to Brody (1977) "internalized guilt-inducing injunctions against placing an elderly spouse or parent regardless of the most reality-based determinants of that placement [p. 115]." Cath (1972) labeled the institutionalization of a parent, "a nadir of life," because one of the most unhappy times in life may be when a child must make a decision to institutionalize a parent. Children themselves are likely to be old. In Brody's (1966) study of applicants to a voluntary home, the Philadelphia Geriatric Center, in the early 1960s, 40% had at least one child 60 or over, and children's ages ranged up to 74. The family, however, is not simply involved in the decision for institutional placement but is likely to move the older person into their home to avoid institutionalization. Townsend (1962) reported that 45% of the older people who were institutionalized in England had moved in with the family until they were no longer able to provide care at home. In the 1976 Survey of Institutionalized Persons (1978), 29.1% of those 65 and over who were residing in institutions had lived with family before admission. Newman (1975) reported that among a national probability sample, more older people moved to a child's or other relative's home or to a home that was better or closer to a child or relative than moved into institutions. For those who enter proprietary nursing homes, Miller and Harris (1964) found that 45% of the 90 patients at Rockland Nursing Home and Cottages, a proprietary nursing home in New York, lived with their children or other relatives immediately prior to placement, and 20% of the families in the York and Calsyn (1977) study of nursing homes in Minnesota had also done so. It is not surprising, therefore, that Dobroff (1976) found that admission to five long-term care facilities in the New York area related to age-associated changes in the family situation of children. The median age of children was about 50 years of age and the patients, 84. The types of changes she reported were the retirement of a son or son-in-law and the decision to move to a warmer climate, and the incapacity or death of a care-giving child. Brody (1966) reported that in half of her sample of applicants, application was precipitated one fourth of the time by death or severe illness of an adult child or child-in-law. Whatever the circumstances, families can do little to avoid feeling guilty and the elderly feeling abandoned.

THE EFFECTS OF INSTITUTIONAL LIFE

If before admission the experience is of being abandoned with an associated psychological portrait not unlike those who have resided in institutions, what changes could we expect to find when following the same people from preadmission to after entering and living in the homes? Before answering this question, it is essential to return to how our longitudinal design provides different answers than the cross-sectional design that has been invariably employed to assess the effects of living in long-term care institutions. Unfortunately comparisons between "matched" samples of elderly living in the institutions with elderly living in the community who have neither considered nor applied for institutional care do not permit a differentiation between effects preceding admission and effects from living in the institution. Differences between the two samples, that is, may not only be a result of the institutional environment but also of effects preceding admission, as well as population differences and effects of relocation. In following the same individuals from before to after entering and living in the institutional environment, effects preceding admission and population differences are controlled. Relocation effects, however, cannot be so readily dismissed but, as will soon be apparent, the prediction of differential vulnerability—preadmission characteristics that covary with the adverse outcomes of extreme deterioration and death assessed 1 year after admission—sheds light on relocation effects. Still, by following the same individuals from an average of 4 months before admission to 2 months after admission to the best of contemporary long-term care facilities, we can come closer to answering: What are the irreducible effects from entering and living in long-term care institutions?

By 2 months after admission the typical institutional resident has been through the *first month syndrome*, the transient but severe behavioral changes usually evidenced during the initial period after admission. By 2 months postadmission, our data gathered both before and after admission suggests more stability than changes. Constrictions in cognition and affective responsiveness persisted and also there was a continuation (or stability) of moderate levels of well-being, anxiety, and depression. Changes found were limited to an increase in hopelessness, an increase in bodily preoccupation, a perception of less capacity for self-care and a lessening of affiliation in interaction with others. The *self-system*, however, remained remarkably intact and stable—in contrast to the deselfing process which Goffman (1961) has described as occuring when entering a state mental hospital. Rosner (1968) found, for example, on an interpersonal self-sort task, using a pool of 48 self-descriptive items, that respondents who entered the homes were similar to respondents in the community and institutional contrast groups in selecting 4 or 5 items the second time that had been selected the first time. Even when those items selected by 75% or more of respondents were eliminated, the percentage of items chosen after admission that had been chosen before was very high: 3 or 4 self-descriptive items. On this index of the more idiosyncratic items, there was also no apparent effect on the consistency of the self-view as a result of entering and living in the homes. The only shift that did occur was on the dimension of affiliative–hostile, which suggests a perception of less friendliness and more hostility toward others.

RESIDENTS AND THE FAMILIES

We then asked ourselves whether this diminution in affiliation toward others suggests a decline in interaction with others. On one instrument, the Personal Resources Questionnaire, an 11-item scale that requires the respondent to mention the names of one or more specific others who can, for example, be turned to when lonely, for help, or when happy, suggests that residents interact with a range of peers and staff, and also with family —at least in the homes we studied. Regarding family, there is an amelioration of feelings of abandonment reflected in diverse parts of our data, and a tendency toward "mythicizing" of living children, reflected specifically in reminiscent data, which apparently is an exaggerated expression of an age-associated process of mythicizing significant figures from the past (Revere & Tobin, in press). The function of this type of reminiscence activity may be to make the past more real, more poignant and, in the myth becoming the reality, the older person finds a justification for his or her life. Although a child may still be alive and a frequent visitor, the increased psychological distance created by institutionalization and the need to maintain self-consistency in the face of institutional demands and distance may cause an exaggertion in this adaptative process of mythicizing the child. The exaggerated response is probably reinforced by the institutional environment where the coin of the realm is famous offspring who are attentive and caring and where family attention provides leverages for personal prestige and also for more attentive staff caring. Family members, however, are present not only in memories and conversations with other residents and with staff but also as visitors. In the 1978 Survey of Institutional Persons, for example, three of five residents were receiving weekly visitors. Visiting is actually more prevalent at the homes we studied because visiting depends, as noted by Dobroff (1976), "in part on the degree to which the institution and its staff made the families feel welcome in the institution and encouraged their efforts on behalf of aged relatives [p. vii]." These homes indeed welcome visitors. The family is thus not only involved in the process of entering homes but also involved afterwards, a topic that has recieved too little attention (see the Tobin & Kulys review, in press).

THE LATENT MEANING

We summarized our major findings:

> Entering and living in the institutional environment was not associated with changes that would support belief in the "destructiveness of institutions." The changes that were found did not suggest institutional effects of destructiveness; changes such as a lessening of hopefulness, in the absence of an increase in depression, or the adoption of the patient role. Apparently the institution forces the adoption of the patient role, including increasing the preoccupation with bodily concerns and personal vulnerability, which, in turn, reduces the elderly resident's expectations for future gratifying experiences that can give purpose to life [Tobin & Lieberman, 1976, p. 132].

The shift at the more latent level was not, however, as modest as the manifest changes in psychological status. The earliest memories revealed a significant shift toward the introduction of themes of mutilation and death. This shift in recollection sometimes occurred when the same incident was reported at both times. For example, before admission one elderly woman offered the following earliest memory: "I remember my mother. She had hair like braids, open and falling upon her shoulder. She was sitting up in her bed and near her on her table was a bottle of honey and I remember asking her for honey. That's all I remember—nothing before and nothing behind. I still can see her sitting in bed. I must have been 2 years, 2 or 3. Closer to 2, I guess. But that's a picture I have." After admission she recalled: "I remember my mother's death. I remember at least one moment of it. She had honey on her bed and I wanted some of that honey. I didn't really understand that she was dying. I was almost 3 years old. That's all I remember. I can see her face clearly even now. She had two braids hanging down. This picture is all I remember of her." The contrast between the two memories suggests that a breakthrough of repression had occurred in which previously withheld, archaic material was now being expressed. It would appear that in the first report the pain of mother's death is defended against, but breaks through in the second telling of the same incident. In the reconstruction of the same incident at both times, there is a central theme of oral deprivation (e.g., wanting, but not getting, the honey), as well as the personally meaningful symbolism of mother's braids.

More often, however, the increase in loss of becoming institutionalized was associated with a shift in the incident, as in the following example of the repeat earliest memory. When on the waiting list: "I liked to go swimming and mother wouldn't let me. Once I stood on the pier and fell in. I remember how they took me out and took me to my mother. That's all I remember. I wasn't sick." And after admission: "Didn't have coffins in the old country like they do here. My father died. I remember my sister was still a breast baby . . . It was a cold day. My mother said don't go. But he was a stubborn man and so he got pneumonia and died."

Contrasts with thematic changes in the control groups suggest that one-third would not have shifted to these themes of more narcissistic loss had they not entered the homes. This shift is, apparently, specifically related to entering and living in the homes, and to living in a total institutional environment with sick elderly in a home that is to be the last one. With such a significant shift, from abandonment to increased vulnerability, it was indeed surprising that so little change was observed in psychological status. Most likely the ability to successfully contain, to defend against, the latent meanings is a function of entering the best of contemporary long-term care facilities. Yet even these facilities exact their toll, as reflected in the latent meaning of institutional life itself, in the adoption of the patient role, a lessening of futurity, and portraying oneself as less affiliative in relation to others.

By the end of 1 year postadmission, more than one-half of the sample had either died (13 of the 85, or 15%) or had extremely deteriorated (28, or 33%). Those we were able to interview again showed only a lessening of affiliation in relation to others and a lessening of body preoccupation. All other measures did not show a change. This pattern of stability with only focal changes in affiliation and body preoccupation among the intact survivors masks the above noted global outcomes: Forty-one of the 85 had died or had become extremely deteriorated. To what extent these 41 would have shown these outcomes had they not entered and lived in the houses is impossible to know. Although similar outcomes were found for 18% of the community sample, such outcomes were found for 47% of the institutional control sample. The latter statistic suggests no excess morbidity and mortality for those who entered the homes. This issue will be incorporated into the discussion of differences between the deteriorated or dead and the intact survivors; that is, into the discussion of predictors of vulnerability to the stress of institutionalization.

PREDICTING VULNERABILITY TO THE STRESS OF INSTITUTIONALIZATION

Intact and the nonintact respondents did not differ on age, for example, but they did differ in living arrangements prior to admission. Of the 85 respondents, 17 had lived in nursing homes prior to admission, the other 65 were living with others or alone in noninstitutional settings. Of the 17 admitted from nursing homes, 13 (77%) were in the nonintact group as opposed to only 4 (23%) in the intact group. Relocation from a nursing home to a home for the aged is obviously associated with more negative outcome than relocation into the home from independent community living. Yet those admitted from nursing homes were similar to those admitted from the community on most of our measures. Neither, for example, did they differ on functional adequacy nor with the severity or number of events leading to the decision to seek institutional care. It is also possible that their deterioration partially resulted from the earlier relocation. They had to adapt to the stress of two relocations in a rather brief time interval. This double relocation may explain the few differences that were found between those elderly who lived transitionally in a nursing home and those who did not. The elderly admitted from the nursing homes tended to be more passive, to use denial more, and to have a lowered sense of futurity, characteristics that in many ways reflect an institutional profile. Their lower anxiety and greater comfort in relating to the interviewers may have related to their assurance of care while in the nursing home and to their being further along in their resolution of the issues of loss and abandonment than the respondents who were admitted directly from the community.

As implied, we determined the psychological predictors of morbidity and mortality, by using as baseline measures, assessments made while on the waiting list. Measures were sorted out into nine dimensions that have either been explicitly discussed as, or inferred to be, predictions of outcome to stress: functional capacities, affects, hope, the self-system, personality traits, reminiscence, coping with the impending event, interpersonal relations and accumulated stress (see, also Lieberman, 1971, for further elaboration on selection of these variables). We then contrasted the two outcome groups—the intact survivors and the nonintact—on these measures, and simultaneously, we contrasted the corresponding two outcome groups for the two control samples. Thus any measure that differentiated, or predicted, for the sample that underwent the stress of institutionalization and also predicted for the sample not undergoing this stress could not be a predictor of vulnerability to the stress of institutionalization but, rather, would be a characteristic that is associated with survival. Stated another way, only if a measure predicted for the sample undergoing stress could the attribute being measured be considered a sensitizer to the stress of institutionalization and not associated with survival per se. Measures in several dimensions were associated with survival: functional capacities, affects, hope, self-system, coping, and interpersonal relations. Only one dimension, and then only one type of measure within the dimension, was a sensitizer to the stress of institutionalization: *passivity* among the personality traits. Passivity, that is, was associated with morbidity and mortality among those entering the homes but not with morbidity and mortality for those in stable environments (also see Turner, Tobin, & Lieberman, 1972).

PASSIVITY AS A PREDICTOR OF OUTCOME

How should we interpret this association between passivity and negative outcomes? Turner (1969) interpreted the finding as a reflection of how the lack of *congruence* with the adaptive demands of the institutional setting leads to heightened stress. (This hypothesis has been explored further by us in the study of the therapeutic relocation of state mental hospital patients to nursing homes and boarding houses [Lieberman, Tobin, & Slover, 1969], and by Kahana [1974] in the institutionalization of elderly in long-term care facilities.) Passivity as a predictor, because of the congruence between the trait in individuals and institutional adaptive demands, had

saliency because the homes we studied rewarded aggressiveness. Assertiveness, even nastiness and distrust, were assumed by staff to reflect appropriate responses to institutional life and engagement with them, as well
as with the program and peers. More aggressive residents, therefore, have
less of a need to modify characterological coping style when adjusting to
the relocation enviornment. The new resident who is passive may, in experiencing greater stress, react in more severe and dramatic ways. When
very old people—our sample averaged 80 years of age—react severely to
the initial shock of relocation, they are likely not to recover because of the
lack of residual homeostatic capacity. The greater the stress, the more
likely that the additional taxation will exhaust integrating capacities,
leading to extreme deterioration and hastening death.

The inability to maintain biological integrity is also the mechanism used
to explain why passivity relates to negative outcome when passivity is
postulated to hinder the mobilization of those internal resources necessary
for survival under stress. Passivity in this alternative explanation, is not
only pertinent for the elderly, although it may be more critical for the
elderly. Gutmann (1977) had discussed the psychodynamics of the increasing passivity in normal aging and the consequent importance of "externalizing aggression, to turn potential debilitating inner conflicts into external
struggles [p. 309]." As Gutmann further notes: "the capacity to externalize
anger might be a survival asset at any age [p. 309]." Nardini (1952), in the
same vein, observed that in Japanese prison camps, passivity was a most
frequent precursor of death and Cannon (1942), in his classic work on
"voodoo" death, suggested that even the most healthy of individuals may
succumb to death if passivity is extreme.

Passivity as a characteristic that generally predisposes to disintegration
or, alternatively, passivity as a characteristic that heightens the experience
of stress because it is incongruent with environmental adaptive demands
may both be valid explanations for passivity as a predictor of outcome. If
so, the source for the effects on passive individuals resides more in environmental dislocation than in institutional life per se: in either how
dislocation as a stressor augments the tendency for passivity to lead to
disintegration, or how dislocation leads to heightened stress because of
person–environment incongruity.

RELOCATION STRESS

Environmental discontinuity, or relocation, is too broad a topic to
cover here. Fortunately, Lieberman (1975) at a West Virginia conference, in
a paper entitled "Adaptive Processes in Later Life," discussed our institu-

tionalization study as one of our four studies of relocation. The other three studies were of relocations from one institution to another. These studies, of relocations from the community to institutions or from institutions to institutions, as well as from the community to other community settings, suggest the types of variables associated with negative outcomes. Quality of environments are associated with outcome, as well as are personal characteristics. Physical debilitation is, for example, associated with heightened mortality rates. Regarding psychological variables, many are critical to adverse outcomes such as the attachment to the prerelocation interpersonal world and its objects, the degree that the relocation is involuntary, and perceiving little control of the relocation situation. Because our study of institutionalization was of less impaired elderly, all of whom were relocated voluntarily to a common and better environment, we were unable to reaffirm the importance of many of these variables as predictors of outcome.

Yet we have determined that some variables assumed to be predictors of vulnerability must first be considered for their relationship to survivorship per se. When this is done, the residual variables—those that predict for institutionalization but not when this intervening stress is not present—can emerge. In our study, passivity emerged. However the obverse of passivity is conceptualized—as assertiveness, aggressiveness, or grouchiness—it very well may be that psychological mobilization is more important than such other widely accepted predictors such as the need to be familiar with the institutional environment, to be realistic and not use denial to cope with the event, to have control over the situation, and to be hopeful regarding the relocation. Only through further studies shall we be at all able to understand why in some studies adverse relocation effects were found and in others not. Most studies of mortality as an outcome of institutional relocation of the elderly, as collated by Borup, Gallego, and Heffernan (1979), do not, however, reveal *excess mortality*. These authors argued that because studies that have revealed excess mortality in institutional relocation have generally relied upon baseline rates rather than control groups, "there is a need to counter the myth . . . that relocation brings about an onslaught of death" and "relocation does not cause an increase in mortality [p. 139]." To assess the diverse institutional relocation studies in this way, unfortunately, diminishes the complexity of the phenomenon. Our study of psychological predictors reflects one way of approaching the understanding of institutional relocation effects by focusing on psychological predictor variables. One caveat: Institutional relocation is not the most frequent relocation among the elderly but, rather, moving from one community dwelling to another occurs with much greater frequency and with minimal adverse effects (see Chapter 10, this volume).

A Forward Look

At the time we launched our study (as noted earlier, more than a decade ago), about two-thirds of new residents entered long-term care facilities from community dwellings whereas now about one of two enter from acute hospitals (1976 Survey of Institutional Persons, 1978). The factors accounting for the increasing admissions from acute hospitals include changes in reimbursement practices, secular trends in attitudes of the elderly and their families, and an increase in the development of community based social and health services ("alternatives to institutional care")—all of which have changed the terrain of long-term care facilities and increased the percentage of admission from acute hospitals. Deflecting elderly mental patients from state mental hospitals, for example, can decrease the percentage of institutionalized persons admitted from the community if, that is, these elderly are not admitted directly to nursing homes. Voluntary (sectarian and nonsectarian) homes have largely been transformed from congregate residences for the isolated and less impaired to approximating nursing homes in serving, almost exclusively, the mentally and physically impaired who are more likely to be admitted directly from the acute hospital.

These, as well as other changes, may have important implications for practice and policy, but they do not invalidate the findings of our study. Admission from the acute hospital, more sudden and with less preparation than when deciding to apply for admission and then awaiting admission for 4 months, does not dispel the experience of being abandoned that is associated with becoming institutionalized. Indeed the experience may be more intense with less time to cope with it, delaying the intensified experience until after admission. Moreover, hospitalization may encourage or deepen passivity (as was found to occur among those of our respondents who lived transitionally in nursing homes before entering the sectarian homes) with subsequently greater morbidity and mortality; and even when entering the best of contemporary long-term care facilities. Another example pertains to the experience of being vulnerable—expressed in themes of mutilitation and death in projective, reminiscence, measures used to assess latent experiences 2 months after admission. Admitted rather abruptly from an acute hospital to a facility with a residential population that is largely confused and extremely frail, will certainly evoke the experience of being personally vulnerable, but it is to be expected that this experience too will be intensified. Also behavior and affects at more manifest levels will be reinforced, including the more apparent adoption of the patient role, being increasingly preoccupied with bodily functions, a deeping of hopelessness, a lessening of the capacity or willingness for self-care, and perceiving oneself as more hostile in relationship to others. Yet, it also must be considered that the process may be different qualitatively—that among those who survive intactly through the first year, for example, there will neither be an amelioration in painful affects nor an ability to maintain self-consistency. If indeed the process does differ for those currently experiencing becoming institutionalized when old, we shall only know through longitudinal studies in which elderly are intensively assessed before entering, and then reassessed after living in, long-term care facilities.

References

Blenkner, M. Social work and family relationships in later life with some thoughts on filial maturity. In E. Shanas & G. Streib (Eds.), *Social structure in the three generation family.* Englewood Cliffs, N.J.: Prentice–Hall, 1965.

Borup, J. H., Gallego, D. T., & Heffernan, P. G. Relocation and its effects on mortality. *The Gerontologist,* 1979, *19,* 135–140.

Brody, E. M. The aging family. *The Gerontologist,* 1966, *6,* 201–206.

Brody, E. M. *Long term care of older people.* New York: Human Science Press, 1977.

Cannon, W. B. "Voodoo" death. *American Anthropologist,* 1942, *44,* 169–181.

Cath, S. H. The institutionalization of a parent: A nadir of life. *Journal of Geriatric Psychiatry,* 1972, *5,* 25–46.

Dobroff, R. The care of the aged: A shared function. Unpublished Doctoral Dissertation, Columbia University School of Social Work, 1976.

Goffman, E. *Asylums: Essays on the social situation of mental patients and other inmates.* Garden City, N.Y.: Doubleday, 1961.

Gutmann, D. The cross-cultural perspective perspective: notes toward a comparative psychology of aging. In J. E. Birren & K. W. Schaie (Eds.), *Handbook of the psychology of aging.* New York: Van Nostrand Reinhold, 1977. Pp. 302–326.

Heyman, D. K., & Jeffers, F. Observations on the extent of concern and planning by the aged, for chronic illness. *Journal of the American Geriatrics Society,* 1965, *13,* 152–159.

Kahana, E. Matching environments to the needs of the aged. In J. Gubrium (Ed.), *Late life—communities and environmental policy.* Springfield, Ill.: Charles C. Thomas, 1974. Pp. 201–214.

Kastenbaum, R., & Candy, S. The four percent fallacy: A methodological and empirical critique of extended care facility population statistics. *International Journal of Aging and Human Development,* 1973, *4,* 15–21.

Kulys, R., & Tobin, S. S. Interpreting the lack of future concerns among the elderly. *International Journal of Aging and Human Development,* 1980–1981, *11,* 138–145.

Kuypers, J. Elderly persons en route to institutions: A study of changing perceptions of self and interpersonal relations. Unpublished doctoral dissertation, University of Chicago, 1969.

Lieberman, M. A. Some issues in studying psychological predictors of survival. In E. Palmore & F. C. Jeffers (Eds.), *Prediction of life span.* Lexington, Mass.: Heath Lexington Books, 1971. Pp. 167–179.

Lieberman, M. A. Adaptive processors in late life. *Life span developmental psychology: Normative life crises.* New York: Academic Press, 1975. Pp. 135–159.

Lieberman, M. A., Tobin, S. S., & Slover, D. The effects of relocation on long-term geriatric patients (Final report to the Dept. of Mental Health, State of Illinois, Project No. 17–328), 1969.

Mendelson, M. A. *Tender loving greed.* New York: Knopf, 1974.

Miller, M. B., & Harris, A. P. Family cognizance of disability in the aged on nursing home placement. *Social Casework,* 1964, *45,* 150–154.

Nardini, J. Survival factors in American prisoners of war of the Japanese. *American Journal of Psychiatry,* 1952, *109,* 241–248.

Newman, S. Housing adjustments of older people: A report of findings of the first phase. Ann Arbor: University of Michigan Institute of Social Relations, March, 1975.

1976 survey of institutionalized persons: A study of persons receiving long-term care. U.S. Dept. of Commerce. Bureau of the Census. Washington, D.C.: U.S. Government Printing Office, 1978.

Office of Nursing Home Affairs, *Long term care facility improvement study.* Washington, D.C.: U.S. Government Printing Office, 1975.

Palmore, E. Total chance of institutionalization among the aged. *The Gerontologist,* 1976, *16,* 504–507.

Pincus, M. A. Toward a conceptual framework for studying institutional environments in homes for the aged. Unpublished doctoral dissertation, University of Wisconsin, 1968.

Revere, V., & Tobin, S. S. Myth and reality: The older person's relationship to his past. *International Journal of Aging and Human Development,* 1979, in press.

Rosner, A. Stress and the maintenance of self-concept in the aged. Unpublished doctoral dissertation, The University of Chicago, Committee on Human Development, 1968.

Shanas, E. *The health of older people: A social survey.* Cambridge, Mass.: Harvard University Press, 1962.

Shanas, E., Townsend, P., Wedderburn, D., Friis, H., Milhoj, P., & Stenhouwer, J. *Old people in three industrial societies,* New York: Atherton Press, 1968.

Tobin, S. S. The earliest memory as data for research. In D. Kent, R. Kastenbaum, & S. Sherwood (Eds.), *Research, Planning, and action for the elderly: Power and potential of social science.* New York: Behavioral Publications, 1972.

Tobin, S. S. Social health services for the future aged. *The Gerontologist,* 1975, *15,* 32–37.

Tobin, S. S., & Etigson, E. C. Effects of stress on the earliest memory. *Archives of General Psychiatry,* 1968, *19,* 435–444.

Tobin, S. S., & Kulys, R. The family and services. In C. Eisdorfer (Ed.), *Annual review of gerontology and geriatrics.* New York: Springer, in press.

Tobin, S. S., & Lieberman, M. A. *Last home for the aged: Critical implications of institutionalization.* San Francisco: Jossey–Bass, 1976.

Townsend, P. *The last refuge—a survey of residential institutions and homes in England and Wales.* London, England: Routledge and Kegan Paul, 1962.

Turner, B. F. Psychological predictors of adaptation to the stress of institutionalization in the aged. Unpublished doctoral dissertation, University of Chicago, 1969.

Turner, B. F., Tobin, S. S., & Lieberman, M. A. Personality traits as predictors of institutional adaptation among the aged. *Journal of Gerontology,* 1972, *27,* 61–68.

U.S. Bureau of the Census, *U.S. Census of the Population: 1970.* Subject Reports. Persons in Institutions and Other Group Quarters. Washington, D.C.: U.S. Government Printing Office, 1973.

York, J. L., & Calsyn, R. J. Family involvement in nursing homes. *The Gerontologist,* 1977, *17,* 500–505.

Subject Index

A

Abilities, significance of, 8
Adaptability, at a social level, 23–24
Adaptation
  conservatism as, 19–20
  intellectual, 8
  population or social-system level defini-
    tion of, 14
  to society, 13
  as trade-off process, 23
  of youth, 23
Adaptation level
  environmental change and, 173, 174
  press and, 174
Adjustment, defining, 27–28
Adolescence
  egocentricity of, 17
  flexibility in, 12
  pure logic of, 13
Adolescent egocentricity, 13
Adolescents, development potentials of, 122
Adult cognition, 3–24
  rigidity versus stability in, 19–20

Adult cognitive maturity, commitment as
  onset of, 12
Adulthood
  cognitive deficits of, 22
  commitment and responsibility in, 12
  competence in, 65–66
  Piaget model of, 15
  processing of information in, 20–21
  reality of, 68
  structural change in, 13
  structural transitions of, 16
Adult life
  contradiction in, 13
  transition to post-parental phase of, 121
Adult resistance to change, 19
Adults
  attention to detail in, 21
  encoding processes in, 20
  intellectual capacities in, 8
  mnemonic system functioning in, 22
  psychomotor functioning loss in, 10
  sensory functioning loss in, 10
Age
  as definition of role behavior, 44

213

DATE DUE

AUG 6 1982		
JAN 2 0 1984		
OCT 1 2 1984		
NOV 2 3 1984		
NOV 6 '87		
MAY 13 '88		